THE SOLITARY EXPLORER

THE SOLITARY EXPLORER

Thomas Merton's Transforming Journey

ELENA MALITS, C.S.C.

Harper & Row, Publishers, San Francisco
Cambridge, Hagerstown, Philadelphia, New York
London, Mexico City, São Paulo, Sydney
1817

Grateful acknowledgment is made for permission to reprint excerpts from the following books by Thomas Merton:

Conjectures of a Guilty Bystander, copyright © 1965, 1966 by The Abbey of Gethsemani; *Contemplation in a World of Action,* copyright © 1965, 1969, 1970, 1971 by the Trustees of the Merton Legacy Trust. Reprinted by permission of Doubleday & Co., Inc.

Disputed Questions, copyright © 1953, 1959, 1960 by the Abbey of Our Lady of Gethsemani; *Mystics and Zen Masters,* copyright © 1961, 1962, 1964, 1965, 1966, 1967 by the Abbey of Gethsemani; *The New Man,* copyright © 1961 by the Abbey of Gethsemani. Reprinted by permission of Farrar, Straus & Giroux, Inc.

The Seven Storey Mountain, copyright © 1948 by Harcourt Brace Jovanovich, Inc. (renewed 1976 by the Trustees of the Merton Legacy Trust); *The Sign of Jonas,* copyright © 1953 by The Abbey of Our Lady of Gethsemani. Reprinted by permission of Harcourt Brace Jovanovich, Inc.

The Asian Journal, copyright © 1968, 1970, 1973 by the Trustees of the Merton Legacy Trust; *Breakthrough to Peace,* copyright © 1962 by New Directions Publishing Corporation; *Gandhi on Nonviolence,* copyright © 1964, 1965 by New Directions Publishing Corporation; *The Geography of Lograire,* copyright © 1968, 1969 by the Trustees of the Merton Legacy Trust; *New Seeds of Contemplation,* copyright © 1961 by The Abbey of Gethsemani, Inc.; *The Way of Chuang Tzu,* copyright © 1965 by The Abbey of Gethsemani, Inc.; *The Wisdom of the Desert,* copyright © 1960 by The Abbey of Gethsemani, Inc.; *Zen and the Birds of Appetite,* copyright © 1968 by The Abbey of Gethsemani, Inc. Reprinted by permission of New Directions Publishing Corporation.

The Monastic Journey, edited by Brother Patrick Hart, copyright © 1977 by the Trustees of the Merton Legacy Trust. Reprinted by permission of Andrews & McMeel, Inc., and the Trustees of the Merton Legacy Trust.

Faith and Violence, copyright © 1968 by University of Notre Dame Press. Reprinted by permission of University of Notre Dame Press.

FIRST EDITION

Designed by Jim Mennick

Library of Congress Cataloging in Publication Data

Malits, Elena.
  THE SOLITARY EXPLORER.

  Includes bibliographical references and index.
  1. Merton, Thomas, 1915–1968.   2.   Trappists in the United States—Biography.   3.   Poets, American—20th century—Biography.   I.   Title.
BX4705.M542M34 1980   271'.125'024   80–7744
ISBN 0–06–065411–2

80 81 82 83 84 10 9 8 7 6 5 4 3 2 1

To my companions on the journey

Contents

Preface

Thomas Merton's *The Seven Storey Mountain* came too early in life to encompass his whole story. He lived—indeed, very intensely—for twenty years beyond the publication of the autobiography in 1948. That book, which made him famous, was an account of a young man's search for God and meaning in the midst of a disordered, self-seeking life. Merton's quest had culminated in his conversion to Catholicism at age twenty-three while a student at Columbia University. Three years later, he became a Cistercian (Trappist) monk. *The Seven Story Mountain* appeared just seven years after Thomas Merton, now Frater Louis, O.C.S.O., had entered the Abbey of Gethsemani in Kentucky. It was written from the perspective of someone who had found what he was looking for and whose life was now shaped by certain definitive decisions. In coming to the monastery, Merton had reached the end of one journey and was launched on another. Appropriating Dante's images, Merton expressed his life story prior to conversion as a journey through hell and spoke of his experience since that turning point as climbing up the mountain of purification.

If the arduous ascent to the vision of God had begun with his baptism, it was intensified by the very nature of the monastic vocation. For Merton, to be a monk was precisely to be a man consciously and totally given over to the processes of transformation. *The Seven Storey Mountain* traced the story of Thomas Merton's coming to the mountain; it went on to chart the changes wrought within him during the initial stages of the spiritual journey. But the autobiography represented only the beginning of his conversion story. He underwent genuine religious growth all the years of his monastic life, right up to his untimely death at fifty-three by accidental electrocution while on a trip to Asia.

As Merton experienced it, conversion was neither merely the term of an action nor a static condition. Rather, he understood it as a continuing movement, a constant dynamism of the human spirit responding to God and following wherever his Spirit led. Some twelve years after his becoming a Catholic, Thomas Merton put it this way:

> It is evident that the story of my life up to the day of my baptism is hardly the adequate story of my "conversion." My conversion is still going on. Conversion is something that is prolonged over a whole lifetime. Its progress leads it over a succession of peaks and valleys, but normally the ascent is continuous in the sense that each new valley is higher than the last one.[1]

Then and always, Merton articulated his experience of conversion as an open-ended process, an ongoing development, a dynamic thrust forward and upward. His favorite expression for describing it was the metaphor of a journey.

The title of Merton's autobiography was an obvious allusion to the classic Christian story of the quest for God. And the last manuscript Merton completed before his death in 1968 was a long poem called "The Geography of Lograire." This, too, maps a journey through the poet's imagination, the country where he searches to locate himself in relation to other peoples and places. The poem is a sustained metaphor for Merton's task of finding his true self, which for him was ever the route to God. And as we shall see, in between these early and late writings, he repeatedly expressed the story of his continuing conversion through the imagery of an unceasing journey. His life was, indeed, conceived of and lived out as a journey of relentless discovery.

But Thomas Merton's ongoing conversion was exercised as he followed several different paths. There were various developments, involvements, aspects to his life. Several distinct, although not unrelated, stories should be noted in order that we might understand fully this man's quest for transformation. There is the story of his progressive move into contemplative solitude, the story of his becoming a social critic and prophetic figure, and the story of his interest in Eastern religious and philosophical traditions. Merton's progress as a monk, as a man of mystical prayer, as an authoritative voice in the American Catholic Church—each constitutes its own account. Then there is the story of his great friendships with intellectuals and artists and ordinary folk, the story of his influence as a spiritual director, of his artistry as a photographer, and of his role as a humanist. Not least is the story of Merton the writer: autobiographer, religious essayist, poet, novelist, satirist, humorist, and man of belles-lettres.

It was the writer who was able to catch up the threads of all these stories and weave them into the verbal tapestry that shows us Thomas Merton. As a writer, he knew how to follow the patterns of different stories; he possessed the craft of shaping the disparateness of experience into a coherent narrative. Merton was endemically an autobiographical writer, always telling us in one way or another his own story. Not only in his one formal autobiography but also in his journals, topical essays, poetry, and assorted literary forms, he was engaged in recounting the events—inner and outer—of his life. And the man sought to make his very existence the story of someone being refashioned in the image of his Maker.

Merton's journey was motivated and sustained by Christian faith. What he undertook was the pursuit of God within his own depths and the search for manifestations of the divine in all creation. To remain faithful to such a journey, Thomas Merton would need to be purged of all that obscured his vision of the divine action and its source. He would have to be progressively purified of his tendency to agitated activity and his ambivalent desires regarding accomplishments. The spiritual denseness that kept him from seeing the social and political implications of contemplation would need to be cut through. His ignorance and lack of sensitivity to the significance of other religious traditions must be overcome. He had to be opened to the power of his own tradition and learn how to communicate its riches to contemporary people. Most of all, Merton's transformation would demand confronting his inner demons, discovering his real self before God, and embracing his unique destiny. Insofar as he consented to these tasks and wrote about his struggles along the way, Merton's journey is accessible to us. It can illuminate our darkness and empower us to set out on our own journey. That, at least, is what Merton hoped to do by sharing his story of continuing conversion.

Thomas Merton was a complex man with many levels, myriad dimensions, numerous stories. He became known through an autobiography, *The Seven Storey Mountain,* and remained essentially an autobiographical writer all the rest of his life. It is the project of this book to sort out the various developments in Merton's continuing conversion, to see how he integrated and communicated them, and to probe the significance of this multistoried man for contemporary people. Originally I wanted to call the book *The Seven Storey Merton,* because that title nicely suggests the image of the man and his life that my study hopes to elucidate.

Undoubtedly Merton would have enjoyed the pun, but more cautious advisers thought it too cute for a serious book, and possibly confusing to the public. I finally settled on *The Solitary Explorer,* not only because that metaphor clearly was one of Merton's own favorites for himself but also because it captures his distinctiveness as a monk-writer who experienced his paradoxical vocation as a lonely journey into the unknown. Both as a monk and as a writer, Thomas Merton was an adventurer not afraid to travel alone.

This book has been in progress for a year, but the work really began with research for my doctoral dissertation on Merton nearly ten years ago in the theology department of Fordham University. More people than I could mention have helped me along the way; I want them all to know that I am grateful.

My sisters and brothers in the Congregation of Holy Cross have been a never-ending source of support, stimulation, and service. They shared the burdens and joys, the work and excitment of my project from beginning to end. The sisters in my local community saw me through the hard days, putting up with my erratic work habits with much patience. Eva Mary Hooker, C.S.C., and Mary Louise Gude, C.S.C., offered not only encouragement but helpful criticisms of the text. David Burrell, C.S.C., my long-time companion on the journey for which Merton has served both of us as a guide, was willing to hear out my half-formed ideas and read all the rough drafts, always making wise and helpful suggestions.

The monks of the Abbey of Gethsemani have been gracious and most helpful in all sorts of ways. No one could do a book on Merton without being forever grateful to Brother Patrick Hart, O.C.S.O., that indefatigable facilitator and friend of Merton students. The Sisters of Loretto, with whom I lived while doing the initial research, welcomed me warmly into their Kentucky home near the monastery.

My colleagues in the religious studies department at Saint Mary's College and in the theology department of the University of Notre Dame showed sustained interest and provided a stimulating forum for discussion. The Saint Mary's administration offered every possible assistance to help me get the work done. And I want to thank all the students from Saint Mary's and Notre Dame who have participated in the courses where I have used Merton; we learned much from him together.

Sister Francis Clare, C.S.C., was most generous in helping with the typing; Mrs. Linda Guyton worked long hours at the typewriter with great care and good results.

Dr. Rita Cassidy's editorial suggestions, proofreading prowess, and indexing skills proved invaluable.

My mother is always there, wondering what I am up to and sure that it will be better than it is. She probably remembers me curled up with *The Seven Storey Mountain* as a high school girl sometime in the early 1950s.

1

Writing as Temperature

Reviewing Roland Barthes' *Writing Degree Zero* in 1968, Thomas Merton summed up the view of the French structuralist: "When the choice is completely lucid, when the writer chooses simply to *write,* and renounces all the rest ('message', 'expression', 'soul', 'revolution'), the writing itself stands out clearly as writing."[1] That might have applied to Merton himself, because his own writing certainly involved a conscious choice. Indeed, he spent a good part of his life struggling with the implications of what writing meant for a contemplative monk. He had come to accept writing as ingredient to his vocation, even saying in his journal, "If I am to be a saint, I have not only to be a monk, which is what all monks must do to become saints, but I must also put down on paper what I have become."[2] Merton would agree with Barthes, moreover, that authentic writing eschews "using" it for self-aggrandizement, propaganda, or any form of manipulation of others. But Merton's similarity to Barthes' ideal ended there. In "Writing as Temperature," Merton described what writing, according to Barthes, was supposed to accomplish:

A distance is established which reminds the reader not to get lost in the writer or in the writing, not to immerse himself in false complicities with the message or the emotion, not to get swept away by illusions of an inner meaning, a slice of life, a cosmic celebration, an eschatological vision. When writing is just writing, and when no mistake about this is possible because the very writing itself removes all possibility of error, then you have "writing degree zero."[3]

Thomas Merton never practiced writing in this icy condition. Although he wanted his readers to approach him with critical distance, he nevertheless wrote in such a way that people profoundly identified with him and his capacity to articulate the deep desires of the human heart. Merton was wary of his own facility with words, for he was acutely sensitive to the danger of spinning verbal illusions for oneself and catching others up in them. Yet Merton wrote so as to do precisely what "writing degree zero" disavowed: to reveal "inner meaning," to show a real "slice of life," to engage in a "cosmic celebration," to communicate and affirm "an eschatological vision." The temperature of Thomas Merton's writing was frequently near the boiling point. It was full of conviction in the presence of anguished searching. Writing energized Merton for his ongoing journey. He hoped it would release power in the reader to undertake his or her own quest.

If Merton's writing tells us the temperature of his concerns, it also provides a kind of map charting his lifelong journey as a monk and writer. His books and articles have a history; their genesis, progress, and publication make a fascinating story. Tracing what Merton was producing at certain periods of his writing career points to where he was going in his personal itinerary.

It seems appropriate to begin a study of Thomas Merton's continuing conversion by sketching an account of his writings. A comprehensive list is not necessary, but a discussion of certain works can illustrate tendencies manifested in a given stage of the monk's development. We will follow the story of the man as he became known in print. Although Merton produced much material that he kept private,[4] our consideration will be limited to what he published.

When Merton submitted something for publication, he was showing a part of himself to the world; at that point, his interior journey assumed a shape that others could identify. And, because part of the story of Merton as a writer includes the response of people to him and to what he wrote, some assessment of his readers' reactions is in order. Those responses reflect, in fact, what was transpiring in the larger story of the Catholic Church and American society through three decades of cultural and religious change.

Nearly ten years before writing *The Seven Storey Mountain*, Merton had published a few reviews and contributed to literary magazines as a graduate student at Columbia University and as an English instructor in upstate New York. Later, after joining the monastic community at the Abbey of Gethsemani, he wrote (anonymously) texts for several books and pamphlets connected with the monastery. As a young monk, he even got together two books of poetry: *Thirty Poems* (1944) and *A Man in the Divided Sea* (1946). Robert Lowell favorably reviewed *Thirty Poems*, remarking: "Unfortunately, Merton's work has attracted almost no attentive criticism: the poet would appear to be more phenomenal than poetry."[5] Until 1948, however, this "phenomenal" young writer was known only to a relatively small and rather elite reading audience.

That year the Literary Awards Committee of the Catholic Press Association cited his *Figures for an Apocalypse* as "the most distinguished volume of verse published in English by a Catholic poet in 1948." But far more significant, it was then that Merton's autobiography was published. *The Seven Storey Mountain* catapulted to fame a man who seven years earlier had retired to a Trappist monastery to find solitude.

His story was the tale of a journey from "Prades to Bermuda to St. Antonin to Oakham to London to Cambridge to Rome to New York to Columbia to Corpus Christi to St. Bonaventure to the Cistercian Abbey of the poor men who labor in Gethsemani."[6] The key locations on this journey were Corpus Christi, the church near the campus of Columbia University in New York City where Merton had been baptized a Catholic, and Gethsemani, the Cistercian monastery in the Kentucky hills where he now was living as a contemplative in one of the strictest religious orders. If *The Seven Storey Mountain* was the narrative of a much-traveled young man, however, the real journey it recounted was an interior one. The autobiography was essentially a conversion story.

One of the most influential Catholics of the day, Bishop Fulton J. Sheen, praised Merton's autobiography as "a Twentieth Century form of the *Confessions of St. Augustine*."[7] Undoubtedly that comment exaggerated not only the literary excellence of the book but also Merton's character as a "great sinner." Nonetheless, such remarks made the point that Merton surely had scattered some wild oats as a worldly, sophisticated intellectual but also had undergone a profound religious transformation. It was Clifton Fadiman (not a Catholic, or even a religious reviewer) who put his finger on the power of *The Seven Storey Mountain*: "It deals . . . not with what happens to a man, but with what happens inside him—that is, inside his soul. It should hold the attention of Catholic and non-Catholic alike."[8]

The book certainly did capture public attention. The woman who was Merton's literary agent for the autobiography recalls in her journal: "It was unusual for a non-Catholic publisher to bring out a Catholic book. . . . But the story of a conversion? Written by someone who, because of the monastic life, was not likely to write a best selling novel?"[9] Publication of *The Seven Storey Mountain* was a risk, but the book was and still continues to be popular. It has sold well over a million copies; the hard-cover edition went through numerous printings, and there have been three paperback editions by different publishers.[10]

The American reading public in general seemed to like Thomas Merton, but it was the Catholics of the late 1940s and early 1950s, of course, who became his special followers. They were as proud of this convert-become-monk as they were of the Notre Dame football team, and they exhibited something of the same adulation toward him and enthusiasm for his work. The titles of early articles about Merton in the Catholic press tell that story. For instance, there was a review of the autobiography called "The Complete Twentieth Century Man."[11] Occasionally reviewers were cool, like the one who objected that, but for a single comment on Marx and another on the Bomb, *Seeds of Contemplation* (1949) might have been written by a medieval monk.[12] But the first really serious critical note was not sounded until early in 1953.

Dom Aelred Graham, O.S.B., himself a monk and monastic scholar, took Merton to task for preaching a religion that was too other-worldly. He argued that Merton was distracting Christians from their task of redeeming the times by idealizing monasticism and advocating mysticism. Graham criticized Merton's books for lacking theological depth, sufficient reference to the New Testament, and a sound historical sense. There was, Graham claimed, too much self-projection in the Trappist's writing.[13] *Time* considered such searching criticism from so eminent a source as worthy of note.[14] Merton himself took Graham's criticism more seriously and less defensively than did the loyal fans who rose to his defense.[15]

A master's thesis was written on Merton's poetry as early as 1951. In 1954, a doctoral dissertation also had been completed on his poetry, which by that time numbered four volumes, the most recent being *The Tears of Blind Lions* in 1949. But perhaps the single best index of Thomas Merton's importance during this period was the publication of a bibliography compiled in 1954. It listed nearly ninety books, pamphlets, forewords, prefaces, articles, and reviews by Merton, and more than forty articles and reviews about him.[16] By the middle 1950s, Merton was required reading for literature courses in Catholic high schools and colleges and was certainly a favorite on convent and rectory shelves. His poetry was received appreciatively, even ardently, in Catholic periodicals, with a few notable exceptions.[17] Merton's books of meditation and religious reflections, however, drew the most attention in the era of the 1950s.

The period was ushered in with the extraordinary success of *Seeds of Contemplation* (1949), which was promptly compared to *The Imitation of Christ*. That decade witnessed the appearance of such books by Merton as *The Ascent to Truth* (1951), *Bread in the Wilderness* (1953), *No Man Is an Island* (1955), *The Living Bread* (1956), *The Silent Life* (1957), and *Thoughts in Solitude* (1958). These books on prayer and meditation, plus many articles on related subjects, were widely read and evidently provided welcome insight and fresh inspiration for countless people. Reviewers tended to be laudatory; often they were—like Merton himself—people of considerable culture whose background was more literary than theological.[18] It is notable that professional theologians (except a few mavericks like Graham) generally ignored Merton, yet perhaps not surprising, considering the academic hegemony at that time of Neo-Scholasticism with its rigid standards for what could be properly regarded as theological.

During these years, however, Merton was writing on profoundly religious topics such as true and false mysticism, the relationship of faith and reason, the psalms as Christian prayer, the unity of the Body of Christ, the Eucharist, and numerous others of theological import. If Merton did not present himself as a theologian, still he was deeply engrossed in the stuff out of which theology is made. In November 1949, he began teaching a course in spiritual theology to the novices and students at the monastery. Many of his subsequent books grew out of notes for such classes and reflections on his duties as Master of Scholastics, the task to which Merton was assigned in May 1951. In this position, he was in charge of the monks who had recently made simple vows and were engaged in formal theological studies. As Master of Novices, the position Merton held from 1955 to 1965, he became responsible for the monastic formation of the young men preparing to make their first vows, and would continue to give conferences which provided material for his writing.[19]

Theologians of the 1950s may not have been impressed, but Merton's kind of theology deeply affected many people. His ideas were mulled over, meditated on, and approached with utmost seriousness. Merton was for many Catholics—educated only in a desiccated theology, or in none but devotional triviality—their one contact with a rich, vital theological tradition. That tradition came alive to these people because Merton spoke to them "not in the language of speculation, but in terms of personal experience."[20] Merton himself recognized the hazards of such an approach, but he was convinced of its necessity. In his journal covering the years 1946–1952, he noted,

> I found in writing *The Ascent to Truth* that technical language, though it is universal and certain and accepted by theologians, does not reach the average man and does not convey what is most personal and most vital in religious experience. Since my focus is not upon dogmas as such, but only on their repercussions in the life of a soul in which they begin to find a concrete realization, I may be pardoned for using my own words to talk about my own soul.[21]

And it was exactly Thomas Merton's "own words" about his "own soul" that interested people. Arresting as his ideas might be, it was ever the man himself who attracted attention. Of all Merton's books in the 1950s, *The Sign of Jonas* (1953) was surely the most eagerly read and best loved. Undoubtedly, that was because this journal revealed the man more candidly than had anything since *The Seven Storey Mountain.* Thomas Merton simply enticed and captivated readers. *Newsweek* and *Saturday Review* found the random musings of this Trappist monk as worthy of note as did the Catholic periodicals.[22] Indeed, a vast public seemed fascinated by the random thoughts of Thomas Merton scribbled in his notebook behind some barn at Gethsemani.

There were a few attempts to explain Merton's magnetism and the extraordinary appeal of *The Sign of Jonas,* but most comments remained superficial.[23] Writing about his next book, *No Man Is An Island* (1955), Aelred Graham (former critic turned admirer) viewed Merton's attractiveness in the light of the mid-twentieth-century's need of the mystics for people to discover the meaning of religion and life. Graham located the particular power of Thomas Merton in his "rare and attractive combination of gifts."[24]

Graham's understanding of who Merton was and what he was doing proved more perceptive than most, and he nicely identified Merton's strengths and weaknesses (the latter being self-preoccupation and too much stress on asceticism), but even Graham did not account for Merton's power. It seems fair to say that in the decade of the 1950s Merton's popularity was neither sufficiently explained nor his import adequately assessed.

At the outset of the 1960s, Merton was still the darling of the Catholic bookstores. *The Secular Journal of Thomas Merton* (1959) had recently come out and was selling. Published twenty years after the material had been written, the book consisted of selections from a diary Merton had kept as a layman. And the public was definitely still interested in knowing anything and everything about Thomas Merton. More than twenty-five periodicals reviewed the book. *Newsweek* said, "The Journal is of great interest as the record of a youth of spirit, humor, irony, deep distress over the world, and love of his God."[25] Another book, *Spiritual Direction and Meditation* (1960), was a collection of notes and articles written in the 1950s; it showed nothing very different from the kinds of books that had been appearing throughout that period.

But several books published in the early 1960s did reveal a new turn for Merton. *Disputed Questions* (1960) brought together essays on a broad range of topics. Writings such as "The Pasternak Affair," "Christianity and Totalitarianism," and "Notes for a Philosophy of Solitude" represented forays into hitherto uncharted territory. Merton had not been publishing articles on such matters since his entrance into the monastery. Now he was moving into the area of literary and political concerns and was beginning to write about solitude in a new way. A critic in *Saturday Review* observed that *Disputed Questions* signaled a dramatic change in Merton. He found the author of *The Seven Storey Mountain* no longer seeking to convert the world to Catholicism or America to some form of the contemplative life; rather, he said, Merton "quietly knocks on the door of our heart asking 'who are we?' "[26]

The Wisdom of the Desert (1960) marked an important step in Thomas Merton's understanding of the solitary vocation. This book consisted of translations—or rather what Merton called his "free and informal redaction of stories" from the sayings of the Desert Fathers of the fourth century.[27] The long introductory essay showed that Merton was thinking about the meaning of solitude in relation to society, rather than merely in terms of its value for an individual's spiritual development.

The third book appearing at this time that moved beyond what had been Merton's typical writing was *The New Man* (1961). This, like so many books before it, was made up of a series of meditative essays on religious subjects, but a new emphasis could be discerned. Merton was raising "existential" questions. The theme of identity provided the book's unity. The author asked in various ways how contemporary people can overcome the terror of existence and survive in a society dominated by the "Promethean instinct." Reviewing *The New Man*, a *Commonweal* writer accented Merton's progress in grasping the meaning of Christ and the Christian in relation to the basic identity question of modern people: "He has acquired a profound understanding of the peculiarly contemporary questions which demand an authentic Christian answer."[28]

Finally, *New Seeds of Contemplation* (1961), although containing most of the same material as the original *Seeds of Contemplation* (1949), was more than an expansion and revision. Merton called it "in many ways a completely new book."[29] The twelve years that had passed modified the author's solitude "by contact with other solitudes" and had resulted in a "new perspective" regarding people both inside and outside the monastery.[30] The book revealed a Merton not only far richer in contemplative experience but also considerably broadened in his concerns. It was not addressed primarily to Catholics; rather, Merton directed his reflections to "people without formal religious affiliations who will find in these pages something that appeals to them."[31]

Merton had begun reviewing books on Zen in the late 1950s. In 1961, a dialogue with D. T. Suzuki was published.[32] About the same time the first of his many essays on Eastern philosophy and religion, "Classic Chinese Thought," appeared.[33] Such articles marked a significant move for Merton; henceforth he would be publishing more and more on subjects outside the familiar Christian orbit. But an even more dramatic development was in the making. Late in 1961, a short piece appeared concerning a current ethical debate about private bomb shelters. The monk castigated the attitude, generated by the nuclear buildup, that was leading Americans to argue the moral legitimacy of setting up survival enterprises based on private ownership.[34] This was not the first time Merton had written on problems stemming from the nuclear threat (he commented on them in his journals and wrote about such matters to friends), but "The Shelter Ethic" was the first thing of its kind to get into print. A long series of topical essays on similar subjects would be forthcoming.

If 1959–1961 was a transition period, 1962 became the genuine watershed for Thomas Merton the monk, so far as the type of his publications was concerned. February of that year saw the appearance of "Nuclear War and Christian Responsibility," an essay severely criticizing the United States for moral passivity and irresponsibility regarding the nuclear danger. Merton stressed the eschatological character of the nuclear threat and insisted that the Christian must refuse cooperation with a policy inevitably leading to genocide.[35] A rash of strongly worded articles on similar themes followed in rapid succession.[36] "Original Child Bomb," Merton's long prose poem on Hiroshima, and *Breakthrough to Peace* were also published in that eventful year of 1962. The latter, a volume of essays by leading opponents of nuclear war, was edited by Merton, who also wrote the introduction and one essay.

How did Merton's readers react to this turn of affairs? *Commonweal* received some letters of disapproval,[37] but for the most part the articles on war were ignored. Of course, these articles brought Merton into even closer dialogue with notables in the peace movement (he often sent around drafts to friends such as Dorothy Day and James Forest), but the general reading audience Merton had built up over the past thirteen years must have considered the 1962 yield a poor Merton crop. For them, the next year brought *Life and Holiness* (1963).

This little volume was in the more familiar Merton manner, although a sensitive reader may have picked up a somewhat altered orientation. Merton called the book "a meditation on some fundamental themes appropriate to the active life." He viewed the Christian's striving for holiness in a particular context, "the Church's action on the threshold of a new age." And, most significantly, Merton now acknowledged that even the cloistered contemplative "must to some extent participate 'actively' in the Church's work, not only by prayer and holiness but by understanding concern."[38]

Merton certainly would be participating "actively" by his writing during 1963. Although evidencing the new perspective, the meditations in *Life and Holiness* still remained rather traditional and tame. But the essays Thomas Merton was publishing in various periodicals were something else indeed. In the first half of that year, several more articles showed up on themes related to the war issue.[39] In the second half of 1963, there appeared the first of Merton's published essays on racial matters in the United States.[40] Especially his "Letters to a White Liberal" launched Merton into the thick of the struggle for black freedom. Merton was then reading novelists such as James Baldwin and William Melvin Kelly, and he closely followed developments in the civil rights movement, particularly the direction given by Martin Luther King, Jr. The "Letters" constituted a scathing critique of the white's (especially the liberal's) failure to understand that "the Negro problem is really a white problem; that the cancer of injustice and hate which is eating white society . . . is rooted in the heart of the white man himself."[41]

Seeds of Destruction, published in late 1964, contained the now well-touted "Letters," of which Merton wrote in the book's introduction: "The developments that have taken place during 1964 have, if anything, substantiated everything these 'letters' attempted to say."[42] He had predicted that the white liberals of 1963 would soon realize that the black movement was beyond their power to control and, when they did recognize it, would adopt a conservative, semifascist stance. Merton's language may have been exaggerated at times, but "Letters" proved to be one of the most perceptive and literally prophetic pieces on the racial situation to appear in the earlier part of the 1960s.

The reaction? Some of Merton's admirers of the 1950s would be innocent of so worldly a label as "liberal," and, if they read "Letters" at all, could have been only dismayed. But the sophisticated critic Martin Marty accused Merton of being unjustified and too pessimistic in his appraisal of what was happening regarding the civil rights movement.[43] Another liberal, this one a Catholic, was even more critical of "Letters" than Marty had been: "Father Merton's appeals are marred by romanticism, extravagance and scorn for the sinners he would persuade."[44]

Along with *Seeds of Destruction,* some articles appeared in 1964 on a rich variety of religious and literary topics; but others indicated that Merton was preoccupied with the many forms of violence destroying American society.[45] Evidently he was looking more and more to Gandhi for guidance, and he published several essays on the Hindu revolutionary, leading up to *Gandhi on Non-Violence,* which he edited in 1965.

Of the three books Merton published in 1965, two were on men from the Eastern tradition.[46] Besides the book on Gandhi he brought out *The Way of Chuang Tzu,* an assemblage of notes on the Chinese philosopher (third or fourth century B.C.), based on "free interpretative readings of characteristic passages." Smitten by the sayings of the witty Chinese recluse, Merton confessed, "I have enjoyed writing this book more than any other I can remember."[47] A seminal essay on the different schools of Zen, which compared certain Zen ideas with those of Western mysticism, also appeared at this time.[48] Not that Merton had stopped writing on controversial current issues; his publications that year, however, would suggest that he was once again assuming a more contemplative approach.

Such a suspicion is borne out by noting other writings in the mid-1960s. One quietly reflective piece spoke about Thoreau and Philoxenos (a ninth-century Syrian hermit) but mainly celebrated the festival of the rain for "its gratuity and its meaninglessness."[49]

A few years earlier, Merton had received permission to build a little hermitage in the woods, about a quarter mile from the main complex of monastery buildings. He had been moving in by stages; by the summer of 1965, he had been released from his duties as Master of Novices, the office he had faithfully exercised in the monastery for ten years. Now he would be allowed to live in the hermitage full-time. The effects of his increasingly more solitary life were palpable in Merton's writing. Excerpts from a journal he was preparing for publication began to appear.[50] They reflected a Thomas Merton deeply concerned about public affairs and social issues, as well as a man who was developing inwardly over the years. Another essay in 1965 revealed Merton's own assessment of what was happening:

> They [those who read his books] demand that I remain forever the superficially pious, rather rigid and somewhat narrow-minded young monk I was twenty years ago. . . . What has actually happened is that I have been simply living where I am and developing in my own way without consulting the public about it since it is none of the public's business.[51]

In Merton's opinion, it may well have been none of the public's business—but not so to the public. When the journal based on his 1956–1965 notebooks came out, entitled *Conjectures of a Guilty Bystander* (1966), *Life* carried notable excerpts from it.[52] The publication of a Merton journal (the first since *The Sign of Jonas* in 1953) was a public event; and *Conjectures* was an important book.

It was a different sort of journal. Unlike the earlier one, entries in *Conjectures* were not "of the intimate and introspective kind that go to make up a spiritual journal."[53] But this book was significant as a record of the progress of Merton's thinking over a crucial decade; it clearly told what national and world events he responded to and indicated what books and people had influenced him most. *Conjectures* showed how certain tentative observations and judgments had gradually coalesced to form decided views. Unfortunately, entries were not dated in the published version, nor were they arranged in strictly chronological order. Many indications in the text, nonetheless, allowed the reader to approximate the dates of particular comments.

The Sign of Jonas had taken a definite story line, charting Merton's day-to-day experiences and recording principally his spiritual struggles and joy as his religious life unfolded. *Conjectures* reflected something of that, of course, but the book was more "an implicit dialogue with other minds." Merton charcterized this journal as

> A series of sketches and meditations, some poetic and literary, others historical and even theological, fitted together in a spontaneous, informal philosophic scheme. . . . The total result is a personal and monastic meditation, a testimony of Christian reflection in the mid-twentieth century, a confrontation of twentieth-century questions in the light of a monastic commitment, which inevitably makes one something of a "bystander."[54]

Some critics complained of the sketchiness of *Conjectures;* most reviewers, however, were inclined to forgive Merton for his "notebook faults."[55]

Another very important book was published in 1966, *Raids on the Unspeakable.* Not a journal, *Raids* had a "poetic temperament," although it was a collection of recent prose writings.[56] The essays dealt in one way or another with the precarious situation of modern people and expressed Merton's basic concern with the freedom and identity of the person. Manifesting the same contemplative orientation evident in other writings of 1965–1966, *Raids* adopted the indirect modes of parable, myth, and irony for responding to the critical state of contemporary society. In the use of such literary forms, *Raids* was similar to *The Way of Chuang Tzu;* the books were also alike in being Merton's favorites. In the tongue-in-cheek prologue, Merton addressed *Raids* as one might a rather naughty, but much-loved offspring:

> I feel that though you are definitely a bit wild, your intuitions hit a few targets that the other books have missed. Mind you, I do not repudiate the other books. I love the whole lot of you. But in some ways, *Raids,* I love you more than the rest.[57]

Raids on the Unspeakable proved to be a classic example of where Merton was in the middle 1960s: the book expressed a man deeply disturbed by public events and popular attitudes but inclined by the discipline of solitude to adopt a contemplative perspective and prefer poetic irony for coping with the problems.

That contemplative perspective was displayed in articles such as "Love and Solitude," in which Merton spoke of solitude as "a spiritual climate, an atmosphere, a landscape of the mind, a level of consciousness."[58] The preference for irony showed itself in the tone of two major articles, "How It Is—Apologies to an Unbeliever," and "Is the World a Problem?" The latter began with joking but led up to the serious point that "The World itself is no problem, but we are a problem to ourselves because we are alienated from ourselves."[59] And "Apologies" was a sincere acknowledgment of the all-too-typical Christian narrowness and arrogance in which Merton also had participated. His manner eschewed being maudlin: "I recognize that I have been standing on your [the Unbeliever's] foot, and now at last getting off it, with these few mumbled sentences."[60]

Merton's enlarged horizons were evident, too, in his deepening interest in Eastern religions, especially Zen Buddhism. In 1966, two articles appeared indicating his sensitivity to the relevance of Zen for contemporary Christians.[61] The single book to be published in 1967 revealed Merton's involvement with Eastern religion and philosophy even more. *Mystics and Zen Masters* contained some material written as early as 1961 but also included the most recent essays on Zen. This book represented a flowering of many years of study of both Western and Eastern monastic traditions; most of all, it showed how far Merton had traveled on the contemplative route. He was now concerned with "the spiritual family of man seeking the meaning of his life and its ultimate purpose." Merton expressed the book's central concern, which united all the diverse essays: "to understand various ways in which men of different traditions have conceived the meaning and method of the 'way' which leads to the highest levels of religious or metaphysical awareness."[62]

Other publications that year indeed suggested that Merton was taken up with exploring many different traditions. During 1966, he reviewed a number of books on primitives, native Americans, and Japanese art; he produced articles on a vast array of persons and groups from diverse cultural backgrounds.[63] That year also brought forth some writings dealing with that new development within the culture of Christianity—"death of God" theology. The monk sharply criticized the radical theology movement for undermining the potential force of its critique of religion by succumbing to the myth of secular autonomy.[64] The publications of 1967 showed that Thomas Merton's literary interests were as wide as ever; he was working particularly on Camus and Faulkner, as several articles attest.

One bit of writing published in 1967 revealed the inner man more than anything else appearing at that time. "Day of a Stranger" had obviously been taken from one of Merton's journal notebooks. Although a handwritten note on the manuscript indicates that it was written in May 1964, the material had not been included in *Conjectures*. This little piece summed up Merton's perspectives, preoccupations, and attitudes of the middle 1960s. It was written in the hermitage and conjured up an image of his simple life there: "Rituals. Washing out the coffee pot in the rain bucket." A section describes the "mental ecology," the "balance of spirits in this corner of the woods," naming those who (along with the birds) are singing to Merton. His anguish over war and racial conflicts are poetically expressed. But even these bitter concerns can be faced within the hermit life, which Merton calls "cool . . . a life of low definition." The stranger who is describing his day as he lives it half-way through the 1960s gives us the quintessential Merton:

> This is not a hermitage—it is a house. ("Who was that hermitage I seen you with last night? . . .") What I wear is pants. What I do is live. How I pray is breathe. Who said Zen? Wash out your mouth if you said Zen. If you see a meditation going by, shoot it. . . . Up here in the woods is seen the New Testament: that is to say, the wind comes through the trees and you breathe it.[65]

The last year of Thomas Merton's life was 1968. Along with one book of poetry (rather, antipoetry), *Cables to the Ace,* two significant prose collections were published. *Faith and Violence: Christian Teaching and Christian Practice* took in material that had appeared as far back as 1963. The book included essays on nonviolent resistance, Vietnam, and racial conflicts, with a few on "death of God" theology thrown in for good measure. Although there was little new, this volume offered an intriguing account of the development of violence and nonviolence in a critical period for America, as well as presenting the best of Merton's writings on these issues.

The last book to appear before Merton's death was *Zen and the Birds of Appetite.* This, too, contained dated material (some nearly ten years old), but most of the essays were fairly recent. The latest one, "The Study of Zen,"[66] emphasized that Zen was not a system and, therefore, was neither opposed nor not opposed to any given structural forms. "Zen is consciousness unstructured by particular form or particular system,"

Merton wrote, "a transcultural, trans-religious, trans-formed con-sciousness."[67] Another recent essay, "A Christian Looks at Zen,"[68] de-scribed Zen as seeking "not to *explain* but to *pay attention, to become aware, to be mindful.*"[69] It is therefore possible, Merton concluded, to say that both Christians and Buddhists can equally practice Zen. Still another piece, "The New Consciousness," dealt with the question of "a radical shift in the Christian consciousness" and expressed Merton's hesitation about the disconcerting vogue for Asian religions coupled with a strong antimetaphysical prejudice in contemporary Western theology. He ob-served rather gloomily,

> Only the Catholics who are still convinced of the importance of Christian mysticism are also aware that much is to be learned from a study of the techniques and experience of Oriental religions. But these Catholics are re-garded at times with suspicion, if not derision, by progressives and conserva-tives alike.

In some respects, that passage could describe Thomas Merton himself in the late 1960s. He caught the disapproval of conservative Catholics for his serious involvement with Eastern religions and was dismissed by some progressives for a concern with mysticism at a time that de-manded the primacy of action. But never had this monk been more con-vinced of the importance of Christian mysticism than in these years of a "frankly activistic, secular and antimystical" Christianity.[70]

Not one for jumping on bandwagons, in his last year Merton was quietly publishing some dozen articles on themes such as contemplation, solitude, and mystical traditions—certainly against the trend of the popu-lar "liberal" theologians of the day.[71] But this sort of writing did not endear Thomas Merton to the conservatives either. First, his views on such topics hardly resembled those of "these nice 'defenders of the faith,' " as he called the theological foot-draggers.[72] Furthermore, Merton was still writing controversial pieces criticizing the Church's failure to take positive action regarding social issues.[73]

The man who, twenty years earlier, had delighted almost everyone in the Catholic world managed toward the close of his life to alienate quite a few on both sides of the post-Vatican II division in the Church. Nonetheless, to the very last Thomas Merton was loved, respected, and admired by wildly diverse sorts of people. He and his old friend from Columbia, Robert Lax, were still going at it in their zany "Catch of Anti-Letters," and Merton made new friends all along his way through Asia.[74]

News of Merton's shocking accidental death (heart failure resulting from electrocution by a large fan) while at a conference in Bangkok on

December 10, 1968, brought forth immediate responses. Alongside an article on Karl Barth, who had died on the same day, *The New York Times* carried a front-page notice and long obituary. It praised Merton as "a writer of singular grace about the City of God and an essayist of penetrating originality on the City of Man. He wrote of ageless spiritual life and religious devotion with a knowledge of a modern."[75] Tributes were soon to follow in numerous periodicals of all sorts. They praised Thomas Merton as a man, monk, writer, scholar, poet, humorist, keeper of the national conscience, teacher, student, and friend. One way or another they all voiced the sentiment expressed in the title of Naomi Burton's article, "I Shall Miss Thomas Merton."[76]

Some of the best articles in the year after Merton's death appeared in a special issue of *Continuum* called "In Memory of Thomas Merton." These essays represented a modest but real beginning of serious Merton scholarship. Titles such as "The Cistercian," "The Social Catalyst," and "The Peacemaker," suggested the complexity of the man and the scope of his work.[77]

Another form of tribute to Merton was the publication of so much of his writing in the years immediately following his death. In 1969, three books came out: *Contemplative Prayer, My Argument with the Gestapo,* and *The Geography of Lograire.* Merton had prepared the first two for publication; the latter, a long poem completed not long before he left for Asia, had not been finally edited by the author. Thus the same year witnessed the publication of Thomas Merton's latest and earliest literary productions, for *My Argument with the Gestapo* was a novel he had written in 1941 before entering the Trappists. The book included much autobiographical material, although cast in a fictional journal form that has the sequence and quality of a nightmare. Writing the preface in 1968, Merton called the novel "a kind of sardonic meditation on the world in which I then found myself: an attempt to define its predicament and my own place in it." The novel provided access, Merton said, "to my own myth."[78]

The last long poem, *The Geography of Lograire,* Merton had called a "first draft of a longer work in progress." Like *My Argument,* it has a dreamlike, often nightmarish quality. This poem also is a statement of a personal myth, although now more broadly integrated into the larger experience of humanity. The author's note explained, "In this wide-angle mosaic of poems and dreams I have without scruple mixed what is my own experience with what is almost everybody else's."[79]

Contemplative Prayer contained a collection of meditative essays written considerably earlier and certainly not among Merton's best on the subject. Unfortunately, the time of the book's publication, with no indication of when the essays were written, gave the impression that these were Merton's last words on contemplative prayer. One reviewer remarked on the "religious insularity" reflected in these essays.[80] But the magic name of Merton had made even mediocre books sell during his lifetime, and in the year following his death the book was welcomed.

In 1969, a plethora of Merton articles, poems, and letters appeared—some twenty, including various translations. These had obviously been prepared by Merton and slated for publication.[81] But something else also began to show up: articles based on notes from taped conferences or transcriptions of talks given by Merton. This was to continue during the next few years.[82]

A whole series of posthumous articles on the contemplative life was published in 1970 and 1971, followed by a major book, *Contemplation in a World of Action*.[83] It included material Merton himself had put together and wanted published after *My Argument with the Gestapo*. The editor added some other pieces on the hermit life; the book is rather long and repetitious, but (unlike *Contemplative Prayer*) it is an invaluable witness to Merton's latest and most developed thinking on issues that were his central concerns over the years.[84]

Another book—this one small and of a single piece—came out about the same time. Written a year or so before Merton's death, it was to be an introduction for a projected edition of the Bible.[85] *Opening the Bible* exhibits Merton's best free-wheeling theological style in his effort to give some insight into what kind of book the Bible is. He draws on Zen stories, a Faulkner novel, and other diverse sources to illustrate the character of the biblical "Word" and the conditions requisite for receiving it. Merton insists on the demands put on the would-be-hearer: "Any serious reading of the Bible means personal involvement in it, not simply mental agreement with abstract propositions. And involvement is dangerous, because it lays one open to unforeseen conclusions."[86] Like so many Merton comments, that was a thoroughly autobiographical statement.

The very last writing Thomas Merton did was certainly characteristic: he kept a journal of his trip to Asia. Because he never lived to edit these hastily scribbled jottings, the task of preparing the material for publication was arduous, and the book was long in coming. *The Asian Journal*, however, was worth waiting for as an autobiographical testimony of the monk in the final stages of his lifelong journey. One of Merton's entries (December 6, Singapore), made just a few days before his death, poignantly expresses his feelings about the trip after nearly three months of traveling. Ironically, it was a statement symbolic of his entire life:

My next stop will be the Bangkok meeting to which I do not especially look forward. Then Indonesia, a whole new journey begins there. And I am still not sure where it will take me or what I can or should plan on. Certainly I am sick of hotels and planes. But the journey is only begun.[87]

Thomas Merton's earthly journey ended at that Bangkok conference, but his story is not finished. In the decade since his death, a steady stream of Merton's writings has been published. For the most part, these are occasional essays, translations, and introductions to books. Some letters have come out, but only a few from a vast assortment.[88] Several anthologies have appeared, such as *Thomas Merton on Peace* and *The Monastic Journey*.[89] A collection of Merton's photographs was edited by John Howard Griffin, who had taught him how to use the camera. *A Hidden Wholeness* shows us another dimension of Thomas Merton. As Griffin remarks, he used his lenses "primarily as contemplative instruments." Thus Merton's photographs "began to reveal, in a way that nothing else did, certain aspects of his interior vision and his qualities as a man."[90]

A revised and updated edition of the popular *A Thomas Merton Reader* (originally published in 1961) was on the market in 1974.[91] The most important publishing event since *The Asian Journal,* however, came with the appearance of *The Collected Poems of Thomas Merton* in 1977.[92] Along with the ten volumes of his poetry, this work contains many hitherto unpublished pieces. The book displays the incredible range of Merton's poetic modes. It also underscores the seriousness with which Merton took the vocation of the poet and his own participation in that task. As he said in a note on William Carlos Williams in 1967, "on the poet devolves the most vital function of society: to recreate it—the collective world—in times of stress, in a new mode, fresh in every part, and to set the world working or dancing or murdering each other again, as it may be."[93] As *The Collected Poems*—with its wild appendices—shows, Merton was not a "writing degree zero" poet!

There are three published bibliographies on Merton.[94] Marquita Breit's, complied in 1974, lists 1,801 items; 927 are Merton's work, and the rest are books and articles about him and reviews of his books. It is currently being updated, but by 1974 118 books and pamphlets by Merton had been published, along with 81 prose contributions to books, 477 articles in periodicals and newspapers, and 56 translations done by him.[95] One is overwhelmed to realize that Thomas Merton could have written so much, given the routines of the monastic life that he followed faithfully for most of his life.

In the last few years, some little gems have appeared, such as *He Is*

Risen and *Ishi Means Man.*[96] Especially in celebration the tenth anniversary of Merton's death in 1978, a number of older books that have been out of print were reissued.[97] But much Merton material remains unpublished. There are some manuscripts and, of course, his letters. Parts of journals that he had intended for print will eventually appear, pending editing. But Thomas Merton's private notebooks, under the terms of his will, are unavailable even to scholars until twenty-five years following his death. The will permits the official biographer appointed by the Merton Legacy Trust to have access to the classified notebooks and to quote them with discretion. Thus all those interested in Merton eagerly await publication of that authorized biography. It was begun by his close friend, John Howard Griffin, whose health has not allowed him to complete the massive task. The work is presently being done by Michael Mott and eventually will be published by Houghton Mifflin Company.

While the public waits for every scrap of Mertonia to be printed, much writing on the monk of Gethsemani has been and is being done. By the end of 1979, some sixty-seven doctoral dissertations or master's theses on Thomas Merton had been completed with many still in progress.[98] Nearly fifteen books on him have been published since his death; articles, both in scholarly journals and the popular press, are numerous.[99] Merton's works have been translated into twenty-three languages, including Russian, Slovak, Swedish, and Vietnamese. "The Merton Seasonal," a newsletter from the Thomas Merton Studies Center at Bellarmine College in Louisville, recently listed the titles of thirty pieces by Merton that have been translated into Polish, and nineteen into Japanese. There are ten articles on Merton in Japanese.[100]

Along with the flood of publications by and about Merton, another indication of the great interest in him is the existence of several Thomas Merton centers. The central one for research is at Bellarmine College. In 1967, Merton himself began the collection there by directing that his manuscripts, tapes, drawings, photographs, and relevant items not otherwise disposed of should be deposited at Bellarmine. In 1969, the Thomas Merton Studies Center was formally established, and this Louisville facility has been the hub of Merton studies ever since. But other centers have sprung up in New York City, Pittsburgh, Denver, and Magog, Quebec. The emphases differ: some are meeting places for contemplatives of all religious traditions; others are concerned with the ministry of justice and peace. Collectively these centers represent the many sides of Thomas Merton and reflect the various ways contact with his writings have shaped people's lives.

There have been many Merton conferences, symposia, and festivals in the last few years.[101] But 1978, the tenth anniversary of his death, witnessed more Merton happenings than ever before.[102] These gatherings of ecumenical groups, academicians, social activists, literati, contemplatives, and just ordinary folk are testimonies to the depth and breadth of enthusiasm for Thomas Merton. The scope of these conferences demonstrates the significance Merton holds for so many different people.

In the essay with which we began this chapter, "Writing as Temperature," Merton commented on Barthes' idea of writing. But Merton's description of one aspect of Barthes might have been said of Merton himself, for it summed up Thomas Merton as a writer better than Barthes as a thinker. Merton was explaining what the latter contributed as both new and significant about the nature of writing: that it is *gestus.*

> *Gestus* is more than "gesture", more than idiosyncrasy. It is the chosen, living, and responsible mode of presence of the writer in his world. But this *gestus* has been overlaid and corrupted with all sorts of elements which have turned it into posturing. . . .
>
> The authentic *gestus* of writing begins only when all meaningful postures have been abandoned, when all the obvious "signs" of art have been laid aside. . . .
>
> To do this, the "writer" must forget all charismatic exaltation, all aspiration to power, all *numen,* all that would seem to give him some ascendancy over the reader.[103]

That Thomas Merton indeed surrendered "ascendancy over the reader" reveals itself in the spiritual potency he exercises on us. The *gestus* of his writing is the act of the true teacher and authentic guide: in showing us himself, he reveals us to ourselves.

Merton was writing in the period of profound transition for Christians in general and Catholics in particular, the decades from the 1940s through the 1960s. His work is not only a personal testimony but a microcosm of patterns of thought, attitudes, and behavior characteristic of those years. He himself reflected those patterns, but was no devotee of theological fads or current enthusiasms. What stands out about him, both as a man and a writer, is his capacity for discrimination. The "Super-Catholic-Romantic-Monk" of *The Seven Storey Mountain* grew into the Christian pilgrim of *The Asian Journal* who journeyed to the East in search of what it could teach him about his own vocation as a Christian contemplative. The "spiritual writer" of the 1950s became the social critic of the 1960s who took up the prophetic role from what he called "the monastic perspective." Merton attributed these changes to his experience of solitude and faithfulness to the demands of his vocation. The contemplative life had taught him detachment, openness, and compassion. He was enabled to enter into the experience of others quite different from himself, because his own sense of identity had been fashioned through contemplation.

Thomas Merton appeals to many different people for many different reasons. For contemporary Catholics, I think, he stands as a symbol of hope. His life story—what he shared as a writer—embodies the radical transformation of attitudes and orientations that Catholics have experienced in the last few decades. Since Vatican II, many Catholics have been trying to learn what it means to be open to other religious traditions without sacrificing the uniqueness of their own identity. But that is not the concern of just Catholics in this era; it is the quest of all Christians. Likewise, Christians have been attempting to discover how to be genuinely involved in and responsible for the social order, without losing a healthy sense of detachment, and without losing the awareness that the real solutions come not from better programs but from transformed hearts. Thomas Merton managed to do those things. He was both faithful and open. He is a symbol of a life that can embrace paradox, live with tensions, and grow into new realizations through constantly reinterpreting the meaning of one's primary commitments.

Merton's writing articulated his journey, his commitment to continuing conversion. He commands our attention, moves us, prods us to embark on our own pilgrimage. His writings are effective because in them we meet someone who himself has undertaken the journey and can, therefore, serve as as our guide. His life is a witness to the openness of the Christian quest. His story mediates life to us insofar as it exhibits meaning and provides us with a way of appropriating it. Merton said it better:

> Our very existence, our life itself contains an implicit pretention to meaning, since all our free acts are implicit commitments, selections of "meanings" which we seem to find confronting us. Our very existence is "speech" interpreting reality.[104]

Such is the temperature reading on life that Thomas Merton's writing gives us.

2 CHAPTER

Journey into the Unknown

Merton's writing, in the form of either prose or poetry, was essentially poetic. His use of language tended to be more expressive than analytic. Possessed of a rich imagination, he instinctively articulated his insights through metaphor. Although he employed many metaphors to depict his life, one dominates Thomas Merton's story. For him, Christian life—and specifically the monastic vocation—was a journey into the unknown. Entrance into the Christian life "is not the end of a journey," he said, "but only a beginning. A long journey must follow: an anguished and sometimes perilous exploration. Of all Christians, the monk is, or at least should be, the most professional of such explorers."[1] Merton developed that idea:

> The monk is a man who completely renounces the familiar patterns of human and social life and follows the call of God into "the desert" or "the wilderness," that is to say, into the land that is unknown to him and unfrequented by other men. His journey into the wilderness is not a mere evasion from the world and its responsibilities. Negative reasons cannot account for the monastic journey into solitude. Monastic renunciation is the answer to a positive call from God.[2]

Focusing on Merton's metaphor of a journey into the unknown will yield a deeper understanding of his continuing conversion, precisely as he conceived and expressed it.

Given the serious analytic work of recent years, which has shown, as one philosopher puts it, that "truly creative and nonmythic thought, whether in the arts, the sciences, religion, or metaphysics, must be invariably and irreducibly metaphorical,"[3] attention to metaphor in a writer such as Merton needs no justification.

The need for employing metaphor to speak of the divine activity within the human self is the common testimony of saints, mystics, and ordinary believers. It is hardly surprising that the effects of a God who transcends our conceptualizations and our language are not amenable to straightforward description. People who have felt themselves called, transformed, and sent by the Spirit to be an instrument for transformation in others, have been inevitably forced to speak of that reality in terms of poetry and parable. Whenever men and women have wished to articulate something of their perceptions of God's work in themselves and their lives, they have turned to modes of indirect discourse. A few have been so overcome by the incommunicability of religious experience that they have opted for silence altogether; others (more common) apologize for the inadequacy of their language but nonetheless use what is available to them, and sometimes discover or create a whole new idiom for sharing with others the Word that burns within them. The use of metaphor is inescapable for such purposes. One need only think of the Scriptures themselves, as well as the great Christian mystical traditions and personalities: the "darkness" of the apophatic school, the theologians of "light," Augustine's "heart" and "city," Teresa of Avila's "interior castle," and Therese of Lisieux's "little way," to name but a few from a countless list of those who have resorted to metaphors for communicating their experience and their message. Thomas Merton, with his "journey into the unknown" is at home in such company.

We can follow Merton's use of that metaphor—in all its variations— through the stages of his development by considering selections from his autobiographical writings. Although a few other sources will be drawn on, the principal works consulted for this task are *The Seven Storey Mountain, The Sign of Jonas, Conjectures of a Guilty Bystander,* and *The Asian Journal.* Tracing Thomas Merton's journey into the unknown through his accounts of what was happening to him can be a powerful experience. Given the quality of his life and of his imaginative gifts to draw us into his story, the reader who takes Merton seriously will be personally challenged to confront his or her own life. Merton puts us in touch with mysterious powers, raises anguished questions, and sometimes plunges us into struggles analogous to those he went through. The story of Thomas Merton's ongoing journey presents us with what he called "the deep conflict which underlies all Christian conversion—the turning to a freedom based no longer on social approval and relative alienation, but on direct dependence on an invisible and inscrutable God, in pure faith."[4] Pursuing Merton's favorite metaphor is a risky business; his journey into the unknown announces to us an invitation to take up consciously the quest for God.

Thomas Merton was a graduate student in English at Columbia University when he rather suddenly became a Roman Catholic in 1938. He had been a professed, although nonmilitant, atheist who never had much formal contact with religion. He was only twenty-three when he underwent his religious conversion, but Merton had already experienced a full and intense life as a sophisticated Bohemian-type youth.

Part One of *The Seven Storey Mountain* is the exciting tale of Merton's childhood and life as a young man prior to his conversion. It is the story of a person who was quite literally shaped by much traveling. The young Merton never spent much time in any one place. He lived in three cultures—French, English, and American—and variously identified with one or another of them at different times in his life.

Merton's parents came from different parts of the world. Owen, his father, was an artist from New Zealand, a quiet, reflective man. "My father painted like Cezanne and understood the southern French landscape the way Cezanne did," Thomas Merton said. "His vision of the world was sane, full of balance, full of veneration for structure, for the relations of masses and for all the circumstances that impress an individual identity on each created thing. . . . My father was a very good artist."[5] In describing his father's approach as a painter, Merton was articulating the heritage that eventually went into making him a contemplative. His mother, Ruth, was also an artist, but her temperament was much more restive and action-oriented. She was a "liberated" American woman from Long Island who was intensely interested in social reforms and in "progressive" education for her sons. Tom, who would thrive on the independence of mind she nurtured in him, was to one day make this assessment:

> I inherited from my father his way of looking at things and some of his integrity and from my mother some of her dissatisfaction with the mess the world is in, and some of her versatility. From both I got capacities for work and vision and enjoyment and expression.[6]

The expatriate couple had been living in the south of France. Tom was born in Prades in 1915. Rumblings of war made the family hastily leave Europe for America the next year, so Tom was scarcely a year old when he took his first journey. They went to live near Ruth Merton's parents in Flushing, Long Island. A second son, John Paul, was born in 1918. Then, in 1921, Ruth died of cancer.

Owen Merton never quite got hold of himself after his wife's death.

He packed up and took his small sons off to Cape Cod for a while;
then they went to Bermuda. Six-year-old Tom was in and out of schools—
mostly out—and spent his time exploring the seashores alone or drawing
pictures of ships. Sporadically the children lived with their maternal
grandparents, Pop and Bonnemaman. Tom loved to go to Pop's office
at Grosset and Dunlap's, publishers then specializing in cheap adventure
novels, and to curl up for a whole day with Tom Swift or the Rover
Boys. The Merton boys learned to worship at Pop and Bonnemaman's
shrine, the local movie house, and Tom more or less consciously acquired
his grandfather's Masonic prejudices and suspicion of Catholics. When
he was ten, Tom's father suddenly announced that they were going to
live in France.

Tom attended the Lycée de Montauban in the Midi. He detested it
and sought desperately to distract himself during this unhappy period.
The eleven-year-old boy found a group of friends who were, like himself,
intelligent, witty, and precocious. Merton recalled that "we were all furi-
ously writing novels. . . . We would get together, walking in a superior
way, with our caps on the backs of our heads and our hands in our
pockets, like the great intellectuals that we were, discussing our novels."[7]
Tom resisted the stern discipline of the French Calvinist school, and found
mandatory religious services cold and unmoving. Regarding his exposure
to religious and moral values, Merton commented,

> The only really valuable religious and moral training I ever got as a child
> came to me from my father, not systematically, but here and there and more
> or less spontaneously, in the course of ordinary conversations. Father never
> applied himself, of set purpose, to teach me religion. But if something spiritual
> was on his mind, it came out more or less naturally.[8]

When he was thirteen, Tom's father decided that his sensitive, precocious son was becoming hard-boiled in the harsh environment of the
lycée, and sent him to England. His education would be under the supervision of Owen Merton's relatives. Tom spent his early adolescence at
Ripley Court, a proper British preparatory school, where he went through
a short-lived "religious phase." Then he was sent to Oakham, an obscure
but rather good public school, to get ready for the university. At Oakham,
Tom endured three painful years of adolescent self-discovery. He was
wildly undisciplined, exercising his imagination to break every possible
school rule. He read voraciously (exactly what he wanted); at fifteen,
as he listened to his Duke Ellington records, Tom devoured Hemingway,
Joyce, Lawrence, Waugh, Celine, Gide. He delighted in escaping from
Oakham during holidays to tramp alone through Germany or Italy, taking

only a rucksack filled with delicious, avant-garde books. Tom spent his summers with his American grandparents—seeking to avoid any supervision and to discover whatever adventures New York could offer, amorous or otherwise.

Thomas Merton's father died from a brain tumor when the boy was sixteen. That humiliating death was a bewildering experience for Tom. The son genuinely loved his father, whom he regarded as "a man with a wonderful mind and a great talent and a great heart." At first Tom was listless, but soon he returned to his self-centered round of activities:

> The death of my father left me sad and depressed for a couple of months. But that eventually wore away. And when it did, I found myself completely stripped of everything that impeded the movement of my own will to do as it pleased. I imagined that I was free. And it would take me five or six years to discover what a frightful captivity I had got myself into. It was in this year [1931], too, that the hard crust of my dry soul finally squeezed out all the last traces of religion that had ever been in it.[9]

The death of his father was a watershed for the youthful Tom. His most significant tie was cut; the boy felt himself possessed of an uninhibited freedom, whose exercise was a form of worshipping his "own stupid will." Merton described it this way:

> And so I became the complete twentieth-century man. I now belonged to the world in which I lived. I became a true citizen of my own disgusting century: the century of poison gas and atomic bombs. A man living on the doorsill of the Apocalypse, a man with veins full of poison, living in death.[10]

During the next few years, Tom not only pursued his literary tastes but also became concerned about social issues. He began to fancy himself a great political rebel and grew intellectually interested in communism. He also developed a fascination for Freud, whose sexual theories allowed Tom to justify his promiscuity to himself. At eighteen, he entered Cambridge to read modern languages. His guardian advised him to prepare for a diplomatic career, but Tom envisioned himself becoming a journalist and novelist.

The year at Cambridge was a disaster. Tom was often drunk and depressed, thanks to stormy love affairs or the brooding atmosphere of an unsettled Europe in 1933. Some of his friends were expelled from school; one committed suicide. Tom Merton was utterly disgusted with Cambridge, with life—most of all, with himself. He later admitted that the only good thing that happened that year was reading Dante, even though he could appreciate only the *Commedia's* esthetic value, not its moral implications. Merton described himself at that time:

> I was armored and locked in within my own defectible and blinded self by
> seven layers of imperviousness, the capital sins which only the fires of Purga-
> tory or of Divine Love (they are about the same) can burn away. But now I
> was free to keep away from the attack of those flames merely by averting
> my will from them: and it was by now permanently and habitually turned
> away and immunized. I had done all that I could to make my heart untouchable
> by charity and had fortified it, as I hoped, impregnably in my own impenetrable
> selfishness.[11]

Word of Tom's disreputable conduct reached his guardian, who suggested that he cool his heels for a while with his grandparents in America.
Merton took the advice and sailed from England in November 1934.
Rumors of war were raging throughout Europe. Tom Merton was upset
about leaving someone with whom he was emotionally involved. The
writer of *The Seven Storey Mountain* looked back on that crossing of the
Atlantic as the beginning of his real journey into the unknown, and addressed a prayer to the Mother of God:

> I was not sure where I was going, and I could not see what I would do
> when I got to New York. But you saw further and clearer than I, and you
> opened the seas before my ship, whose track led me across the waters to a
> place I had never dreamed of, and which you were even then preparing for
> me to be my rescue and my shelter and my home. And when I thought
> there was no God and no love and no mercy, you were leading me all the
> while without my knowing anything about it, to the house that would hide
> me in the secret of His Face.[12]

During that same crossing, Merton underwent a change. He called
it a "conversion," although "it was not the right conversion." He was
becoming a communist. Reflecting on that episode, Merton said, "I suppose, my Communism was about as mature as my face—as the sour,
perplexed, English face in the photo on my quota card. However, as far
as I know, this was about as sincere and complete a step to moral conversion as I was then able to make."[13] While Merton's interest in social
revolution, indeed in Marxism, was to last throughout his life, this involvement with communism was hardly more than a romantic flirtation
lasting but a short time while he was in college.

Thomas Merton became an undergraduate at Columbia University
in 1934. From the first, he loved the place and the people he encountered
there. "Compared with Cambridge, this big sooty factory was full of
light and fresh air. There was a kind of genuine intellectual vitality in
the air—at least relatively speaking."[14] Merton had the good fortune to
get into—quite by accident—Mark Van Doren's course on Shakespeare.
Merton said that it "was the best course I ever had at college. . . . It

was the only place where I ever heard anything really sensible said about any of the things that were really fundamental—life, death, time, love, sorrow, fear, wisdom, suffering, eternity."[15] The non-Catholic Van Doren would become a profound spiritual influence on Merton and remain a life-long friend.

Merton pledged a fraternity, but his real friends came from the literary, arty set of budding intellectuals who inhabited the "Fourth Floor" of John Jay Hall where all the offices of the student publications were located. Here was the environment young Thomas Merton loved: noisy, seething with frenetic activity, filled with passionate commitment to various causes, bursting with vitality and zany projects. "The campus was supposed to be, in that year, in a state of 'intellectual ferment.' Everybody felt and even said that there was an unusual number of brilliant and original minds in the college."[16] Merton was one of them. And he was right at home with his new friends in that set: Bob Lax, Ed Rice, Bob Giroux, Bob Gibney. They lived a fast-paced, exotic, overstimulated existence, trying every experience to get grist for their literary mills. Merton had his share of hangovers and romantic entanglements. One day he collapsed from exhaustion. "I suppose it was a sort of nervous breakdown. In connection with it I developed gastritis," Merton wrote, "and thought I was beginning to get a stomach ulcer."[17] But this collapse proved to be a turning point. "I had come very far, to find myself in this blind-alley. . . . And it was my defeat that was to be the occasion of my rescue."[18]

From that point in 1936, events moved rather rapidly to alter profoundly Thomas Merton's life. By chance, he discovered Etienne Gilson's *The Spirit of Medieval Philosophy,* a book that introduced him to the first intellectually respectable concept of God he had ever encountered. Merton was very impressed. Then he came in touch with Aldous Huxley's *Ends and Means,* an eclectic book on asceticism and mysticism that opened up a new world for Merton, because it argued that "we were using the means that precisely made good ends impossible to attain: war, violence, reprisals, rapacity." Thomas Merton was very personally touched by Huxley's insistence that the reason it was impossible for moderns to use proper means was that "men were immersed in the material and animal urges of an element in their nature which was blind and crude and unspiritual."[19] Merton's reading patterns began to change. The things he now wanted to talk about were something quite new to him: God, the reality of the human spirit, the search for truth, the meaning of life.

Merton finished college and immediately entered the graduate English program. He decided on William Blake as a topic for his master's thesis. Studying Blake sensitized Merton to the possibilities of a spiritual vision.

By the end of the summer of 1938, Merton could say that he had become "conscious of the fact that the only way to live was to live in a world that was charged with the presence and reality of God."[20] Merton went on to read some spiritual classics and various Catholic books, started attending Mass in Corpus Christi Church, and talked to his friends about Catholicism. In September, while reading a life of Hopkins, the great Jesuit poet, Merton went through his conversion experience:

> I took up the book about Gerard Manley Hopkins. The chapter told of Hopkins at Balliol, at Oxford. He was thinking of becoming a Catholic. . . .
>
> All of a sudden something began to stir within me, something began to push me, to prompt me. It was a movement that spoke like a voice.
>
> "What are you waiting for?" it said. "Why are you sitting here? Why do you still hesitate? You know what you ought to do? Why don't you do it?"[21]

He did it. Thomas Merton took instructions and was baptized into the Catholic Church on November 16, 1938.

The Journey to Gethsemani

Following his conversion, Merton experienced the deepest peace and happiness he had ever known. But within a year he entered on a period of moral confusion and self-doubt about what for him was God's will. The autobiographer described that experience as a journey into the unknown:

> I had come, like the Jews, through the Red Sea of Baptism. I was entering into a desert . . . where I would have a chance to give God great glory by simply trusting and obeying Him, and walking in the way that was not according to my own nature and my own judgment. And it would lead to a land I could not imagine or understand.[22]

This time of painful testing would terminate only with Thomas Merton's decision—two years in the making—to enter the Trappist monastery of Gethsemani in December 1941. Merton summed up what was really going on during that time: "I had to be led by a way that I could not understand, and I had to follow a path that was beyond my own choosing."[23]

In *The Seven Storey Mountain,* Merton carefully charted every step of his journey to Gethsemani. The event that set him on that path took place in September 1939. After a night of wandering around Greenwich Village with his friends, Tom Merton found himself overtaken with a startling thought: "While we were sitting there on the floor playing records and eating this breakfast the idea came to me: 'I am going to be a priest.' " He was unable to turn away from this new awareness, which "was a strong and sweet and deep and insistent attraction that suddenly made itself felt." From the beginning, Merton realized that this was no fleeting romantic urge nor "a reaction of especially strong disgust at being so tired and so uninterested in this life I was still leading." Rather, he intuitively grasped that this idea about his becoming a priest "was something in the order of conscience, a new and profound and clear sense that this was what I really ought to do."[24] Merton spent the whole day walking alone and trying to take in what was happening to him. That evening he went into a church in Greenwich Village while Benediction was going on:

> I fixed my eyes on the monstrance, on the white Host.
>
> And then it suddenly became clear to me that my whole life was a crisis. For more than I could imagine or understand or conceive was now hanging upon a word—a decision of mine. . . .
>
> I looked straight at the Host, and I knew, now, Who it was that I was looking at, and I said:
>
> "Yes, I want to be a priest, with all my heart I want it. If it is Your will, make me a priest—make me a priest."[25]

This account from *The Seven Storey Mountain* is significant because it incorporates all the elements that form a pattern in Merton's experience of responding to God's call to embark on that most fundamental of this man's journeys into the unknown, his monastic vocation. There is a dawning awareness of a gratuitous invitation; that engenders a crisis of doubt; the crisis is resolved when vague desire becomes conviction; and decision brings a liberation and releases in Merton the power to act.

The next episode that seems particularly important at this time in Merton's life is his trip to Cuba in the spring of 1940. While attending Mass in a Havana church, Merton underwent a profoundly transforming inner event that he described as both "ordinary" and yet utterly extraordinary. Hearing the children shout "Creo en Dios" (I believe in God) at the Consecration, Merton said "there formed in my mind an awareness, an understanding, a realization of what had just taken place." In richly metaphorical language reminiscent of the mystics, he described this sudden awareness of God as a "thunderclap," a "light that was so bright it had no relation to any visible light and so profound and so intimate that it seemed like a neutralization of every lesser experience."[26] He obviously regarded this as a first "ecstatic" encounter, his initial step on the mystical path. Characteristically, Merton stressed the experiential, not intellectual, nature of his realization, and pointed up the long-range implications rather than the immediate psychological effects.

The space and detail that the writer of *The Seven Storey Mountain* gives to the overall process culminating in his decision to enter Gethsemani are clear indications of the importance Merton attached to it. Everything suggests that he regarded the period between his baptism and becoming a Trappist as his second conversion—one that concretized, validated, and made existentially effective the promise of the first. The very structure of the autobiography points to this as the decisive sequence of experiences.

Before Merton was able to make such a decision, however, he had to go through a very dark phase of the journey. Once having chosen to seek the priesthood, Merton thought he would become a Franciscan. He was preparing to enter the novitiate when he had a very unsettling experience that undermined his resolve. While reading the Book of Job, suddenly he felt "something deep and disturbing . . . something personal" in the Lord's accusations against Job. At that moment, Merton became conscious that something was disrupting his now familiar mode of thinking of himself as one called to the priesthood and possessed of the requisite qualities. All he could grasp now was that the new understanding of himself to which his religious conversion had brought him was being threatened. He had, the autobiographer asserted, gotten sidetracked from the arduous journey by envisioning himself as a Franciscan—a life that was utterly compatible with his natural romantic inclinations. "I had fallen asleep in my sweet security. I was living as if God only existed to do me temporal favors."[27]

Thus the time of Merton's spiritual childhood and make-believe journey was abruptly ended. Now he would have to make a thoroughgoing reassessment of himself. Deprived of the supports he had come to take for granted and disabused of a facile self-image, Merton experienced himself as "once more out in the cold and naked and alone." The expressions he used to describe this painful period from the late summer of 1940 until December 1941 play on the journey theme. The question God asked about his vocation had thrust Merton "into the darkness of this cold solitude." When he was alone and in that darkness, however, he began to see: "I suddenly remembered who I was, who I had been." And this seeing that was a remembering initiated a search that became a journey to an unknown destination. On the short trip back to New York City from the country where he had been vacationing, Merton said "It seemed like a long, long journey as the train crawled along the green valleys." Once more in his life he felt himself en route, without a dwelling place. Watching a boy being called home by his mother, Merton remarked poignantly, "I became vaguely aware of my own homelessness."[28]

Thomas Merton immediately went to tell his Franciscan counselor the whole story of his sinful past. From the young convert's present perspective, his past appeared sordid. Indeed, that was too negative an evaluation of his behavior; nonetheless, Merton's previous life had certainly been different from that of the ordinary candidate for the Franciscan novitiate! Tom had not deliberately concealed his story, but it had seemed unnecessary to go into details about the sins of which he had repented. Now, however, he told everything, and was advised to forget about entering the order. He accepted the demolition of his cherished dream. Then he made another decision. Purchasing a set of breviaries, he resolved to "try to live in the world as if I were a monk in a monastery."[29] There was no way back for him now. Merton had to go forward alone and in the dark, finding a way uniquely his. He described his recognition of this situation in the language of the upward journey: "It was difficult and uncertain business, and I was starting again to make a long and arduous climb, alone, and from what seemed to be a great depth."[30]

In the spring, the idea came to Merton to make a retreat during Holy Week at Gethsemani, the monastery that Dan Walsh liked so much. Tom had taken a course in Scholastic philosophy from Walsh, a visiting professor at Columbia, who was a fervent and knowledgeable Catholic. Merton had gone to him for advice about religious orders when he first had the idea of becoming a priest. Walsh had then suggested the Trappists, but Merton thought that such an austere life was too much for him. He felt that the Franciscans would be more to his measure. Now Tom remembered Walsh's description of Gethsemani and thought that would be the ideal place for his retreat. Merton wrote and received word to come. At the same time, he got a notice from his draft board. It was a coincidence that had some important implications for him. Precisely at the point when Merton was to have a taste of the life that represented to him the firmest basis for any peace, he would be forced to think through his own position regarding war and take a stance.

When he took that first journey to Gethsemani, Thomas Merton had come a long way since his baptism in knowing who he was and what he wanted from life. Everything at the monastery communicated peace and spoke of God to him. He felt a profound desire to embrace this life, although there was still a trace of fear that should he pursue that desire he would be hopelessly disappointed again. Nonetheless, he was impelled beyond fear: "There was something in my bones that told me that I ought to find out whether my intense desire to lead this kind of life in some monastery were an illusion."[31] By the time he finished the retreat, Merton was at least inchoately aware that he belonged at Gethsemani and would end up there.

But during the summer and fall of 1941 Thomas Merton would have to struggle through one more serious conflict before he could recognize with conviction his vocation to the Cistercian life. It was the type of conflict that only somebody already along the way of transformation experiences: one between two genuine values. While Merton's attraction to Gethsemani grew, he now felt the pull to serve Christ in the poor and down-trodden humanity of Harlem. He was impressed by Baroness Catherine de Hueck, the Russian emigrée who had fled from communism and was dedicated to work for justice among blacks in New York City. She came to speak at St. Bonaventure's University in upstate New York while Merton was teaching there, and her message regarding the social responsibility of Catholics toward the poor, especially black people in America, moved him deeply. He began going into the city on weekends to do volunteer service with her at Friendship House in Harlem.

Merton resisted the urge to give himself full time to the work in Harlem, feeling at that time that he should be writing. The Baroness de Hueck encouraged him and wrote to Merton using his favorite metaphor of travel: "Go on. You are on the right path. Keep on writing. Love God, pray to Him more. . . . You have arisen and started on the journey that seeks Him. You have begun to travel that road that will lead you to sell all and buy the pearl of great price."³² It was the baroness, in fact, who eventually asked the questions that triggered events leading to Merton's full acknowledgment that he belonged to Gethsemani: when was he coming to Harlem for good, and was he thinking about becoming a priest? Merton replied that he had no vocation. The next day he agreed that at the end of the semester he would leave St. Bonaventure's and go to Friendship House for good.

Within the next few days, however, several other people asked if Merton were thinking about the priesthood. This question precipitated a dramatic conflict that was Thomas Merton's last crisis of resistance. He was torn, he later wrote, between the vivid conviction that "the time has come for me to go and be a Trappist," and his fear that he was not called to that life; "in the way, stood hesitation: that old business."³³

The decisive scene took place in a garden—not unlike the setting of Augustine's conversion. Merton found himself running literally in all directions but psychically immobilized. He was suspended over the chasm between knowing what he should do and having the facility to do it. Thomas Merton did not yet possess the strength to make the leap of decision. But just then there occurred what we might call a redemption through imagination. Augustine, on the brink of surrendering the last tie that held back his conversion—sexual attachment—had experienced a fantasy in which continence was personified as a chaste, beautiful woman beckoning him to cross the barrier that kept him from God.[34] Merton, paralyzed by a conflict between negative feelings of unworthiness about himself and the strong, positive attraction of his will to monastic life, heard a bell summoning him to Gethsemani. The symbol arose in his consciousness and released in him the power to act. He described that inner event like this:

> Suddenly . . . in my imagination, I started to hear the great bell of Gethsemani ringing in the night . . . as if it were just behind the first hill. The impression made me breathless, and I had to think twice to realize that it was only in my imagination that I was hearing the bell of the Trappist Abbey ringing in the dark.

Merton interpreted this fantasy as a signal. "The bell seemed to be telling me where I belonged—as if it were calling me home."[35] The symbol, welling up from his feelings, allowed Merton to recognize and accept his true vocation. As an image, it could be the bearer of a message concerning himself to himself; it was a clarion waking him out of illusion and sending him on his journey into the unknown. Henceforth, his affectivity could be used to reinforce decision, rather than thwart it. Now Merton would be able to say that all his doubts about his vocation "had been mostly shadows,"[36] and act accordingly.

In less than a week, Merton was on the train to Gethsemani. "This journey, this transition from the world to a new life was like flying through some strange new element—as if I were in the stratosphere. And yet I was on the familiar earth."[37] The difference was in himself. "I was free. I had recovered my liberty. I belonged to God, not to myself."[38]

The author of *The Seven Storey Mountain,* writing with several years of experience behind him, drew his autobiography to a close by returning to the metaphor of his life as a journey into the unknown:

> The life of each one in this abbey is part of a mystery. . . .
> In one sense we are always travelling, and travelling as if we did not know where we were going.
> In another sense we have already arrived.
> We cannot arrive at the perfect possession of God in this life, and that is why we are travelling and in darkness. But we already possess Him by grace, and therefore in that sense we have arrived and are dwelling in the light.
> But oh! How far have I to go to find You in Whom I have already arrived![39]

Indeed, Merton would have to go far in the next few years by struggling with the tensions created in his contemplative life by the very success of *The Seven Storey Mountain*. He ended his autobiography with a passage that projected the voice of God addressing the writer:

> "I will give you what you desire. I will lead you into solitude. I will lead you by the way that you cannot possibly understand, because I want it to be the quickest way. . . .
>
> "You will have gifts, and they will break you with their burden."[40]

Merton had been gifted with exceptional talent as a writer. By temperament and training writing was, so to speak, his natural vocation. But he had also received the gift of a special call to the life of solitude and contemplation. He would feel the burden of these gifts as they came into conflict when the reception of his autobiography made Thomas Merton into a famous writer.

A Voyage Inside the Whale

Merton's journal of the years between 1946 and 1952, *The Sign of Jonas*, was taken up with the paradox of being a monk and writer.

> The sign Jesus promised to the generation that did not understand Him was the "sign of Jonas the prophet"—that is, the sign of His own resurrection. The life of every monk, of every priest, of every Christian is signed with the *Sign of Jonas*, because we all live by the power of Christ's resurrection. But I feel that my own life is especially sealed with this great sign, which baptism and monastic profession and priestly ordination have burned into the roots of my being, because like Jonas himself I find myself traveling toward my destiny in the belly of a paradox.[41]

Right from the start of this book, Merton alerts us to the journey theme. The journal recounts an adventure story—the adventure of a soul pulled in seemingly contradictory directions. "Like the prophet Jonas, whom God ordered to go to Niveveh, I found myself with an almost uncontrollable desire to go in the opposite direction. God pointed one way and my 'ideals' pointed in the other."[42] Merton wanted ever more solitude and interior stillness, but found himself in the midst of endless activity. In 1947, he had been peacefully working on the autobiography and a history of the Cistercian Order while preparing to take solemn vows. But then came 1948. Thomas Merton said that "the publication of *The Seven Storey Mountain* at the end of the summer brought a change in my whole life."[43]

Dom Frederic was the Abbot who, Merton acknowledged, had formed and shaped his whole monastic identity by deciding he should write books. For Merton to say that the Abbot had launched him on a path of perpetual tensions, however, was not to blame his religious superior. Although Merton wrote under obedience, he well knew that it was his own inner compulsions that pushed him to ceaseless intellectual and literary activity. And he was sufficiently self-aware to appreciate Dom Frederic's astuteness in recognizing that Thomas Merton simply had to have an appropriate outlet for all that creative energy.

Already, in *The Seven Storey Mountain,* Merton had recognized the problem that his propensity to write created for him as a contemplative. He characterized the situation in negative terms:

> There was this shadow, this double, this writer who had followed me into the cloister. He is still on my track. He rides my shoulders sometimes like the old man of the sea. I cannot lose him. He still wears the name of Thomas Merton. Is it the name of an enemy?[44]

In *The Sign of Jonas,* the writer appeared increasingly the monk's enemy. By late 1948, Merton remarked that his life had begun to change more than he realized. "I did not at once become aware that my writing, which had once been a source of imaginary problems, was now becoming a real problem and that the problem was reaching a crisis."[45]

In Lent of 1949, Merton found himself with a new kind of problem: he was utterly paralyzed and unable to write at all as he attempted his first theological book, *The Ascent to Truth.* He bogged down in the effort to elucidate rationally the classic theological account of the soul's mystical ascent. While Merton was struggling mightily to produce this book, his fan mail from the autobiography increased enormously, and he became involved in a demanding correspondence. In the journal, he commented that "a deep spiritual reaction against all this involvement occurred when I was ordained deacon."[46]

All else paled, however, before Thomas Merton's ordination on May 26, 1949. That event was a real landmark on his journey into the unknown. He expressed its meaning thus: "My priestly ordination was, I felt, the one great secret for which I had been born."[47] Now Father Louis, he described the ecstatic happiness of the days that followed and rejoiced in the peaceful summer after ordination. Then he observed that "Ordination is only the beginning of a journey, not its end. The beginning was easy and pleasant. But when summer was over the serious business of being a priest began."[48] By the fall of 1949, Merton was into a dry, dark period that lasted through most of 1950.

Merton characterized this change as "a sort of slow, submarine earthquake which produced strange commotions on the visible, psychological surface of my life." Unable to write until December 1950, suddenly

Thomas discovered "completely new moral resources, a spring of new life, a peace and happiness that I had never known before and which subsisted in the face of nameless, interior terror."[49] This episode bears the marks of a classic purification, which, when terminated, opens out into an altered awareness and previously unrealized joy. Merton had reached a new plateau in the spiritual quest. And he came away from the crisis with more than a renewal of his creative powers. His whole understanding of the solitary vocation had been affected. "And now, for the first time," he said, "I began to know what it means to be alone."[50]

One of the consequences of this painful period of 1949–1950 was Merton's new insight into the meaning of his writing. Although still desiring to escape from so much activity, he realized that writing could be his means for discovering solitude. Having just signed a long-term contract to do four books, he wrote in his journal with a certain confidence, as well as resignation:

> That probably means the final renouncement forever of any dream of a hermit-age. God will prepare for me His own hermitage for my last days, and mean-while my work is my hermitage because it is *writing* that helps me most of all to be a solitary and a contemplative here at Gethsemani.[51]

That period from 1950 to 1952 Merton described as one "in which many more things happened and in which I had less time to write."[52] By far the most consequential of those things was Merton's appointment as Master of Scholastics in May 1951. Now he had to take charge of the recently professed young monks, directing their spiritual growth and supervising their programs of study. These new responsibilities entailed much work and considerable organization of the externals of his life. But the real significance of the appointment was the change the monk said it brought about in his understanding of solitude. Thomas Merton came to see that the kind of work he had feared as interfering with solitude was "the only true path to solitude." That path had led him into a new desert: "The name of it is compassion."[53] With this deepened realization of the implications of solitude for him, Merton felt as if he were "beginning all over again to be a Cistercian" and affirmed: "Thus I stand on the threshold of a new existence."[54]

The Sign of Jonas, whose prologue was called "Journey to Nineveh," closed with an epilogue alluding to another symbolic journey into the unknown. In "Fire Watch, July 4, 1952," Merton has us accompany him on rounds of the dark monastery while he takes his turn as night watch-man. Walking through the deep stillness of Gethsemani when the monks are asleep occasions a journey into his memory to touch what Merton's years in this community have meant:

It was this silence, this darkness, this emptiness that I walked into with Brother Matthew eleven years ago this spring. This is the house that seemed to have been built to be remote from everything, to have forgotten all cities, to be absorbed in the eternal years. But this recovered innocence has nothing reassuring about it. The very silence is a reproach. The emptiness itself is my most terrible question. . . .

With my feet on the floor I waxed when I was a postulant, I ask these useless questions. With my hand on the key by the door to the tribune, where I first heard the monks chanting the psalms, I do not wait for an answer, because I have begun to realize You never answer when I expect.[55]

Merton recalls what he has learned during his time in the monastery, but he not only goes back to the past. The epilogue is an affirmation of the present. It expresses Thomas Merton's conviction that his life is, and will continue to be, a journey into the unknown. The more he knows of God and the spiritual life, the more he appreciates that he is a pilgrim making his way through the infinite realms of mystery:

Although I see the stars, I no longer pretend to know them. Although I have walked in those woods, how can I claim to love them? One by one I shall forget the names of individual things.

You, Who sleep in my breast, are not met with words, but in the emergence of life within life and of wisdom within wisdom. You are found in communion: Thou in me and I in Thee and Thou in them and they in me: dispossession within dispossession, dispassion within dispassion, emptiness within emptiness, freedom within freedom. I am alone. Thou art alone. The Father and I are One.[56]

Merton's next journal, *Conjectures of a Guilty Bystander* (1966), included materials taken from notebooks he kept from 1956 through 1965. That means there was an autobiographical blank from 1952, when *The Sign of Jonas* ended, until 1956. In a few scattered places, Merton spoke of the events of these years, but he really told us very little. In the preface for an anthology of his writings, Merton wrote, long after the fact, that his appointment as Master of Scholastics in 1951 "entailed a fair amount of work preparing conferences and classes." He also mentioned that in 1955 he was made Master of Choir Novices, "an office involving considerable work and responsibility. No writing of any account was done in 1956, but after that it was possible to produce short books or collections of essays, and some poetry."[57]

There was an incident in Merton's life at this time that not only has a bearing on the journal silence of these years but that also deeply affected his understanding of the direction his interior journey should take. In 1956, on a rare trip outside the monastery, Merton attended a conference at St. John's, Collegeville, Minnesota, in the company of his

Abbot and another monk. While there Thomas Merton met and had long discussions with Dr. Gregory Zilboorg, a well-known Catholic psychiatrist who also was at the meeting. Zilboorg apparently gave Merton a warning concerning tendencies the doctor had observed in his writings. The psychiatrist said that Merton was in danger of falling into "verbalogical" writing: substituting words for reality; that his words must, rather, become incarnate. Merton never mentioned in his published writing this meeting with Zilboorg. John Howard Griffin, Merton's biographer, who has access to his private notebooks, says that the episode was significant for the monk, who commented in one of those notebooks that where he was most verbalogical was in his writing on religion.[58]

Something else that might account for the journal silence of 1952–1956 is Merton's problem concerning his desire for more physical solitude and what that implied for his relationship to Gethsemani. That desire, and the personal struggle it entailed, was nothing new, of course.[59] The longing for solitude that had been present from the beginning of Thomas Merton's life as a Trappist seemed destined to persist, even to intensify. Although in 1951 he was enthusiastic about the prospects of his appointment as Master of Scholastics for enlarging and enhancing his understanding of solitude, one readily suspects that the burdens of spiritual direction and teaching would soon produce a crisis in a man of Merton's temperament and inclinations.

Merton's desire for solitude manifested itself in two different inclinations. Sometimes he expressed a wish to transfer to an eremitical order such as the Carthusians or the Camaldolese; at other times, he wanted to build a hermitage of his own somewhere on the grounds of Gethsemani, which would allow him still to share in the Trappist life. That Merton was taken up with these concerns is at least indirectly attested to by various writings concurrent with this 1952–1956 period of journal silence.[60] The journey theme appears in Merton's treatment of the monastic life—and especially its eremitical form—as a sojourn in the desert and a return to paradise.[61]

Peregrinations of a Bystander

Put together from Merton's notebooks covering 1956 to 1965, *Conjectures of a Guilty Bystander* once again picks up Merton's story, although the chronological sequence of this journal is not straightforward. The book reflects a man who has been and continues to be on a journey. It is the writing of someone who experiences changing perspectives and is traveling along a new route.

Merton had become Master of Novices in 1955. Within a few years, in spite of increased responsibilities in the monastery, he was venturing into areas such as Chinese philosophy and nuclear war. Merton claimed that the essays written in the late 1950s were the ones most significant to him:

> Maybe one reason for this is that, to me at least, they represent a successful attempt to escape the limitations that I inevitably created for myself with *The Seven Storey Mountain,* a refusal to be content with the artificial public image which this autobiography created.[62]

If those essays began to undermine Merton's "artificial public image," *Conjectures* displaced it. The writer of this journal was convinced that "a man is known better by his questions than by his answers," and the concerns he expressed were those "appropriate to an age of transition and crisis, of war and racial conflict, of technology and expansion."[63] *Conjectures* revealed a monk much more explicitly related to life outside of Gethsemani.

Merton paid considerable attention to an experience on a street corner in Louisville in 1957 or 1958, when he felt he had awakened from a "dream of separateness, of spurious self-isolation in a special world, the world of renunciation and supposed holiness." He was enabled to see with startling clarity that, although monks are "out of the world," they are still "in the same world as everybody else, the world of the bomb, the world of race hatred, the world of technology, the world of mass media, big business, revolution, and all the rest." (This listing names almost all the social problems with which Merton henceforth would be preoccupied.) His narrative of the incident ends with a prayer of gratitude: "Thank God, thank God that I *am* like other men, that I am only a man among others." Then Merton reflects on what is implied in that awareness, astounded that for sixteen or seventeen years he has been taking seriously "this pure illusion that is implicit in so much of our monastic thinking."[64] Everything about the way he narrates the episode indicates that Merton regarded it as crucial. This insight appears to mark a real turning point on his journey. Certainly his comments on social and political crises in *Conjectures* would confirm that, from the middle and late 1950s onward, Thomas Merton was deeply concerned with the problems of the contemporary world.

Merton's awakened consciousness of the world outside the monastery, however, in no way lessened his interest in the task of being Novice Master. He commented in *Conjectures* that there is an intimate connection between his involvement with the novices and his sense of responsibility to the world. Thinking over his relationships with the novices, Merton remarked how good it was to have loved and been loved by them "with such simplicity and sincerity, within our ordinary limitation, without nonsense, without flattery, without sentimentality, and without getting in one another's business." Merton made an important link between this work in the community and his larger concerns: "From this experience one can, after all, recover hope for the other dimension of man's life: the political."[65] Thus Thomas Merton's involvement both within and outside the monastery during these years was integrally related in his mind.

His horizons were also broadening in other ways as he journeyed into new intellectual and spiritual territory. In 1959, Merton sent a copy of his book on the Desert Fathers to the well-known Buddhist scholar, D. T. Suzuki, and an extended exchange of views between them took place. This marked the beginning of an ongoing dialogue on points of contact in Christian mysticism and the Zen tradition.[66]

In the early 1960s, then, the monk who called himself a "bystander" was traveling on many fronts, apparently at peace. As one of Merton's fellow monks at Gethsemani remarked, "In spite of his steady complaints about being too busy with writing, direction, and teaching it was evident that he enjoyed all three."[67] The old hankering for solitude persisted but now would begin to find fulfillment. Merton secured permission to make his dream for a hermitage at Gethsemani into brick and mortar—rather, cement block. The simple building was constructed gradually and Merton moved into it by degrees over nearly a five-year period.

Much of the material that went into *Conjectures* was written or edited in the hermitage; it was here that Merton developed that "personal version of the world of the 1960s"[68] that the book articulated. And the posture of a "guilty bystander" was consciously assumed, reflected on, and reckoned with in the deep silence of the little building that had started out to be a place for ecumenical gatherings and ended up as Merton's precious retreat.

Journal entries were not only typical Merton-style reflections on people, nature, and books, but also musings on various world events. These looked different from the vantage point of the hermitage. On his forty-sixth birthday (January 31, 1961), Merton remarked with marvelous irony the "feat" of technology that put an ape into space. The race in space was one journey for which Merton had nothing but contempt. Even more, he continually lamented the nuclear buildup in 1962, experiencing the frustration of being unable to do anything. Yet Merton could still say, "Even though one may not be able to halt the race toward death, one must nevertheless choose life, and the things that favor life."[69]

In the early 1960s, Thomas Merton remained in his hermitage as much as possible and chose life—listening to woodpeckers, or reading Barth, Bonhoeffer, and Brazilian poets (among countless other writers). He recorded the dreams that revealed his life, even one that he took as a premonition of death. "I think sometimes that I may soon die," he commented after describing a dream in which he was walking "toward the center" of a great city.[70] Of course, choosing life in such a solitary setting entailed facing death more directly. Merton recalled "the flow of events" and thought of his brother's death at sea twenty years earlier.[71] And he took notice of changes in his "own inner climate," the changes that inevitably pose the questions of one's own death. "I must begin to face the deepest of all decisions," he wrote, "the 'answer of death'—*the acceptance of the death sentence*—and with joy, because of the victory of Christ."[72] Never one to be morbid, as time passed Merton reminded himself of the task that lay ahead and of his unfinished journey into the unknown:

> So I, too, come to a turning point of some sort, not knowing yet what it is. More than the nice thought about Chartres and the eternal banquet. More serious. But still a matter of coming up out of Egypt into my own country. I have work to do: to get free within myself, to work my way out of the cords and habits of thought, the garments of skins (as if I could do that by myself). But one must want to begin. Even if the thought of it comes clothed in a good coat of nonsense and imagination.
>
> Meanwhile there is work to be done in the Church: and we are beginning a novena before the first session of the Second Vatican Council.[73]

The work that Merton took on in the hermitage—getting free within himself—certainly included social concerns. During these years, Thomas Merton was not indulging in what he disparagingly termed "pure soliloquy." Rather, he was excercising his conviction that "what a man truly is can be discovered only through his self-awareness in a living and actual world."[74] That living and actual world, for Merton, consisted of the social and political situation outside, as well as his responsibility to the novices. He was actively implicated in the former by the large number of articles he was writing during the early 1960s on war, race, and poverty. Although Merton may not have been participating personally in the ban-the-bomb marches or sit-in demonstrations of the time, he was deeply engaged in social issues. That engagement, however, was always within the context of his monastic life, which, as the middle of the decade approached, was becoming increasingly more solitary.

Around the time he was editing *Conjectures,* Merton wrote an important autobiographical piece as a preface to the Japanese edition of *The Seven Storey Mountain.* He said that the occasion for such a preface invited reflection on the nearly twenty years since the autobiography had been written. The author would let the story stand—but had the author changed? "I have never for a moment thought of changing the definitive decisions undertaken in the course of my life: to be a Christian, to be a monk, to be a priest," he declared. Thomas Merton insisted that his decision to renounce modern society had to be reaffirmed many times and "has finally become irrevocable." But he indicated that the assumptions behind that decision had changed in many ways.[75] Commenting on the rumors about his leaving the monastery that were always circulating, Merton asserted, "I am still in the monastery and intend to stay there." And then Merton expressed the sentiment that links writings such as this with *Conjectures* and reveals the direction in which his life was moving:

> If I have ever had any desire for change, it has been for a more solitary, more "monastic" way. But precisely because of this it can be said that I am in some sense everywhere. My monastery is not a home. It is not a place where I am rooted and established on earth. It is not an environment in which I become aware of myself as an individual, but rather a place in which I disappear from the world as an object of interest in order to be everywhere in it by hiddenness and compassion.[76]

In the middle 1960s, Merton would be in process of "disappearing" as he lived in the hermitage. Yet, as always, the paradox was evident: this was a time of rich human contacts and significant public utterance. Thomas Merton might say he was disappearing, but he would be conversing as he went!

The years 1964 and 1965 were a time of transition for Merton who, while still Master of Novices at the monastery, was allowed to spend more time in the hermitage.[77] During this time, Merton was mainly seeking solitude. He was, nonetheless, tempted by several invitations to ecumenical meetings and various other conferences. He was seriously interested in a few of them, and he was much chagrined at the Abbot's refusal to let him attend. Merton appeared ambivalent about people coming to the hermitage but clearly delighted in conversations with the many who did. Among them (to mention but a few) were a Polish poet, Jewish rabbis, a concert musician, an archbishop, and the farmer from down the road. Merton eagerly sought news of Vatican Council II, of the Vietnam War, of developments among revolutionary Latin American poets, and of what was happening in other monastic communities undergoing renewal. Generally Merton avoided groups that visited the monastery, although occasionally he did meet them.

One gathering was of marked significance. In November 1964, a group assembled for a retreat centered on the theme Merton called "The Spiritual Roots of Protest." This was a small group of peace movement notables, both Catholic and non-Catholic, whom the monk had collected to reflect on the grounds for religious dissent and commitment. Merton was interested not in formulating any kind of program but in examining the bases for whatever courses of action might be decided on by individuals. He found the experience lively and fruitful, and the discussions made a deep impression on Merton. That the other participants were also much affected is not hard to surmise: among them were the Berrigan brothers and members of what would become the "Cantonsville Nine" and the "Milwaukee Fourteen."[78]

Another meeting of considerable import for Thomas Merton's journey had been held slightly earlier in 1964. In October, a conference of Cistercian Abbots and Novice Masters met at Gethsemani. Merton gave a talk using the resources of his research over the years on the place of hermits in the monastic tradition in general, and the Cistercians in particular. Although he did not exactly win the day, Merton's presentation helped pave the way for his eventual full-time retirement to the hermitage.[79]

But 1964 was, of course, not all talk. Merton was reading (everything from Celtic nature poetry to Karl Jaspers and Jacques Ellul) and writing copiously. He was quietly reflecting, perhaps even more searchingly, now that he was spending more time in the hermitage. In the fall, he began sleeping there from time to time. He noted that in his fiftieth year solitude allowed fewer evasions. Merton wrote of his simple joys—singing and dancing by himself around the hermitage—and of his frustrations, especially some disagreements with the Abbot. Although he frequently commented on aspects of life at Gethsemani he disliked, Thomas Merton clearly saw himself as committed to staying there.

Of all the experiences Merton wrote about in 1964, one dominates the narrative. He took a real journey to New York City to visit D. T. Suzuki. It was the first time he had been there since entering Gethsemani twenty-three years earlier, and his first significant trip out of the monastery since 1956 and the meeting with Zilboorg.

An invitation had come for a private meeting with the Buddhist scholar in June of that year. Merton received permission to go, although his activities were restricted. He stayed on the Columbia campus and was obviously delighted to see the city and his old haunts once more. There were two long talks with the ninety-four-year-old Suzuki, whom Merton found charming in every way. They spoke of Merton's Zen writings, of which the Buddhist highly approved. The two exchanged ancedotes and thoughts on many subjects. Merton reflected later that it was crucially important for him to experience how profound an understanding there was between them, all the more because Merton so admired Suzuki'a writings.[80]

Another kind of journey engendering a different sort of conversation would take place in 1965. In August, Merton was allowed to resign as Master of Novices and live in the hermitage. There he would be free to pursue his reflective dialogue uninterruptedly. Moving into the hermitage made Merton happy, almost giddy with delight. But what comes through his writings immediately after the move is Merton's decided conviction that this is what God wanted him to do and what Thomas Merton *must* do to fulfill his destiny. Although notably excited by the prospects of his new life, Merton was deeply at peace. His whole psyche seemed to relax. He remarked that after only a few weeks of solitude his recurring health problems (stomach disorders and severe skin irritations) had cleared up. By the fall of 1965, Merton's journey had taken him into the profound rest of a truly solitary life.

Although there is no journal material for reference from this point until 1968, it is possible to piece together significant events of these years from various sources, principally Merton's essays. This period of taking up life in the hermitage was not without its problems. The exquisite peace of that first autumn did not last long. In November 1965, a dramatic incident triggered a frightened, almost panicked reaction in Thomas Merton.

He had been associated for some time with various groups that formed the Catholic Peace Fellowship. When a young member of the Catholic Worker staff set himself aflame and died protesting the Vietnam War in front of the United Nations building, Merton became seriously alarmed. He wired the Fellowship to express his fear that "the peace movement in its search for results and passion for improvisation was 'fanning up the war fever rather than abating it.' " Always wary of organized movements, this tragic event supported Merton's worst suspicions that demonstrations would exert a "pathological attraction." His first reaction was to ask that his name be removed from the list of Catholic Peace Fellowship sponsors, but eventually Merton rescinded the request and things were patched up.[82]

In 1966, among other concerns, Merton was very much taken up with Eastern religions, especially Zen. Having finished the book on Chuang Tzu the year before, he was now engaged in putting together the essays for *Mystics and Zen Masters*. His interest in Zen was developing intellectually; more important, living as a solitary allowed him to experience more profoundly what Zen was all about. In the preface to *Mystics,* for instance, Merton said that he was attempting not merely to look at the Eastern traditions from the outside but, more, "to share in the values and experience which they embody."[83] Such experience gave Merton a deep sense of solidarity and brotherhood with Asian monks. Not infrequently, he commented on the affinity he felt with them.

Life in the hermitage also affected Merton's sense of his relationship to those who professed no religious belief. While his own faith continued to develop, Merton came to feel more acutely the situation of the unbeliever. He poignantly expressed his "apologies" for the attitude of Christians—himself included. And Merton stressed his affinities with the unbeliever: "I have a tendency to slip out of my rank among capital B-Believers, and even to edge over a little toward your side. . . . because things sometimes seem to me a little quieter and more thoughtful where you are."[84] His desire for reflective depth, as well as Merton's sense of his mission, was articulated through the journey metaphor in this 1966 essay, "Apologies to an Unbeliever:"

> My own peculiar task in my Church and in my world has been that of the solitary explorer who, instead of jumping on all the latest bandwagons at once, is bound to search the existential depths of faith in its silences, its ambiguities, and in those certainties which lie deeper than the bottom of anxiety. In these depths there are no easy answers, no pat solutions to anything. It is a kind of submarine life in which faith sometimes mysteriously takes on the aspect of doubt when, in fact, one has to doubt and reject conventional and superstitious surrogates that have taken the place of faith.[85]

Merton was obviously wrestling with many difficulties. Among them was the old struggle to live down the image he himself created in his autobiography. That had plagued him for many years, but at this juncture it seems he needed to reaffirm his rejection of what Merton called "a sort of stereotype of the world-denying contemplative." Writing in 1966, he made efforts to demolish that image, which obviously hindered his effectiveness as a prophetic voice: "I want to make clear that I speak not as the author of *The Seven Storey Mountain,* which seemingly a lot of people have read, but as the author of more recent essays and poems which apparently very few people have read." Even more, however, at this time Merton needed to speak to others (and undoubtedly to himself) in "the voice of a self-questioning human person who, like all his brothers, struggles to cope with the turbulent, mysterious, demanding, exciting, frustrating, confused existence."[86]

Thomas Merton was, nonetheless, still more concerned with living than with living down a stereotype that was almost twenty years old.

But around 1966 he was engaged in a deeper search for his own identity. There was more questioning, self-doubt, and personal revision evident in his writing. Perhaps a year in the hermitage had provoked a crisis of some sort of ego disintegration. That would hardly be surprising, given the psychological rigors that sustained solitude necessarily entails. Also, Merton's health was not good at this time. In 1966, he was hospitalized for back surgery.

The next year brought more anguish, although in different forms. What Merton called "the hot summer of sixty-seven," marked by racial explosions in Newark, Detroit, and other American cities, distressed him deeply. Merton acknowledged that, although he had been pessimistic in 1963, then he at least was hopeful that blacks and whites could pool resources and "work together for a radical and creative change in our social structure." By the critical summer of 1967, however, he felt "the time was just about running out," and that the murders of civil rights workers and the event of Watts "were all steps in the direction of hopelessness." He was also weighed down by "the gradual, irreversible escalation in Vietnam," which he felt had much to do with the continuing violence at home.[87] Thus Thomas Merton was very much caught up in the larger crises of his country as he lived in the hermitage and faced his personal trials.

Although he may have weathered certain ordeals, in the middle of 1967 Merton was evidently going through another distressing experience as he pursued his solitary journey. An essay written that August reflects a basic struggle to make sense out of his existence, as well as a certain disillusionment about the possibility of communication. There is a strong tone of anguish over the problems of the contemplative life and a rather blatant sarcasm regarding monastic orders. Even the Pope comes in for some jabs from Merton's pen in an essay that he had been requested by the Holy Father to submit as a message to modern humanity from a contemplative monk. Throughout this piece, Thomas Merton makes intensely personal statements. He says it is true that he came to the monastery in revolt against the confusion of a meaningless world, but then affirms, "I have no right to repudiate the world in a purely negative fashion, because if I do that my flight will have taken me not to truth and to God but to a private, though doubtless pious, illusion." Straightforwardly, Merton expresses his present state of anguished seeking: "When I first became a monk, yes, I was more sure of 'answers.' But as I grow old in the monastic life and advance further into solitude, I become aware that I have only begun to seek the questions."[88] This important article draws to a close with a statement of the problem that a modern person—

Merton himself—experiences: "It is not that we hate God, rather that we hate ourselves." Could "the value of our own self" be realized, there would be a way out. But, Merton insists, that realization only comes through the love of all human beings. "It is the love of my lover, my brother or my child that sees God in me, makes God credible to myself in me."[89] Perhaps Merton was concretely experiencing the pangs of having no lover and no child, or maybe he felt separated from his friends (such as the Berrigan brothers) who were in the front lines of the battle for brotherhood.

Merton was also dissatisfied with institutional practices at Gethsemani, and his persistent difficulties with the Abbot had come to a head by 1967. There were serious communication problems between the monk and his religious superior. The monk often chafed at what he regarded as Dom James Fox's overly tight rein on him. Merton could be caustic in his criticism of the Abbot's policies that he disliked, such as the "big business" cheese industry that largely supported the monastery. More fundamentally, Merton took issue with the Abbot's conception of certain structures of the monastic life, such as enclosure and religious obedience. During this time Merton obviously entertained serious doubts about remaining at Gethsemani. He was considering other possibilities for living the contemplative life to which he felt himself called, possibilities that would entail real journeys to other places. At least the problem with his Abbot was solved late in 1967 when Dom James announced his intended resignation.

The Last Journeys

On January 1, 1968, Father Flavian Burns was elected Abbot of Gethsemani. The most significant year of Thomas Merton's life had an auspicious beginning. The new Abbot had been a student under Merton and became his personal confessor. Merton felt that the man shared his own view of the monastic vocation, was favorably disposed to the hermit life (himself having actually lived it), and personally understood him. With the tragic irony that good fortune sometimes works, it was this superior who gave Merton permission to go on the trip from which he never returned.

Two journeys dominated 1968, although other things were happening to Merton and it was a year of extraordinary literary productivity. In the spring, Merton visited the Trappistine monastery near the California coast and the monastery of Christ in the Desert, a small Benedictine foundation in New Mexico. The second journey in the fall took him back to those two places, also to Alaska, and on to Asia for an extended tour.

Merton's earlier journey began on May 6 with a flight to San Francisco.[90] He spent a week alone on the Pacific shore before going to Our Lady of the Redwoods. He enjoyed enormously his stay with the Trappistine nuns. Then Merton flew to Albuquerque and was driven to the almost inaccessible monastery where two Benedictines and a Trappist hermit lived. Thomas Merton was delighted with the setting of Christ in the Desert, and he was deeply impressed by the primitive form of monastic life he found there. He enjoyed time out in the canyons taking pictures. The Monastery of Christ in the Desert was a place Merton considered as a possibility for spending periods of solitude in the future.

After Merton returned to Gethsemani on May 20, he wrote a long reflection on the trip, calling to mind his most vivid impressions and asking himself where his life should go from this point on. His answer: nowhere. What Merton meant was that he should not determine on a certain way of seeking transformation. Rather, he told himself that he should cultivate leisure, while remaining moderately productive. Above all, he must not make a "project" of conversion—just allow change to come. Go for walks, Thomas Merton counseled himself. Within just a few months, he would take a longer one than he had anticipated.

The trip that the monk embarked on in the fall of 1968 covered far more territory and provided a dramatic contrast to the serenity of the spring venture. Of course, he would keep a journal during his travels. Merton thought of the Asian expedition as his great journey into the unknown. What he did not know was that it would take him beyond earthly existence.

The monk had received some invitations to conferences in Asia scheduled for the fall and early winter, and the new Abbot gave him permission to attend. Shortly before departing, Merton sent a circular letter to his friends. He clearly announced that he had no intention of going anywhere near Vietnam, and that anything he did on the trip would be "absolutely nonpolitical."[91] Later he would describe what he was doing in Asia as "not concerned with talking but with learning and with making contact with important people in the Buddhist monastic field."[92] Merton did, however, give his share of lectures, which helped to pay his way.

En route to the East, he returned to New Mexico, visited Alaska, then made two stops in California: at the Center for the Study of Democratic Institutions in Santa Barbara and at the Trappistine monastery in the Redwoods. Merton was evidently enjoying these settings and the people, but in his letters back to Gethsemani he said that he was impatient for India. He wrote to his secretary requesting items he needed and asked him to dispatch copies of Merton's books to people whom he met along the way. Apparently Merton was concerned about the rumors his trip might start. In one letter to Brother Patrick Hart, he said, "Give my regards to all the gang and I hope there are not too many crazy rumors. Keep telling everyone that I am a monk of Gethsemani and intend to remain one all my days."[93]

Once actually off to Asia, he went first to Calcutta, where he spoke at a meeting of world religious leaders at the Temple of Understanding. Thomas Merton straightforwardly stated where he stood and why he had come:

> I speak as a Western monk who is preeminently concerned with his own monastic calling and dedication. I have left my monastery to come here not just as a research scholar or even as an author (which I also happen to be). I come as a pilgrim who is anxious to obtain not just information, not just "facts" about other monastic traditions, but to drink from the ancient sources of monastic vision and experience.[94]

After another talk in Calcutta to the Conference of Religious of India on the topic of prayer, he went on to Thailand—and to what he considered the really important part of his journey. Going up into the Himalayas, at Dharamsala he made a retreat given over to reading and meditating and meeting Tibetan masters. Then he visited the Dalai Lama and enjoyed three long discussions with him, focused mainly on meditation and higher forms of prayer. Merton made numerous other contacts: Tibetan lay people who practice a special type of contemplation called Dzogtchen, Cambodian Buddhist monks of the Theravada tradition, and representatives of Moslem Sufism. He also went to Darjeeling and met many lamas. While making another retreat near there on a tea plantation, he took photographs of the majestic Mount Kanchenjunga.[95]

The culminating moment of Merton's journey was an experience in Polonnaruwa, an ancient city in central Ceylon. There in a rocky hollow surrounded by trees, he encountered enormous stone figures of two Buddhas, one seated and the other reclining. Merton was alone in the charged atmosphere of the temple ruins: "I am able to approach the Buddhas barefoot and undisturbed, my feet in wet grass, wet sand. Then the silence of the extraordinary faces. The great smiles. Huge and yet subtle. Filled with every possibility, questioning nothing, knowing everything."[96] He stared, transfixed. Something profound happened:

> Looking at these figures I was suddenly, almost forcibly, jerked clean out of the habitual, half tied vision of things, and an inner clearness, clarity, as if

exploding from the rocks themselves, became evident and obvious. . . . The thing about all this is that there is no puzzle, no problem, and really no "mystery." All problems are resolved and everything is clear. The rock, all matter, all life, is charged with dharmakaya . . . everything is emptiness and everything is compassion.[97]

Reflecting on this experience a few days later, Merton accorded it immense significance: "I don't know when in my life I have ever had such a sense of beauty and spiritual validity running together in one aesthetic illumination." He even saw in this event the fulfillment of his journey to the East:

Surely, with . . . Polonnaruwa my Asian pilgrimage has come clear and purified itself. I mean, I know and have seen what I was obscurely looking for. I don't know what else remains but I have now seen and have pierced through the surface and have got beyond the shadow and the disguise.[98]

What remained was but two days in Singapore, then a few more in Bangkok. He wrote home that he missed the quiet of his own hermitage and was hoping for some silence at Rawa Senega, the monastery in Java where he planned to go after the Bangkok conference of Christian monastic leaders.[99] On December 6, in Singapore, Merton noted in his journal that he was uncertain about the future, but knew that "the journey is only begun."[100]

The monk arrived in the city of Bangkok on December 8. Before going to the conference, he checked into a downtown hotel, wrote some letters, and took a photograph from the window. The letter to Gethsemani suggested some weariness and a little nostalgia: "I think of you all on this Feast Day and with Christmas approaching I feel homesick for Gethsemani. But I hope to be at least in a monastery. . . . Best love to all. Louie."[101] The photograph he took showed a bustling city and a splendid bay viewed from a height, with the water below and distant hills bathed in sunlight. Merton's last photograph was strangely reminiscent of a dream he had recorded in *Conjectures,* one he somehow associated with his death:

I dreamt I was lost in a great city and was walking "toward the center" without quite knowing where I was going. Suddenly I came to a dead end, but on a height, looking at a great bay, an arm of the harbor. I saw a whole section of the city spread out before me on hills covered with light and snow, and realized that, though I had far to go, I knew where I was. . . .

I think sometimes that I may soon die, though I am not yet old (forty-seven).[102]

December 10, 1968, happened to be the twenty-seventh anniversary of Thomas Merton's entrance into the Abbey of Gethsemani. That was the day he gave his last talk, the day he died. His final presentation was given from notes.[103] Merton said that this talk might have been entitled "Marxist Theory and Monastic Theoria," for it was concerned with the "identity crisis" of the monk in comparison with the Marxist mystique. The lecture focused on "the monk . . . who questions himself in the presence of the Marxist . . . trying to find where he stands, what his position is, how he identifies himself in a world of revolution."[104]

Merton narrated an incident told him by a Tibetan lama. This monk, fleeing for his life during the communist takeover of Tibet, asked an Abbot friend what he should do. The reply: "From now on, Brother, everybody stands on his own feet." That summed up Merton's message to the Christian monks and nuns he was adressing, as well as saying something about Thomas Merton himself. "To my mind," he said, "that is an extremely important monastic statement. If you forget everything else that has been said, I would suggest you remember this for the future: 'From now on, everybody stands on his own feet.' "[105] Standing on one's own feet as a monk, for Merton, meant not relying on structures of any kind. "What is essential in the monastic life," he asserted, "is concerned with this business of total inner transformation. All other things serve that end."[106]

In his final public utterance, Merton affirmed a kind of monastic life that does not depend on cultural, sociological, or psychological factors, but goes far deeper. He was saying—in indirect fashion—that his life had been precisely this search for freedom and transcendence. "If you once penetrate by detachment and purity of heart to the inner secret of the ground of one's ordinary experience, you attain to a liberty which nobody can touch, which nobody can affect, which no political change of circumstances can do anything to." Then Merton concluded: "I believe that our renewal consists precisely in deepening this understanding and this grasp of that which is most real."[107]

So often in his autobiographical writings Merton had announced his plans or indicated what he thought he would have to do in order to continue growing and keep to the path of his journey into the unknown. As he walked from the podium, the monk made one last prophetic statement: "I believe the plan is to have all the questions for this morning's lectures this evening at the panel. So I will disappear."[108] Thomas Merton was found dead on the floor of his room that afternoon with a large floor-standing fan—from which he had received 220 volts of direct current—lying across his chest.

Not quite two months earlier, flying out of San Francisco to begin the Asian journey, Merton had described his feeling about the significance of this trip: "The moment of take-off was ecstatic. . . . We left the ground—I with Christian mantras and a great sense of destiny, of being at last on my true way after years of waiting and wondering and fooling around."[109] His charred remains were returned to the United States (with a final irony) on an Air Force plane coming back from Vietnam. Undoubtedly that flight home was the only journey for Thomas Merton that was not a new quest. At that point, he knew the unknown.

As a man with a lively imagination, Merton came up with potent metaphors to capture the unfolding character of his life. Articulating his experience as a journey into the unknown was not merely a literary device for him. Rather, like all good metaphors discovered by autobiographical writers to express their sense of themselves, Merton's metaphors served to situate and empower him. They disclosed to him his present reality and enabled him to go on.

In a study of the meaning of autobiography, James Olney nicely describes the function of metaphors for autobiographical writers:

> A metaphor . . . through which we stamp our own image on the face of nature, allows us to connect the known of ourselves to the unknown of the world, and, making available new relational patterns, it simultaneously organizes the self into a new and richer entity; so that the old known self is joined to and transformed into the new, the heretofore unknown, self. Metaphor says very little about what the world is, or is like, but a great deal about what I am, or am like, and about what I am becoming; and in the end it connects me more nearly with the deep reaches of myself than with an objective universe.[110]

Merton's metaphor of the journey into the unknown surely expressed what he felt was transpiring in his life. But, more than that, the metaphor pointed him in a certain direction. It revealed to him new possibilities for his development and kept alive within him an attitude of openness, courage, and willingness to take risks. His use of that metaphor related Merton's psyche profoundly to the great journey images of the Judeo-Christian tradition: Abraham, the Exodus, the Exile, Jesus Christ's Passover from death to life. The monk's articulation of his life in terms of that metaphor was thus an exercise of faith. And faith, for Thomas Merton, always required "that in order to be true to God and to ourselves we must break with the familiar, established and secure norms and go off into the unknown."[111]

3

The Solitary Explorer

Whatever else he was, Thomas Merton thought of himself and lived as a solitary. He possessed a gregarious temperament and delighted in lively exchange with people, yet his need for solitude was more fundamental. Indeed, he chose solitude as his way of life, perceiving his monastic vocation as an ever deepening invitation to become solitary and to discover what that meant. Merton stated unequivocally that "a monk is, etymologically, a *monachos* or one who is isolated, alone."[1] Whether living the more mitigated common observance of a monastic community or in eremitical retirement, the monk is called to solitude. Merton was quintessentially a *monachos.* He understood solitude as a spiritual exigency and necessary condition for finding God, for becoming his true self, and for attaining genuine unity with others. His own experience of solitude was a decisive factor in shaping Merton's insight into and expression of Christian faith. And his reflection on that experience is one of his richest gifts to us nonmonks.

Merton's capacity to show us the significance of solitude is pertinent to the religious quest of many contemporary people. It bears on our struggle to discern the presence of God in the world and in ourselves. Merton lived most of his life in the silence of a contemplative monastery and spent the last few years in a hermitage tucked away on the grounds. Few of his readers would or could replicate that lifestyle! Yet what Merton wrote concerning his own solitary life speaks to people in very different circumstances. He makes us more aware of the solitary dimension of every human life and each Christian vocation, no matter what concrete form it assumes or how much physical solitude is possible. He reminds us forcibly of simple truths that the pressures of modern society and our own inertia conspire to suppress: that we need to learn how to be alone in order to be human; that we overcome alienation from each other by overcoming it within ourselves. Merton startles us into realizing that solitude confronts us with "the disconcerting task of facing and accepting one's own absurdity" and that "it is only when the apparent absurdity of life is faced in all truth that faith really becomes possible."[2] Thomas Merton's solitude was occupied with that painful task. His explorations help to cut down our pretentions to control reality by imposing our definitions on it. His example as a solitary asks us to see, to be, to respond to life differently.

It is not so much what Merton said about solitude that compels us, but rather what he understood and expressed about Christian life because he explored it in solitude. He was convinced that his vocation as a monk enjoined on him a solitary quest and that fidelity to this solitary searching was precisely his social role. Merton's journey was undertaken in solitude, but what he did was not for himself alone. He called himself "the solitary explorer," a man "bound to search the existential depths of faith in its silences, its ambiguities, and in those certainties which lie deeper than the bottom of anxiety."[3] Although he was invited "to explore the inner waste of his own being as a solitary,"[4] it was for the sake of discerning "the great pattern of the whole experience of man, and even something quite beyond all experience."[5] The story of Merton's solitary exploration is thus the story of his growth in realizing his monastic call not only as his own destiny but also as a contribution to the quest for meaning of men and women in the contemporary world.

"The solitary explorer" was no casual metaphor. It captured Merton's sense of himself as someone on a journey into the depths of the human spirit. The metaphor expressed the paradox of his venture—its challenge and anquish, its fascination and monotony, its power and frustration. For Merton, to be a solitary explorer meant to become "a man who, in one way or another, pushes the very frontiers of human experience and strives to go beyond, to find out what transcends the ordinary level of existence."[6] But if that metaphor suggested the pioneering quality of Merton's search, it was no romantic image. Rather, it conjured up the relentless stamina and courage such a life entails. Merton was acutely aware that his lonely exploring was "a bitter and arid struggle to press forward through a blinding snowstorm. The hermit, all day and all night, beats his head against a wall of doubt."[7]

Thomas Merton was willing consciously to endure doubt and face the characteristic difficulties of the contemporary believer: insecurity, uncertainty, dislocation, and meaninglessness. He shared the worst temptations of modern religious people and encountered them head on. "I have been summoned to explore a desert area of man's heart in which explanations no longer suffice, and in which one learns that only experience counts,"[8] the seasoned explorer wrote in his hermitage. Solitude taught him to relinquish the defenses that shield a person from the terrifying questions "Can a man make sense out of his existence? Can man honestly give his life meaning merely by adopting a certain set of explanations which pretend to tell him why the world began and where it will end, why there is evil and what is necessary for a good life?"[9] The experience of this solitary explorer—lived through, savored, and valued—led Merton to appreciate that "faith sometimes mysteriously takes on the aspect of doubt when, in fact, one has to doubt and reject conventional and superstitious surrogates that have taken the place of faith."[10] Merton struggled in solitude to identify those false substitutes, let go of them, and be healed by the naked power of truth. What he learned from that purifying process was that "one cannot truly know hope unless he has found out how like despair hope is."[11]

The search for authentic faith and hope in which the solitary explorer engaged was not devised by Merton's own ingenuity. He drew on the monastic tradition, which he had thoroughly studied and appropriated. Nonetheless, Merton's personal experience and imaginative creativity gave a particular twist to the story of his development in solitude. In writing about this journey, he often used old terms in new contexts, translated standard phrases into a contemporary idiom, and devised an original vocabulary when necessary. Carefully attending to Merton's way of speaking about his monastic vocation will reveal the direction of his growth over three decades and help us see a transforming process at work, because his insight into that vocation unfolded as Merton's experience of solitude intensified. His life as a solitary explorer shaped Merton's self-understanding and his perspectives on reality. Such searching progressively yielded new perceptions of the Gospel for him.

We can trace that movement by examining three recurrent phrases Merton used for describing the vocation of a monk; he is called "to leave the world"; he lives in "the desert"; and his purpose is "to seek God." Merton's solitary reflections enabled him to reinterpret those classic monastic metaphors in creative ways that make them relevant to Christians who are not monks, as well as to those who are. The fresh meanings

Merton gives that language make a rich contribution to contemporary religious understanding. The unfolding of those meanings through Thomas Merton's years as a monk makes his story as a solitary explorer.

The Monk's Call "to Leave the World"

In *The Seven Storey Mountain* and other early writings, Merton all too easily confused the ordinary social settings in which most people live with the New Testament sense of "the world." *Seeds of Contemplation* advised the reader: "Do everything you can to avoid the amusements and the noise and business of men. Keep as far away as you can from the places where they gather . . . to mock one another with their false gestures of friendship. Do not read their newspapers."[12] Withdraw from created things as much as possible; shun social involvements. Life in the world is deflected toward evil because sin organizes itself into "the unquiet city of those who live for themselves and are therefore divided against one another."[13] Egoism, greed, and lust for power become embodied in social processes. It is this structure that represents "the world" Christ condemned and that the Christian flees in becoming a monk.

In a positive sense, during the first decade of his monastic life Merton thought of leaving the world as a "flight from disunity and separation, to unity and peace in the love of other men."[14] But there were negative connotations; to leave the world implied some repudiation of the human condition and an escape from the anguish of history. The young monastic writer could say that leaving the world to become a monk "takes a man above the terrors and sorrows of modern life as well as above its passing satisfactions. It elevates his life . . . to the peace of the spiritual stratosphere where the storms of human existence become a distant echo."[15]

Merton eventually came to admit that there was an element of unhealthy rejection of society in his early notion of being called to leave the world. In *The Sign of Jonas,* he acknowledged that he had been unduly harsh and often unfair in his appraisals of the world outside the monastery: "Perhaps the things I had resented about the world when I left it were defects of my own that I had projected upon it."[16] Significantly, Merton attributed the capacity for such insight into himself to his experience of solitude. That had enabled him to discern his own psychic complicity with the world he rejected. Solitude disclosed to Merton his complaints about the world as "a weakness" and his reaction to it as "too natural" and "too impure." It led him to the assessment that "the world I am sore at on paper is perhaps a figment of my own imagination."[17] Solitude provided the therapy Thomas Merton needed to revise his understanding of what leaving the world really demanded. "To leave the 'world,' then, is to leave oneself first of all and to begin to live for others."[18] It meant renouncing egoism and the kind of activities that sustain one's illusions about himself. So understood, leaving the world could only be for the sake of discovering a person's real relation to the world through love.

Toward the end of that first decade as a monk, Merton expressed in paradoxical language the sense of his vocation that had developed: "It is clear to me that solitude is my vocation, not as a flight from the world, but as my place in the world because for me to find solitude is only to separate myself from all the forces that destroy me and history."[19] The solitary explorer found himself charged with learning how to make more discriminating judgments. "It would be a grave sin for me to be on my knees in this monastery," he wrote, "and spend my time cursing the world without distinguishing what is good in it from what is bad."[20] But for Merton, the way to distinguish those creative and destructive powers in the world was to recognize and accept them within himself.

Throughout the 1950s, Merton was engaged in that process. He was seeking to understand his call to leave the world in a manner that would open him to love his brothers and sisters in the world more genuinely. The monk was convinced that solitude must engender not isolation but union with others. "Isolation in the self, inability to go out of oneself to others, would mean incapacity for any form of self-transcendence."[21] Merton was groping for a conception of his life of solitude that was neither individualistic nor negative. He found help in his study of the Desert Fathers. These men who had fled the cities of the late Roman Empire when it became officially Christian were expecially appealing to Thomas Merton. He regarded himself as being in a situation not unlike theirs. He was especially attracted to their insistence on "the primacy of love over everything else in the spiritual life"[22] and to their quest for simplicity and authenticity. Merton saw the Desert Fathers' withdrawal from ordinary society as an expression of their need to become whole, and to let themselves be healed of the divisive forces within the human heart. These men sought "to be themselves, their *ordinary* selves, and to forget a world that divided them from themselves."[23] That was the very condition for doing anything of spiritual significance for the world. For "thus to leave the world is, in fact, to help save it in saving oneself."[24]

Merton would continue to develop that paradoxical theme during the 1960s. His desire for greater solitude, just when he was most passionately concerned about the destructive forces unleashed in contemporary society, was strengthened by what he recognized in the Desert Fathers. Writing of their motivation for leaving the world, Merton articulated his own intuition. "They knew that they were helpless to do any good for others as long as they floundered about in the wreckage," he remarked. "But once they got a foothold on solid ground, things were different. Then they had not only the power but even the obligation to pull the whole world to safety after them."[25]

This seminal essay, "The Wisdom of the Desert," was soon followed by another creative piece on related themes. In "Notes for a Philosophy of Solitude," Thomas Merton employed a different metaphor to explain his sense of the vocation of the solitary in relation to others. "Such men, out of pity for the universe, out of loyalty to mankind, and without a spirit of bitterness or resentment, withdraw . . . to heal in themselves the wounds of the entire world."[26] As he more and more agonized over the world's wounds, he was convinced that solitude invited him to discover how he might let the healing process take place in himself.

The monk reflected on the destructive forces causing those wounds. His journal *Conjectures of a Guilty Bystander* was occupied with probing them. Merton struggled to confront the roots of violence, power, totalitarianism, materialism, competition, class and race hatreds, technological servitude, and mass manipulation. He sought to identify those forces not only in their large-scale manifestations but also insofar as they were operative in his own attitudes. Although he had made some progress in leaving the world, he knew that he was still in collusion with it. In the preface to his journal in 1965, Merton assessed where he was: "Though I often differ strongly from that 'world,' I think I can be said to respond to it. I do not delude myself that I am not still part of it."[27] Indeed, Merton's spiritual quest in the later years of his monastic life was the effort to allow all his illusions to be unmasked. He must discover how his own failures to consent to the liberating power of truth made him an accomplice in the world's destructive forces.

He developed a clearer conception of the world that the monk of the 1960s was called to leave. "My particular concept focuses on the sham, the unreality, the alienation, the forced systematization of life, and not on the human reality that is alienated and suppressed."[28] Merton asked anew an old question: "What did I leave when I entered the monastery?" His answer reflected the perspective on himself that the critical distance of solitude provided. "What I abandoned when I 'left the world' . . . was the *understanding of myself* that I had developed in the context of civil society—my identification with what appeared to me to be its aims."[29] Merton's writings were increasingly hard on "the society that is imaged in the mass media and in advertising, in the movies, in TV, in best-sellers, in current fads, in all the pompous and trifling masks with which it hides callousness, sensuality, hypocrisy, cruelty, and fear."[30] This was "the world" that projected its fictions of human reality on the naive, the weak, the unfree. This was the world the monk was called to abandon in order to encounter his own personal freedom as the image of God.

Yet during the mid-1960s the mature Thomas Merton also spoke of the world in quite another fashion. In various essays, he discussed the world that he had left and must continue to leave as a monk and the world for which he was responsible and to which he must remain open if he were to be faithful to his calling. The solitary explorer insisted that the world is not a "pure object" that is "out there." He made some crucial distinctions:

> We and our world interpenetrate. If anything, the world exists for us, and we exist for ourselves. It is only in assuming full responsibility for our world, for our lives and for ourselves that we can be said to live really for God. . . . The way to find the real "world" is not merely to measure and observe what is outside us, but to discover our own inner ground. For that is where the world is, first of all: in my deepest self. But there I find the world to be quite different from the "obligatory answers."[31]

For Merton, it was the function of solitude to put him in touch with his "inner ground." That was where the real struggle for freedom took place. On that ground alone could the solitary take his stand against those "obligatory anwers." Merton called the battle fought on that terrain "spiritual protest."

In a society dominated by "the mass brutality of war and police oppression" and strangled by "the inhumanity of organized affluence,"[32] such protest was essential. Merton came to think of his call to leave the world as simultaneously a religious declaration of belief and a form of political noncooperation. In the violence-torn era of the middle 1960s, he translated the traditional language of the monk's flight from the world into the contemporary idiom of protest: "For my own part, I am by my whole life committed to a certain protest and nonacquiescence, and that is why I am a monk."[33]

Merton's equation of leaving the world with spiritual protest was owed largely to his experience of solitude. On his own testimony, he had become "all the more sensitive" to the "conformism and passivity" of American society over a twenty-year period, "because I have spent this time in the isolation of a contemplative monastery."[34] Toward the end of his life, the monk affirmed that his desire "for a more solitary, more 'monastic' way" brought him to a new understanding and a new set of decisions regarding his vocation:

> To adopt a life that is essentially non-assertive, non-violent, a life of humility and peace is in itself a statement of one's position. . . . It is my intention to make my entire life a rejection of, a protest against the crimes and injustices of war and political tyranny which threaten to destroy the whole race of man and the world with him. By my monastic life and vows I am saying NO to all the concentration camps, the aerial bombardments, the staged political trials, the judicial murders, the racial injustices, the economic tyrannies, and the whole socio-economic apparatus which seems geared for nothing but global destruction.[35]

Did this odd sort of protest accomplish anything? Merton would answer only for himself. He looked back over the years since he had left the world and described what he felt had happened to him:

> I have learned, I believe, to look back into that world with greater compassion, seeing those in it not as alien to myself, not as peculiar and deluded strangers, but as identified with myself. In breaking from "their world" I have strangely not broken from them. In freeing myself from their delusions and preoccupations I have identified myself, none the less, with their struggles and their blind, desperate hope for happiness.[36]

Solitude had allowed Thomas Merton to identify with people in the world in their deepest, often unrecognized and unarticulated longings. He did not share the patterns of their lives; to that extent, the solitary explorer was free to discern the common ground of his and their humanity. Solitude taught the monk how to pursue "the deep desire of God that draws a man to seek a *totally new way of being in the world*."[37] That new way of being in the world empowered Merton to speak out of a lived experience of human solidarity. "I am less and less aware of myself simply as this individual who is a monk and a writer. . . . It is my task to see and speak for many, even when I seem to be speaking only for myself."[38] Leaving the world had meant fleeing from delusions and disunity to find a selfless place in which to stand and from which to see. Merton called that living in the desert.

Living in "the Desert"

To be "called into the desert" is an image deeply embedded in the Judeo-Christian tradition. In the biblical narratives, the wilderness is the place of testing, of learning to trust and to depend on God alone, of openness to divine revelation. The desert is where the demons must be confronted if the Lord will be encountered. Christian ascetical-mystical literature has used "the desert" as a metaphor for the stripping away of human securities so that God's power and mercy might be acknowledged. Thomas Merton appropriated it to express his understanding of what the solitary life asked of him and what it bestowed; what he shared of his experience serves to orient the rest of us who now and then are invited to sojourn there.

Throughout his writings, Merton frequently characterized the monastic vocation as a form of wilderness existence. "The monk is a man who completely renounces the familiar patterns of human and social life and follows the call of God into 'the desert' or 'the wilderness,' that is to say, into the land that is unknown to him and unfrequented by other men."[39] To be a *monachos*—whether in a community regulated by silence and solitude or as a hermit—meant to be summoned into an empty, barren, uncharted territory of the spirit. Merton himself felt the full force of that imperative. He used the metaphor of living in the desert to discover the implications of his own vocation. It was a dynamic vehicle for his growth as a monk. That metaphor linked him to the actual origins of the monastic life; it provided Merton with an interpretative image for his own experience, and it functioned as a means of symbolic communication with people who did not live or understand the monastic tradition.

The metaphor remained constant, although at various stages of Merton's development his description of life in the desert of solitude assumed quite different nuances. His earlier reflections stressed its chastening aspects: indigence, deprivation, tediousness, unproductiveness. Later he focused on the liberating potential of life in the desert. Merton's conviction regarding the centrality of the desert metaphor to the monastic tradition guided his studies and inspired his proposals to restore the eremitical life within Cistercian practice to those so called. Above all, his own experience in the hermitage during the later years of his life deeply affected Merton's appreciation and explication of the metaphor. It is this more original and creative period of the solitary explorer that we will consider. Merton wrote many expository essays at this time on the monastic vocation as life in the desert, often speaking in the third person. But in typical fashion, "the monk," "the hermit," or "the solitary" is usually no generality, but Thomas Merton himself.

As Merton faced the turbulent 1960s, the metaphor of living in the desert suggested to him a promise of authentic human freedom. Two motifs emerge in his writing about the solitary vocation vis-à-vis a world in crisis. One is that the desert liberates a person to see in a whole new way; it provides a unique perspective. The other deals with the monk as free to risk—to move boldly into regions of self-exploration and prophetic concerns—thanks to an independence from social institutions, conventions, and pressures that the desert offers. These motifs overlap but are sufficiently distinct to trace individually. They converge in Merton's understanding of the desert life as a metaphor for the process of becoming wholly grounded on faith in God's Kingdom.

The monk goes into the desert of solitude to clear his vision and to see himself and the world from a radically different vantage point. When the ordinary supports of social life are withdrawn, Merton claimed, a new way of seeing becomes possible. Solitude compels a person "to face reality in all its naked, disconcerting, possibly drab and disappointing factuality, without excuses, without useless explanations, and without subterfuges."[40] Through that painful ordeal, one can begin to acquire "a perspective from which the mystifying, absurd chaos of human desires and illusions gives place . . . to a concrete intuition of providence and mercy at work in the natural constitution of man himself, created in the image of God."[41] This perspective allows for a new attitude toward life to develop. It both recognizes sin and accepts grace.

Such a perspective does not spring from any theory but from a wrenching experience that calls into question all of one's self-definitions and expectations. In the desert, one's confidence in external validations of the self is seriously undermined. The solitary is deprived of that sense of importance and usefulness that is ordinarily conferred by playing certain social roles. Comfortable assumptions are challenged, and evasions of the truth become manifest. An awareness of one's contingency, impotence, and radical need breaks through. This dislocating process creates the possibility for a solitary to acknowledge the real grounds for hope:

> The desert is for those who have felt a salutary despair of conventional and fictitious values, in order to hope in mercy and to be themselves merciful men to whom that mercy is promised. Such solitaries know the evils that are in other men because they experience these evils first of all in themselves.[42]

The desert induces anguish, but for Merton it also provides the conditions for a cramped spirit to relax and become open. The capacity to see the truth of the human situation involves more than intellectual perspicacity; it requires attentiveness, expansiveness, receptivity. In silence and solitude, the monk's "mind and heart can relax and attain to a new perspective: there too he can hear the Word of God and meditate on it more quietly, without strain, without forcing himself without being carried away in useless and abstract speculations."[43] This relaxed posture is peaceful, but, for Merton, never passive. Rather, it is alert, watchful, ready. Such an attitude is open to discover and free to respond to the truth. The desert awakens a capacity for discernment. One can begin to see reality with new eyes because the desert liberates a person from "the ignorance and error that spring from the fear of 'being nothing,' " Merton insists. "The man who dares to be alone can come to see that the 'emptiness' and 'uselessness' which the collective mind fears and condemns are necessary conditions for the encounter with truth."[44]

A genuinely new perspective can emerge for the solitary because certain constraints of mind and heart are eased in the desert. Distance tends to loosen the hold of fixed patterns of thought or ideologies on the intelligence. Under the discipline of solitude, the person may become critically aware and able to think independently of collective opinions for the first time. The desert relentlessly disabuses an individual of socially reinforced ideas and accustomed explanations. Merton called it being "spiritually 'born' as a mature identity . . . from the enclosing womb of myth and prejudice."[45] In the desert, new questions, deeper questions, will arise. One becomes detached from the aspirations and conventional goals of society. Without the pressure of ordinary social arrangements, collective values cannot so easily be taken for granted. The solitary must face finding out what really matters to him or her. For Merton, then, the desert clears the head and liberates the heart to uncover its own deepest desires. A sharper, cleaner vision of the self in all its relationships can be gained in the desert, and so "some men will seek clarity in isolation and silence, not because they think they know better than the rest, but because they want to see life in a different perspective."[46]

That perspective is not a private privilege. It is, rather, the gift to humanity of a special awareness able to identify the real sources of conflict and reconciliation in the world. "In facing the world with a totally different viewpoint," Merton claims, the monk "maintains alive in the world the presence of a spiritual and intelligent consciousness which is the root of true peace and true unity among men."[47] Thus if the monk is absolved from direct engagement in struggles over particular problems, for Merton "it is only in order that he may give more thought to the interests of all, to the whole question of the reconciliation of all men to one another in Christ" and "to get a better view of the whole problem and mystery of man."[48]

The better view of that mystery has to do with seeing through one's individual and collective illusions and recognizing the grounds for peace. Merton is talking about the perspective of a person who fully accepts the human condition in him- or herself and with others. That realization may come about in many ways—but living in the desert should engender, hasten, and complete the process. The solitary explorer described it this way:

> It is in the desert of loneliness and emptiness that the fear of death and the need for self-affirmation are seen to be illusory. When this is faced, then anguish is not necessarily overcome, but it can be accepted and understood. Thus, in the heart of anguish are found the gifts of peace and understanding: not simply in personal illumination and liberation, but by commitment and empathy, for the contemplative must assume the universal anguish and the inescapable condition of mortal man. The solitary, far from enclosing himself in himself, becomes every man.[49]

Merton was convinced that the desert offered such a perspective on the human situation, but it provided still something more. The metaphor of living in the desert suggested to him a distinctive opportunity for taking risks essential to spiritual growth. "The essence of the solitary vocation," Merton affirmed, "is precisely the anguish of an almost infinite risk."[50] The desert frees the monk to let go of his social, psychological, even religious bases for security; it disciplines him to endure their breakdown. A crisis is occasioned that discloses what is at stake in the life of the spirit. For Merton, in fact, "the whole point of monastic 'desert' life is precisely to equip the monk for risk, for walking with God in the wilderness, and wrestling with Satan in vulnerable freedom."[51]

The desert presents the risk of undergoing a dissolution of the external self in order to discover one's true identity as a unique person called by God to an unknown destiny. Solitude inevitably forces the monk to confront the *persona* that ordinarily insulates him from his deepest self. "The Christian solitary is left alone with God to fight out the question of who he really is, to get rid of the impersonation."[52] That existential question can emerge, that struggle will occur, because in the desert, "all the masks and disguises are stripped off."[53] Divested of socially sustained self-pretenses and fabrications, the solitary finds him- or herself exposed, defenseless, and vulnerable. This searing experience, however, is the condition for a dawning realization of authentic personal identity. An awareness of one's own truth and inviolable reality can be born in the desert, where protective shells disintegrate. Merton describes it as a process of becoming conscious of one's inner self—the self created in the image of God and capable of freely responding to him. The individual who has not risked being alone does not possess a real identity:

> Because he is willingly enclosed and limited by the laws and illusions of collective existence, he has no more identity than an unborn child in the

womb. He is not yet conscious. He is alien to his own truth. . . . To have
an identity, he has to be awake, and aware. But to be awake, he has to accept
vulnerability and death. Not for their own sake . . . only for the sake of
the invulnerable inner reality . . . to which we awaken only when we see
the unreality of our vulnerable shell. The discovery of this inner self is an
act and affirmation of solitude.[54]

The inner self that is discovered in the desert is not an isolated self.
Consciousness of one's identity as a person before God includes awareness
of being with others also summoned into the desert to learn who they
are, not just as individual persons but as members of a people. The model
for understanding what kind of community the Lord forms for himself
is, of course, Israel in the desert. As Merton reminds us, "it was in the
desert and hazard of Sinai that the People of God acquired its identity,
its full consciousness of the covenant relationship which the prophets
later described as an 'espousal' with Yahweh."[55] To be his people means
to risk living in "complete and continual dependence on God alone."[56]
That is the most radical of risks, but to refuse it would be to deny the
very identity that the covenant bestows:

> Failure to trust Yahweh in the wilderness is not simply an act of weakness:
> it is disobedience and idolatry which . . . seek to shorten the time of suffering
> by resort to human expedients, glossed over with religious excuses. . . . For
> Israel, the desert life was a life of utter dependence on a continued act of
> grace which implied also a recognition of man's own propensity to treachery
> and to sin.[57]

Merton regarded Israel's experience as the paradigm for what every
generation of God's people has to pass through to realize its identity.
To know that identity is to know oneself as loved and as liberated to
respond with love. The *monachos* consciously chooses to live in the desert
where God fashions a people for himself and where human awareness
of what that involves can continually be renewed. His going into the
desert of solitude is a symbolic action that affirms for himself and to
others that God's merciful love is revealed only when one rejects resorting
to human expedients.

The risk the solitary takes is certainly his or her own, but it is also
representative. The solitary explores not a singular, esoteric experience
of faith, but something quite typical of believers. "He can recognize his
own situation in the trials and temptations which many of his fellow
Christians are undergoing. He can understand their sufferings and discern
the meaning of them."[58] Thomas Merton was particularly sensitive to
the plight of so many contemporary people who acutely feel the absence

of God in their lives and are tempted to atheism. Living in the desert, he felt, allowed him to enter into that experience. He shared the risk of this terrible condition and acknowledged its significance for faith: "The desert strips our hearts bare. It strips us of our pretensions and alibis; it strips us, too, of our imperfect images of God. It reduces us to what is essential and forces us to see the truth about ourselves, leaving no way of escape."[59] Such anguished stripping was, for Merton, analogous to the experience of those who have lost the sense of God's presence in their lives. To dwell in the desert meant to go through that suffering, but to recognize that "this can be a very beneficial thing for our faith, for it is here, at the very heart of our misery, that the marvels of God's mercy reveal themselves."[60]

The witness of the desert life was particularly urgent in the Catholic Church, given the developments following Vatican II. In both theology and practice, there was a new awareness of the Church as a pilgrim people journeying through the wilderness. It was imperative, Merton thought, that those actually living the desert experience help the larger community really to grasp what the metaphor implied for the Church. The monk is free from the overorganized, highly institutionalized, bureaucratic, and pragmatically oriented forms of life in the Church. In the desert, "he is liberated from the routines and servitudes of organized human activity in order to *be free*. Free for what? Free to see, free to praise, free to understand, free to love."[61] The monk is in the position, then, to remind the Christian community that the source of its freedom is reliance on God, not prevailing cultural norms. That is precisely what Merton did.

In the 1960s, Thomas Merton was very vocal in his criticism of the Church and monastic orders for their triumphalism, bureaucracy, and inertia. Writing from the hermitage—his desert—he risked his reputation as a loyal Catholic and an obedient monk. He risked something far more significant to him: the possibility of losing his own contemplative equilibrium. Merton knew how perilous it was to take up the task of prophetic criticism. The danger was not having his quiet interrupted, but that he might get caught up in institutional reform to the detriment of personal conversion. Yet when his criticisms were most stinging, even sarcastic, about failures to change institutional patterns, Merton kept a sharp critical eye on himself. The solitary explorer did not fail to observe the dark side of his ringing calls for recapturing the desert spirit in the Church and monastic life. He was aware of his propensities to get overinvolved in the struggles and sometimes to succumb to the force of his own rhetoric. "I wish I had at least a little charity," Merton wrote in his journal. "I wish I were less resentful of dead immobilism: the ponderous, inert, inhuman pressure of power bearing down on everyone to keep every beak from opening and every wing from moving."[62]

Merton did not back off from the difficult work of scrutinizing ecclesial or monastic structures. That risk had to be taken, no matter what the cost:

It may be the price of sacrificing our security, *sacrificing the psychological stability we have built on foundations that we do not dare to examine.* We have to examine those foundations even though it will mean unrest, even though it will mean loss of peace, even though it will mean disturbance and anguish, even though it may mean the radical shaking of structures.[63]

But the more primary risk of living in the desert was, for Thomas Merton, facing himself squarely and assuming responsibility for his own life. He was adamant about what sort of change his solitary vocation absolutely demanded:

What one needs to do is to start a conversion and a new life oneself, in so far as one can. Thus, my new life and my contribution to a renewal in monasticism begin within myself and in my own daily life. . . . Creativity has to begin with me and I can't sit here wasting time urging the monastic institution to become creative and prophetic. . . . What each one of us has to do, what I have to do, is to buckle down and really start investigating new possibilities in our own lives; and if the new possibilities mean radical changes, all right.[64]

So, if the metaphor of living in the desert suggested for Merton a new perspective on life and the liberty to risk all human securities, even more it expressed the monk's call to conversion. Of course Merton believed that the invitation to total transformation of mind and heart—what the Gospel means by *metanoia*—is not peculiar to the monk; it belongs to everyone. But in a very particular way, Merton claimed, the monk has the task of exploring what that means. He goes into the desert to discern the demands of the call to conversion on the most interior level of the self. By experience, he must learn to discriminate between mere change in behavior patterns and genuine transformation of the person in his whole orientation to life. The monk in the desert attempts to do that in himself but not simply for himself. He spies out the terrain of the spirit so that he and others can know the pitfalls and find the paths. "If a spaceman undergoes certain experimental tests and develops certain skills," Merton argued by analogy, "he does not necessarily imply that he is a superior human being: but this happens to be his job and even his 'vocation.'"[65] The solitary has that kind of exploring function. He lives in the desert seeking "by *metanoia* and inner revolution to deepen his consciousness and awareness in such a way that he 'experiences' something of the ultimate ground of being and . . . the saving power of the Spirit, and witnesses to this in some way."[66]

The desert life had become Merton's shorthand term for the process of transforming the monk's vision and response. It stood for the condition in which a person can hear the announcement of God's Kingdom and be ready to act on it. The metaphor conjured up the whole theological foundation of the monastic vocation as a call to enter the Kingdom. It resonated with the biblical overtones of Israel's journey in the wilderness, John's proclamation of the Good News, and the temptations of Jesus in the desert:

> The monastic life in Christianity is . . . a life of hope and hardship, of risk and penance in the sense of a *metanoia*, a complete inner revolution, renunciation of ease and privilege . . . in order to bear witness to God's Kingdom as was given by John, the "voice crying in the wilderness" and in order to experience in oneself the meaning of the three temptations by which Christ repudiated worldly power in order to build his Kingdom on faith.[67]

For Thomas Merton, the *monachos,* "the desert life" had many rich signficances. Another expression in his lexicon as a solitary explorer was one of the most venerable in the monastic tradition. He found countless ways of interpreting his story as a man called out of the world into the desert "to seek God."

"To Seek God"

From St. Benedict on, the monk has been described as a person whose vocation is "to seek God." Only such a quest could justify the way of life on which he enters. Merton wholeheartedly affirmed that tradition: "This one thing that most truly makes a monk what he is, is that irrevocable break with the world and all that is in it, in order to seek God in solitude."[68] He never changed his conviction that the raison d'être of the monastic life was to enable someone "to give himself exclusively and perfectly to the one thing necessary for all men—the search for God."[69] Over the years, however, Thomas Merton's understanding of his vocation as a seeking for God evolved, and he formulated it differently as the times changed and his own experience deepened. What the solitary explorer came to see and to say about his particular quest can guide others who would embark on their own.

For Merton, the basic question of what one is seeking in life must continually be posed. As Master of Novices, he warned his charges that over and over again they should ask themselves why they have come to the monastery. " 'What are you doing here? Why have you come here?' Not that it is a question whose answer we have known but tend to forget. It is a question which confronts us with a new meaning and a new urgency, as we go on in life."[70] A person's awareness of what seeking God concretely implies will take on various colorings as one actually lives the monastic life. Thomas Merton did not fail to ask himself that question all along the way. His answers were diverse yet consistent, imaginatively original though rooted in a tradition. His explications of the metaphor of searching for or seeking God, like his language about leaving the world and living in the desert, reflect certain stages of Merton's growth.

In the late 1940s, there was an unmistakable accent on withdrawal, renunciation, and rejection of human concerns in Merton's conception of what it meant to seek God. His writings exhibit a characteristic appreciation for contemplative "waiting," but at this point the stress falls on ascetic discipline. Merton expressed his understanding of "what it meant to seek God perfectly" in *Seeds of Contemplation:*

> To withdraw from illusion and pleasure, from worldly anxieties and desires . . . to keep my mind free from confusion . . . to entertain silence in my heart and listen for the voice of God; to cultivate an intellectual freedom from concepts and the images of created things . . . to rest in humility and to find peace in withdrawal from conflict and competition with other men; to turn aside from controversy and put away heavy loads of judgment and censorship and criticism.[71]

Thus interpreted, the metaphor of seeking God has a rather negative connotation. It emphasizes the individual's massive effort to take himself in hand by redirecting all his energies, and "then to wait in peace and emptiness and oblivion of all things."[72] Merton would always insist that to seek God required emptiness, but he certainly did not continue recommending that one wait in "oblivion of all things."

During the next decade, Merton highlighted the paradoxical nature of the monk's commitment to seek God. To undertake the search for God shows that the Spirit is already directing and making fruitful one's aspirations. To seek God is to find him and to be already found by God. That was one of Merton's favorite paradoxes:

> No one on earth knows precisely what it means to "seek God" until he himself has set out to find Him. No man can tell another what this search means unless that other is enlightened, at the same time, by the Spirit speaking within his own heart. In the end, no one can seek God unless he has already begun to find Him. No one can find God without having first been found

by Him. A monk is a man who seeks God because he has been found by God.[73]

In the 1950s, Merton tended to talk about the call to seek God not so much as following a program of ascetic renunciation as moving existentially in the darkness of faith on an uncharted course. To seek God becomes a metaphor for a life that has a shape and a direction, although not an agenda. For the monk to seek God means to be engaged in a process of continual discovery. Because the monastic vocation is a mystery, "it cannot be completely expressed in a clear succinct formula," although Merton assured his fellow monks that "God will reveal Himself to us in the gift of our vocation, but He will do so only gradually."[74] Seeking God is the guarantee of finding him—and likewise of finding the inner meaning of one's own life:

> We can expect to spend our whole lives as monks entering deeper and deeper into the mystery of our monastic vocation, which is our life hidden with Christ in God. If we are real monks, we are constantly rediscovering what it means to be a monk, and yet we never exhaust the full meaning of our vocation.[74]

As a "real monk" himself, Thomas Merton was always rediscovering the meaning of his vocation to seek God and ever looking for richer expressions of this reality that escaped nice definitions. In the late 1950s and early 1960s, he began to speak of the monk—of himself—as "the *monachos*" or "solitary," in order deliberately to discard "everything that can conjure up the artificial image of the monk in a cowl, dwelling in a medieval cloister" and to focus on, as Merton said, "what seems to me to be the deepest and most essential."[76] That was a commitment to seek God and one's true self without the diversions provided by society, and thus to confront the void. Precisely in this effort to seek God the genuine *monachos* experiences "the anguish of realizing that underneath the apparently logical pattern of a more or less 'well organized' and rational life, there lies an abyss of irrationality, confusion, pointlessness, and indeed of apparent chaos."[77] Merton was reinterpreting his monastic vocation not only in terms of the mystical tradition but also through the emphases of existential thought with which he had become familiar.

From the beginning, Merton conceived of the search for God and the real self as one endeavor that necessarily proceeds in darkness and unknowing. But by the turn of the 1960s, the impact of his own experience and his reading made him emphasize the anguish of solitary exploration all the more. Now he would say that to seek God entails the actualization of a faith in which a man takes responsibility for his own inner life. He faces its full mystery, in the presence of the invisible God. And he takes upon himself the lonely, barely comprehensible darkness of his own mystery until he discovers that his mystery and the mystery of God merge into one reality, which is the only reality. That God lives in him and he in God.[78]

To be a solitary is a matter of qualitative awareness and choice; it calls for decision. One who would spend his life seeking God must elect solitude. Thomas Merton had, of course, elected solitude by entering Gethsemani, and he continued to ratify that choice throughout his life there. But his personal experience of seeking God in a contemplative community, and his twenty years' study of monastic history and theology, led him to choose the more complete solitude of the hermitage.

From his early days in the Cistercians, we recall, Merton had been tempted to leave for one of the eremitical monastic orders such as the Carthusians or the Camaldolese. Eventually he resolved the tension of his attraction to the hermit life by convincing the authorities that the Cistercian tradition itself allowed for some monks to become hermits after they had been formed and tested in the community. Merton did his homework and made a well-documented case for reinstituting the practice. His own decision to pursue the possibility of living as a solitary in a hermitage at Gethsemani was the result of prayer, research, and dogged perseverance. Indeed, Merton was convinced that he must become a hermit, not as "a spiritual luxury, but a difficult, humiliating responsibility: the obligation to be spiritually mature."[79]

That was not a theoretical statement. During the 1960s Merton was doing what he had always done as a monk: seeking God. But by this time he had progressed more deeply into solitude, and his taking up of the prophetic burden of social criticism reflected his consciousness of that "obligation to be spiritually mature." Time in the hermitage taught him that the monastic call to seek God required him to accept "the condition of a stranger *(xeniteia)* and a wanderer on the face of the earth, who has been called out of what was familiar to him in order to seek strangely and painfully after he knows not what."[80]

Near the end of his life, writing from the hermitage, Merton came up with a new metaphor to explicate the meaning of his call to seek God. He began to speak of the search for God as a "going beyond the frontiers." It was an adventurous expression for the monastic quest, linked most explicitly to Merton's pervasive metaphor of exploring the unknown. For the monk, to seek God implies that he "pushes to the very frontiers of human experience and strives to go beyond, to find out what transcends the ordinary level of existence."[81] Merton was suggesting, as always, that the boundaries that the solitary must transcend are those deadening routines and conventional standards of society, the accepted habits of thought that insulate against insight, and all the "obligatory answers" that alienate a person from him- or herself. But more specifically, the metaphor of going beyond or pushing back the frontiers pointed to an effort to break through a certain limited conception and experience of the self.

For Merton, the post-Cartesian view of the human self that dominates modern Western consciousness is not only limited and limiting but actually destructive. It relegates others, and finally God, to the category of objects. It tends to create what Merton called a "solipsistic bubble of awareness—an ego-self imprisoned in its own consciousness, isolated and out of touch with other such selves in so far as they are all 'things' rather than persons."[82] To transcend such a mind set was imperative for the contemplative monk, Merton argued, for only then could he discover God as the very ground of true self. "We must in all things seek God. But we do not seek Him the way we seek a lost object, a 'thing.' He is present to us in our heart, our personal subjectivity, and to seek Him is to recognize this fact."[83]

Such recognition, to say the least, is not easy to come by. Going beyond the frontiers of ordinary experience demands that a person plunge into the depths of his or her own spirit, into the unnamed region, the night, beyond the conceptualizations of psychology, philosophy, even theology. Thomas Merton, the solitary explorer, was speaking about his own task of showing that the search for God and for the real self are one quest that pursues the same inner path. To seek for God beyond the frontiers meant for him to go into "an arrid, rocky, dark land of the soul, sometimes illuminated by strange fires which men fear and peopled by spectres which men studiously avoid except in their nightmares."[84] The mystical descent and the monastic exploration beyond the frontiers were not very different for Merton. Both metaphors captured the paradox of the human quest for God:

> The frontiers are dissolved, not from our side but from His. And of course this is a universal truth underlying all the paradoxes about "monastic exploration." In the end, there are no frontiers. We would not seek God unless He were not already "in us," and to go "beyond ourselves" is just to find the inner ground of our being where He is present to us as our creative source, as the fount of redemptive light and grace.[85]

As Merton developed the image of exploring beyond the frontiers in "Renewal and Discipline," an essay written in his last year, it expressed his sense of social responsibility as a monk called to seek God by probing the depths of his own self. For clearly Merton understood that if a solitary explorer goes beyond the frontiers, it is not only for the sake of one's personal adventure in the spirit, but also to blaze a trail for others to follow and to bring back some helpful "information." In short, the metaphor articulated Merton's role as a spiritual guide—in person for a few, through his writing for so many.

For Thomas Merton, there can be no authentic seeking God unless a person knows how to let go, move on, and plunge ahead. Such are the "skills" that the solitary painfully learns to acquire. The discipline of monastic life—and in particular, of solitude—prepares one to go beyond the frontiers. "The real function of discipline," Merton wrote in 1968, "is not to provide us with maps, but to sharpen our own sense of direction so that when we really get going we can travel without maps."[86] Traveling without maps, like moving beyond the frontiers, was a metaphor for the capacities of mind and heart that represented for Merton genuine spiritual development. And, as he understood and exemplified it, such development meant that someone could leave behind what he has outgrown and be open to the challenge of the unknown. "The purpose of discipline is . . . to make us critically aware of the limitations of the very language of the spiritual life and of ideas about that life," Merton boldly asserted. "Discipline develops our critical insight and shows us the inadequacy of what we had previously accepted as valid in our religious and spiritual lives."[87] That statement was made in an expository piece on the monastic life, but it served as an autobiographical testimony. Merton had given himself over to the transforming discipline of solitude and had come a long way in understanding his call as a monk to leave the world, go into the desert, and to seek God.

The solitary explorer of Gethsemani recommended to others something he himself embodied:

> What has to be rediscovered is the inner discipline of "the heart," that is to say, of the "whole man"—a discipline that reaches down into his inmost ground and opens out to the invisible, intangible, but nevertheless mysteriously sensible reality of God's presence, of His love, and of His activity in our hearts. . . . the classics of monasticism and contemplation are there to be reinterpreted for modern readers, and above all the Greek and Russian (hesychast) tradition can infuse a new life into our rationalist Western minds. Oriental ways of contemplation (Zen, Yoga, Taoism) can no longer be completely neglected by us. Sufism and Hassidism have a great deal to say.[88]

Merton's final journey to the East was his concrete enactment of that attitude. He quite literally moved beyond the frontiers of the ordinary patterns of Cistercian life to undertake his quest for God in dialogue with those from other religious traditions.

That journey into the unknown was not a departure from the solitary life for Merton, but rather a confirmation of his commitment to it. He had learned from his study of monasticism that "pilgrimage was to remain a 'form of hermit life' and a logical though exceptional, constituent of the monastic vocation."[89] Not long before his death, Merton used the pilgrim metaphor in an address at the Temple of Understanding in Calcutta. "I speak as a Western monk who is preeminently concerned with his own monastic calling and dedication," he said to the gathering of people from many different traditions. "I come as a pilgrim who is anxious . . . to drink from ancient sources of monastic vision and experience."[90] Merton ended that talk with a restatement of what he understood to be the meaning of the monastic vocation in relation to the contemporary world:

> We find ourselves in a crisis, a moment of crucial choice. We are in grave danger of losing a spiritual heritage that has been painfully accumulated by thousands of generations of saints and contemplatives. It is the peculiar office of the monk in the modern world to keep alive the contemplative experience and to keep the way open for modern technological man to recover the integrity of his own inner depths.[91]

Thomas Merton was expressing his vision of what monks everywhere were called to do. But, intentionally or unintentionally, he was also in fact describing what he himself had done for so many people, especially American Catholics. The solitary explorer had lived and written so as to keep alive a spiritual heritage by reinterpreting it in contemporary and eminently personal terms. He contributed mightily to the renewal of post-Vatican II monasticism. And the nonmonks, the nonhermits, the nonsolitaries who read Merton are reminded of (perhaps introduced to) a reality that belongs to their communal history and that can be a vital part of their own current spiritual seeking. The solitary explorer's imaginative language communicates something of his profoundly committed and creative spirit, a spirit passionately given to the quest for "inner trascendent freedom."[92]

The vision of that solitary explorer was not unrelated to the social influence of the guilty bystander—another of Merton's metaphors for himself and his work.

CHAPTER

A Guilty Bystander

"True solitude," Merton noted in his journal, "is deeply aware of the world's needs. It does not hold the world at arm's length."[1] The solitary who was writing *Conjectures of a Guilty Bystander* certainly did not appear oblivious to or distant from the crises of the world in the 1960s. The book was preoccupied with their import and offered Merton's reflections on a broad range of current problems: racism, violence, the arms buildup, propaganda, political tyranny, totalitarianism, ideological conflict, social revolution, runaway technology, affluence and the consumer society, urbanization, and mass culture. But, despite *Conjecture's* obvious interest in and sensitive probing of social issues, Thomas Merton identified himself in the full title of that 1965 journal as a "bystander"—indeed, a "guilty" one.

That was a tensive metaphor, catching up all the ambiguities of Merton's situation as he then perceived it. It expressed his understanding of where he stood and what was being asked of him in his third decade as a monk, one acutely aware that he lived in "an age of transition and crisis, of war and racial conflict, of technology and expansion."[2] At fifty, Merton was a man deeply disturbed about the quality of life in contemporary society. He had developed a sensitive social conscience and a consuming concern for justice and peace; he could not refuse to pay attention to what was happening nationally and internationally. Nonetheless, Merton maintained that "a confrontation of twentieth-century questions in the light of a monastic commitment . . . inevitably makes one something of a 'bystander.' "[3]

He lived on the sidelines of direct action in society. Merton did not march with Martin Luther King in Alabama; go to jail, as did the Berrigans over Vietnam; or work in the soup kitchens of the Lower East Side with Dorothy Day. He remained at Gethsemani during all the turbulence of the 1960s. In fact, he moved into a hermitage. But Merton read, corresponded, thought, and suffered over the compelling social issues of the era. And he wrote about them passionately and persuasively. This bystander understood himself, paradoxically, as a participant in "the life and experience of the greater, more troubled, and more vocal world beyond the cloister."[4]

Calling himself "a guilty bystander" was not an apology from Thomas Merton for choosing to live as a contemplative monk in an age of great social and political upheaval that solicited Christian involvement. If he regarded himself guilty, it was not for eschewing an activist role in society. The metaphor embodied, rather, a recognition that his vocation as a monk demanded a more thoroughgoing and concrete response to the world's plight than he had hitherto anticipated. He was acknowledging a responsibility to understand his monastic commitment precisely with reference to what was actually taking place in society. Merton was searching for ways to grow so as to stand by the world in its anguish. He was bidding himself discover how to live more authentically the life to which he was called, convinced that "the contemplative life is first of all *life*, and life implies openness, growth, development. To restrict the contemplative monk to one set of narrow horizons and esoteric concerns would be in fact to condemn him to spiritual and intellectual sterility."[5] Merton could not settle for such restriction. His own horizons expanded in turning to the struggles in the contemporary world. And his analyses of the problems and prescriptions for change would awaken the consciences of many.

If he named himself a guilty bystander in the 1960s, others started to call Thomas Merton an astute social critic and a powerful prophetic voice. He could cut through justifications of the status quo, display the hypocrisy of so much political rhetoric, and lay bare the will to power and manipulation disguised as "reasonable positions." For instance, in the controversial book he edited in 1962, *Breakthrough to Peace*, Merton took the unpopular stand that "the massive and uninhibited use of nuclear weapons, either in attack or in retaliation, is contrary to Christian morality."[6] And his "Letters to a White Liberal" in 1963 excoriated those who failed to recognize that "this most critical moment in American history is the providential 'hour,' the *kairos* not merely of the Negro, but of the white man." Merton proclaimed that what was taking place in the civil rights movement provided the graced moment in which "hearing and understanding the will of God as expressed in the urgent need of our Negro brother, we can respond . . . in a faith that faces the need of reform and creative change, in order that the demands of truth and justice may not go unfulfilled."[7]

Such writing surely indicated a change in Merton's conception of his role as a monk and a religious writer. The author of *Seeds of Contemplation* in 1948 had unabashedly announced, "I have very little idea of what is going on in the world," and smugly congratulated himself on that condition: "occasionally I happen to see some of the things they are drawing and writing there and it gives me the conviction that they are all living in ash-cans. It makes me glad I cannot hear what they are singing."[8] But the man who introduced *Seeds of Destruction* in 1964 expressed a very different vision of what was appropriate, even necessary, for the monk:

> The monastic community is deeply implicated, for better or for worse, in the economic, political, and social structures of the contemporary world. To forget or to ignore this does not absolve the monk from responsibility for participation in events in which his very silence and "not knowing" may constitute a form of complicity. The mere fact of "ignoring" what goes on can become a political decision.[9]

Clearly, Merton had made a "political decision" *not* to ignore what was transpiring in the world outside the monastery. And that was simultaneously a religious decision, for he interpreted his speaking out "not only as a monk but also as a responsible citizen of a very powerful nation" as "a solemn obligation of conscience."[10] By the mid-1960s, Merton saw the social and political positions he assumed as not only rooted in the Gospel but also directly related to his particular commitments as a monk. His stand against racial injustice and economic exploitation, for example, became for him specific expressions of his monastic vows. "To have a vow of poverty seems to me illusory," Merton declared, "if I do not in some way identify myself with the cause of people who are denied their rights and forced, for the most part, to live in abject misery."[11] At this point in Merton's life, to "identify" with the cause of the dispossessed did not mean simply to empathize; it signified that he had to take a stand, put himself on the line, and speak out on the issues with the formidable verbal powers at his disposal.

But what led Thomas Merton into the public arena? How did the spiritual writer of the 1940s and 1950s become the impassioned critic of American patterns and policy in the 1960s? What happened between *Seeds of Contemplation* and *Seeds of Destruction* to account for the shift in the author's attitudes and perspectives?

The story of Merton's development as a prophetic figure is intriguing and, perhaps, disconcerting. It is fascinating because it contains some elements of high drama: the man who disappeared into the cloister to contemplate in silence things divine eventually emerged through his writing as a vociferous defender of human rights and a vigorous proponent of radical societal reforms. The process of that development, however, was relatively uneventful. If Merton's appearance on the scene as a controversial commentator on public issues was dramatic, the course of his life in the monastery leading up to it was not. His faithful readers knew that.

In the 1960s, many of them wondered what had unleashed this strong, insistent voice about injustice and war from a secluded monastery in the Kentucky hills. Merton's new consciousness and social concern confronted people with a startling question. Can contemplation really make a difference in and for a world of action?

We need to trace Merton's development as a monk to uncover an answer. The story of this guilty bystander shows us a man undergoing a slow process of learning to make the connections between his Christian faith and the pursuit of peace, justice, and liberation in the world. Merton's story displays the power of everyday experiences like reading, reflecting, doing one's job, and praying to shape a new perception of the social implications of faith. That is, perhaps, why his story offers us hope.

Learning to Take a Position

Thomas Merton's blossoming as a social critic and prophetic figure in the last decade of his life was the terminus of a moral development long in the making. The beginning of that process preceded his conversion to Catholicism and its maturation was the result of ever-deepening religious and monastic commitment. The process involved learning how to take a responsible Christian position on ethical issues in society and learning how to accept the practical consequences of such positions in and for Merton's own life.

As an undergraduate at Columbia in 1935, the young Merton certainly gave evidence of interest in social and political problems. He took the trouble to be informed on issues and participated in various movements for peace and economic equity. Although the writer of *The Seven Storey Mountain* tended to satirize humorously the seriousness of Tom Merton as "a great revolutionary" during his "Communist phase,"[12] the fact remains that this Columbia student nonetheless showed some solicitude for injustice in society and the senseless destruction of war. On the ship from England to New York, Merton had experienced his first real awakening to such matters. The autobiographer called it a "conversion," but "not the right conversion."[13]

The dawning of social consciousness followed by Merton's first uncertain attempts at action was a genuine, if minimal, moral development. During the previous year at Cambridge, Tom had been utterly absorbed in himself and his own insatiable desires. As a communist sympathizer at Columbia, he widened his horizons, thought about larger political issues, and even took a few, mitigated risks in support of his new ideas. But at this point Merton was mainly responding to his own need to feel involved in something significant. Although he was "concerned" about social issues, he was still largely motivated by self-interest. The slightly jaded youth perceived his discovery of sociopolitical involvement to be, as he said, "an open door out of my spiritual jail."[14]

Understandably—given the times (mid-1930s), his age (twenty), and his upbringing (undisciplined)—Merton was acting "more on the basis of emotion than anything else"[15] when he participated in the Peace Strike and similar demonstrations at Columbia. He had not yet formed his own convictions; he could not appropriate any position on social issues authentically as his own. And Thomas Merton would be unable to do so until after his religious conversion and the struggle to discern his vocation that followed on it.

By the end of 1941, with America facing war, the man who had become a Catholic three years earlier and now agonized over his thwarted attraction to the monastic life was certainly capable of assuming an ethical stance on political issues with full personal responsibility. Merton's experience of becoming a religious believer had exercised him in wrestling with values, sorting out his convictions from temperamental inclinations or social pressures, and deliberating about the grounds for his actions. He had learned something about making personal decisions: what needed to be examined, what could and could not be assessed about the risks entailed. In deciding to be a Catholic, Merton was brought in touch with that center of himself from which all authentic choices spring. He came to know firsthand what went into judgments about a potential commitment. He had experienced this most fundamental decision of his life as inherently free, although not autonomous; Merton perceived his religious conversion as a surrender and a response to a transcendent call. What he had experienced in coming to faith and through reordering his life by it would profoundly affect Merton's development in taking social ethical positions. Defining himself as a noncombatant objector in the spring of 1941 is a case in point.

The man who carefully formulated his moral position vis-à-vis World War II when summoned by his draft board was notably different from the youth who had in 1935 sworn the "Oxford Pledge"—a sweeping and simplistic refusal to fight in any war—organized by the Communist Party at Columbia. In six years at this crucial stage of life, of course, Merton obviously had matured intellectually and emotionally. But more had happened to him. Through his religious conversion, he had gained a whole new context for weighing public events and his own actions in relation to them. Now he was aware of grounding his judgments not only on information and insight into the situation but also on the demands of his own capacity to act with moral integrity. Merton felt responsible for measuring events by the Gospel in which he believed. He was accountable to the Lord for his personal conduct with respect to those events so judged according to his honest human efforts.

Thinking about the war already raging in Europe and threatening the United States, Merton critically examined the problem his adopted country faced. "If America entered the war now, would it be a war of aggression?" Merton asked himself. He made a judgment that was uncertain, but it represented the best he could do in the complex circumstances. "I personally could not see that it would be anything else than legitimate self-defence. How legitimate? To answer that, I would have had to be a moral theologian and a diplomat and a historian and a politician and probably also a mind-reader." He considered what was available to him and reached a conclusion: "Since there was such strong probable evidence that we were really defending ourselves, that settled the question as far as I was concerned."[16] In the light of the "just war" theory he accepted as part of Catholic theology, Merton made the decision that if he were called to the armed forces he could not absolutely refuse to go.

But Merton also explored other aspects of the problem that led him to qualify his judgment about the morality of the war and the conditions under which he might take part. "To my mind, there was very little doubt about the immorality of the methods used in modern war . . . methods that descend to wholesale barbarism and ruthless, indiscriminate slaughter of noncombatants practically without defence are hard to see as anything else but mortal sins." He decided to opt for the status of a noncombatant objector: "one who would willingly enter the army, and serve in the medical corps, or as a stretcher bearer . . . so long as I did not have to drop bombs on open cities, or shoot at other men."[17]

Such a nuanced judgment, coupled with Merton's willingness to accept its consequences for himself, indicates a deliberately conscious decision. He had learned how to take a position rather than merely react to the

whirl of events as he had done a few years before. Merton described
what had happend to him in the years since his first antiwar activities:

> I had developed a conscience. If I had objected to war before, it was more
> on the basis of emotion than anything else. And my unconditional objection
> had, therefore, been foolish in more ways than one. On the other hand, I
> was not making the mistake of switching from one emotional extreme to
> the other. This time, as far as I was able, I felt that I was called upon to
> make clear my own position as a moral duty.[18]

If it was a moral duty for Merton to define and stand by his position
on the war, that imperative arose from his religious commitments, not
from adherence to an abstract ethical system. He chose to be a noncombatant objector because, as he put it, "it seemed to me that this was what
Christ Himself would have done, and what He wanted me to do." On
the strength of that conviction, Merton said, "I put down all my reasons,
and quoted St. Thomas for the edification of the Draft Board."[19] The
Gospel and the tradition of Catholic moral theology had informed Merton's action.

But it is interesting to observe that, even at this early stage of Merton's
thinking about war and his own responsibility in the face of it, there is
an incipient tension between the religious sources from which he draws.
On one hand, there are the commands of Jesus against violence, and,
on the other, the traditional teaching of the Catholic Church qualifying
the Gospel prescriptions and setting out the circumstances in which violence may legitimately be employed by the Christian. The young Catholic
convert accepted the theological tradition that had elaborated the "just
war" theory—but, one suspects, never more than theoretically. The ghost
of Thomas Merton's Quaker mother would always remain with him.
And his own continuing reflection on the Gospels would eventually nudge
him more toward an outright pacifist position, although Merton would
always see it as a relative pacifism. In the 1960s, he would reject the
"just war" theology as wholly inadequate for dealing with nuclear war
and advocate total noncooperation with the war in Vietnam, to the chagrin
of many Roman Catholic ecclesiastics and moral theologians. But in Merton's attempts to formulate his position as a noncombatant objector in
1941, the future struggles are already presaged:

> After all, Christ did say: "Whatsoever you have done to the least of these
> my brethren, you did it to me." I know that it is not the mind of the Church
> that this be applied literally to war—or rather, that war is looked upon as a
> painful but necessary social surgical operation in which you kill your enemy
> not out of hatred but for the common good. That is all very fine in theory.

But as far as I could see, since the government was apparently holding out an opportunity to those who wanted to serve in the army without killing other men, I could avoid the whole question and followed what seemed to me to be a much better course.[20]

It was a mark of Merton's spiritual immaturity that he was still willing to "avoid the whole question" of the disparity between Christ's teachings and the implications of the church's conventional views, but at least he had learned how to take a personally responsible position on World War II consistent with his faith. One of the benefits of his monastic experience and the spiritual maturing it engendered was that Thomas Merton would be able to face that larger question for himself and expose the difficulties, while counseling new alternatives, for his fellow Catholics.

We have looked at one example to illustrate the kind of moral development regarding social issues that the younger Merton, both before and after his religious conversion, was undergoing. Something of that same process of assuming positions and living by their consequences would continue throughout his life as a monk.

As it turned out, Merton was classified unfit for the draft because of his bad teeth. The threat of induction, however, had pushed him to review the ethical issues surrounding the war and to determine his own religiously based stance. He entered the Abbey of Gethsemani on December 10, 1941, three days after Pearl Harbor. In becoming Frater Louis, he wanted to devote himself to the quest for peace within his soul, serving the cause of peace and justice in the world through his penitential sacrifices and ardent prayers for the welfare of humankind. Not for almost twenty years would the voice of Thomas Merton resound through the land, directly assaulting the problems of war, technological violence, and racial discrimination. What was going on in his life during that time? What did that silence betoken?

A deeply ingrained spirituality of withdrawal from human concerns pervaded the monastery Merton entered, as it did all Catholic religious orders before the impact of Vatican II in the 1960s. Merton could not but be affected by the theology and practices of this tradition, especially in his fervor as a still recent Catholic convert and in his liberating joy at having discovered a monastic vocation after much suffering. And given the circumstances of life in the cloister during those days, Merton lacked specific information about events "in the world." Such a lack of data certainly hindered him in formulating judgments about what was happening outside the monastery walls. Nonetheless, even under the severe restrictions on the availability of news, Merton remained in touch with friends and correspondents who apprised him of national and international issues.

In the 1940s, this monk was not unaware of political and social trends. He did not know details, but Merton got the gist of what was happening. Rather than attempting to gather more information, he thought about the significance of events. Only much later would he write about Hiroshima, although the cold passion of his ironic "Original Child Bomb: Points for Meditation to be Scratched on the Walls of a Cave" (1962) betrays the imprint of an indelible memory. Merton anguished about the direction of American life, especially the booming economy of the postwar years and the restless drive for power and things. He read disillusionment, despair, and the hunger for God on the faces of the large number of men who poured into the monastery in that period.

If *Seeds of Contemplation* in the late 1940s displayed a certain measure of spiritual isolationism, there were other strands of theology and of Merton's own approaches present. For all its negative assessment of life in the world, the book revealed a writer who cared deeply about the problems that separate human beings from one another and cause barriers to be erected between different groups within a nation or between nation and nation. Merton's thoughts were much exercised by the matter of war, although now he was paying more attention to its source in the human heart:

> At the root of all war is fear: not so much the fear men have of one another as the fear they have of *everything*. It is not merely that they do not trust one another: they do not even trust themselves. If they are not sure when someone else may turn around and kill them, they are still less sure when they may turn around and kill themselves. They cannot trust anything, because they have ceased to believe in God.[21]

During his early years of contemplation, Merton had come to search out different grounds for his judgments about war. This sort of thinking might appear less "practical" than his ethical analyses of 1941, but it finally proved more valuable for the formulation of his mature positions. The contemplative life was teaching Merton to plumb the deeper dimensions of every human problem.

In *The Sign of Jonas,* Merton indicates that he continued to be alert and sensitive to social issues, although at the time Merton was preoccupied with the tensions of his vocation as a monk and writer and with reflecting on his ordination to the priesthood. On a trip to Louisville in 1949 to apply for American citizenship, for example, the monk noticed the poverty of the Kentucky farmers in Nelson County and felt compassion for the people caught in such conditions. He experienced guilt because people thought that *he* had given up so much, when it was poor folks like these who endured the real "headaches and responsibilities."[22] One striking illustration of Merton's developing perspectives during this period can be seen in the March 3, 1951, journal entry. He had just reread, for the first time since he had written it ten years earlier, the manuscript for a novel completed at St. Bonaventure's and called *Journal of My Escape from the Nazis.*[23] Merton reflected on his position with respect to the war when he had written that novel and criticized his own lack of depth and too narrow outlook. He commented on the book and on himself:

> One of the problems of the book was my personal relation to the world and to the last war. When I wrote it I thought I had a very supernatural solution. After nine years in the monastery I see that it was no solution at all. The false solution went like this: the whole world, of which war is a characteristic expression, is evil. It has therefore to be first ridiculed, then spat upon, and at last rejected with a curse.[24]

Merton reminded himself that he had needed then, and now, to be more discriminating. He was too facile in his condemnations before entering the monastery. That tendency had not been eradicated, but Merton hoped that his experience as a monk was tempering it.

> Wars are evil but the people involved in them are good, and I can do nothing whatever for my own salvation or for the glory of God if I merely withdraw from the mess people are in and make an exhibition of myself and write a big book saying, "Look! I am different!" To do this is to die. Because any man who pretends to be either an angel or a statue must die the death. The immobility of that *Journal of My Escape* was a confession of my own nonentity, and this was the result of a psychological withdrawal.[25]

A considerable shift in Merton's bases for making moral evaluations is evident. After a decade in the monastery, he views his earlier attitudes toward events and people as having been shaped by very subjective and ill-founded reactions. Now Merton is able to distinguish between a bad and a good sort of withdrawal on his part and see what a better understanding of himself demands for his relationship to a troubled world.

> Coming to the monastery has been for me exactly the right kind of withdrawal. It has given me perspective. It has taught me how to live. And now I owe everyone else in the world a share in that life. My first duty is to start, for the first time, to live as a member of the human race which is no more (and no less) ridiculous than I am myself. And my first human act is the recognition of how much I owe everybody else.[26]

He could even be specific, situating himself and his responsibility in relation to his geography, nationality, and particular moment in history:

> Thus God has brought me to Kentucky where the people are, for the most
> part, singularly without inhibitions. This is the precise place He had chosen
> for my sanctification. Here I must revise all my own absurd plans, and take
> myself as I am, Gethsemani as it is, and America as it is—atomic bomb and
> all. It is utterly peculiar, but none the less true, that after all, one's nationality
> should come to have a meaning in the light of eternity. I have lived for thirty-
> six years without one. Nine years ago I was proud of the fact. I thought
> that to be a citizen of heaven all you had to do was throw away your earthly
> passport. But now I have discovered a mystery: that Miss Sue and all the
> other ladies in the office of the Deputy Clerk of the Louisville District Court
> are perhaps in some accidental way empowered to see that I am definitely
> admitted to the Kingdom of Heaven forever.[27]

Such changes in Merton's assessments of himself and the significance
of his placing in time and space represent the fruit of what life in a
monastery could provide for him. In a man who had lived in so many
places and cultures that he belonged to no one of them, it nurtured a
sense of having real ties. And that sense of knowing one has ties with
particular peoples and localities is important for developing moral commitments. Gethsemani helped Thomas Merton put down roots in a country
and a culture for which he would assume some responsibility. At the
same time, the nature of monastic life prevented him from simply identifying with a social class, an ethnic group, or a national mystique. The
discipline fosters detachment, and detachment allows for critical appraisals
of the group and the environment one loves. Retirement from immediate
involvement in social and political situations enabled Merton to become
both loyal and discriminating. It generated in him a capacity for acceptance
without acquiescence. Above all, monastic life taught Merton how to
be critical of himself—an essential ingredient of sound social criticism.

If the young man of 1941 had advanced beyond the communist student
of 1935 because he had learned the rudiments of taking a responsible
position, the monk of 1951 was able to anchor his judgments in a deeper
level of the self. He was a more interior person—more self-aware, more
free to respond from his own center. Merton would be able to meet
new demands, make connections he had not previously grasped, and develop in unanticipated directions. Appointed Master of Scholastics in
June 1951, Merton knew he had reached a new stage of his life: "Thus
I stand on the threshold of a new existence. . . . It is as if I were beginning
all over again to be a Cistercian: but this time I am doing it without
asking myself the abstract questions which are the luxury and the torment

of one's monastic adolescence."[28] Taking up that task did not prove incidental to the development of the guilty bystander.

Acquiring the Skills of Political Responsibility

By its very nature, the process of learning how to make mature ethical decisions—particularly those with a social bearing—is a gradual one. As we have already noted, it involves deliberation, decision, and commitment to a course of action. This unfolding process we are tracing in Merton's life is more like acquiring a skill than mastering a theory. It can come about only by meeting the demands for acquiring any skill: repeated practice under requisite conditions. Thomas Merton's assignment as Master of Scholastics in 1951 and then Master of Novices in 1955 offered such conditions for employing his ethical facility. And the level of development that Merton had already attained at that point motivated his continuing practice.

These positions within the monastic community thrust Merton into the situation of having to give advice to people and direction to their lives. People who undertake that seriously will be forced to examine many dimensions of practical problems; inevitably, they will be thrown back on themselves to scrutinize the grounds for the advice they proffer and to assess the bases for their own choices. So, like any spiritual director faithful to his charge, Merton himself grew in several respects. And each of these had a direct bearing on his capacity for mature acceptance of responsibility in the sociopolitical order.

First of all, as a spiritual director his appreciation of the uniqueness of each person was deepened by a privileged access to the secrets of another's heart. Such experience enabled Merton to become more sensitive not only to what was utterly particular to each person—himself included—but also to what is commonly shared by all people. In 1952, Merton wrote in his journal,

> The more I get to know my Scholastics the more reverence I have for their individuality and the more I meet them in my own solitude. . . . Now that I know them better, I can see something of the depths of solitude which are in every human person, but which most men do not know how to lay open either to themselves or to others or to God.[29]

Merton's contact with the young men under his guidance prodded him to ask new questions of himself and to constantly reassess himself. He grew more careful in his pronouncements on what others should or should not do and was continually forced to examine the honesty of what he was recommending. Some years later, looking back on his work with these young monks, Merton would say: "It causes a lot of searching. You have to try and make sure you never say anything you don't mean."[30] Thus Merton became more tentative in evaluating his efforts to exercise responsibility, and yet more sure that fidelity to that very task was accomplishing something of real value within himself. He reflected on the experience:

> It is now six months since I have been Master of the Scholastics and have looked into their hearts and taken up their burdens upon me. I have not always seen clearly and I have not carried their burdens too well and I have stumbled around a lot, and on many days we have gone around in circles. . . . But I know what I have discovered: that the kind of work I once feared because I thought it would interfere with "solitude" is, in fact, the only true path to solitude. One must be in some sense a hermit before the care of souls can serve to lead one further into the desert. But once God has called you to solitude, everything you touch leads you further into solitude.[31]

The circumstances of Thomas Merton's relations with the monks in his pastoral care supplied a new setting for his social and ethical development. This progress took the form of several emerging realizations. Merton came to understand more profoundly the relationship between ethical decisions within himself and the necessity to act in the external social order. That understanding was rooted in his growing awareness that the exercise of responsibility toward others demands that one deliberate and decide more responsibly oneself. That was scarcely an original insight— but Merton's experience as a spiritual director thrust this recognition on him with new force and clarity. And such an awareness included the acknowledgment that fidelity to values has both an interior and an external bearing. Merton was experiencing how responsibility to others required that he "do something" about himself and also that he "do something" about concrete social arrangements if they hindered the realization of those values in the lives of the people in his charge.

Merton's work with these young monks was leading him not only to question himself but also, inevitably, to question and criticize institutional structures at Gethsemani. Thomas Merton was by temperament and education inclined to be critical of any organized social structure— as the story of his student days makes abundantly clear.[32] During the early years of his monastic life, Merton's critical tendencies were directed, first of all, at himself and his need for purification and, secondly, at the structures of "the world" outside the monastery that thwarted the exercise of true freedom. So, in the 1940s, Merton had not turned his attention to criticizing institutional patterns within his own monastery, except in a minor and muted fashion. That is understandable and seems perfectly normal. A person who has entered into a way of life in order to be him- or herself transformed does not ordinarily begin by noticing things that might counteract or retard that process. Only after one has lived the life for some time will the defects of its institutional organization and collective attitudes become apparent—and only after a person both knows the life from experience, and has broadened his or her horizons so as to envision new possiblities, can constructive suggestions for change be prudently offered.

The job of Master of Scholastics assisted Merton in redirecting his critical inclinations away from just himself (though he would always remain self-critical) and away from "the world" as a theological construct. His taking responsibility within the monastery would help Merton to move from a rather moralistic criticism to one more genuinely "political," although for a time the "public sphere" would be confined to the Abbey of Gethsemani.[33]

What such a shift meant was that Merton could now gain facility in "taking action" within a concrete sphere of social arragements where something *could* be done by a person who took the trouble to think about the situation, examine his own motivations, care enough about the welfare of others to act, and be willing to accept the consequences (often unpleasant) of seeking to bring about change. To take a simple example: as a spiritual director and teacher, Merton would have become more aware of how the limited cultural opportunities and restricted reading of the young monks hampered their human—and therefore spiritual—development. So he would be impelled to try a number of actions to remedy the problem. He could, for instance, harp about it to the community, needle the Abbot to loosen up restrictions, give conferences himself, perhaps seek to obtain more and better books for the library. In short, he could take a position on a concrete local problem and act to change it.

A man such as Thomas Merton sooner or later would come to such actions. The point here is that the situation in which he was placed in the early 1950s provided the impetus for the development and brought together many factors that had been at work for a long time in preparing it. Not that the circumstances caused the change; they constituted the right context for allowing the change to come about. Merton's experience as Master of Scholastics was his "apprenticeship" in assuming political responsibility. That is where he acquired the skills for functioning in the *polis*—the public domain where properly human freedom is exercised.

It was but one step (although a large one) from the public sphere of Gethsemani to that of the larger American scene.

What would be needed for Merton to take that one step? It was his realization that the interior life is not a private affair, even a local one, but is precisely a "political" matter—something of public import pertaining to the common good of a people.

Ever since his conversion to Catholicism, Merton had believed in the doctrine of the Mystical Body of Christ and was convinced that fraternal charity belonged essentially to the love of God. But that conviction was brought into relief through his life of prayer and through his relationships in the monastic community. The truth to which he had heretofore given notional assent, Merton had experienced by the time of writing *Conjectures:* the interdependence of one's deepest interior responses and the welfare of other persons. Now he grasped existentially what he had long since believed: "My life and my death are not purely and simply my own business. I live by and for others."[34]

Merton's duties as a spiritual guide for the young monks helped him to criticize and revise his own conceptions of "the spiritual life." He had, after all, inherited a certain skewed tradition that stressed both a body–soul dichotomy and the autonomy of the individual. He observed the damaging consequences of such a disembodied view and reacted strongly against "the damnable abstractness of the 'spiritual life,' " which Merton considered "one of the chief reasons why many modern men and women cannot endure a lifetime in a monastery or convent." He became increasingly convinced that "as long as thought and prayer are not fully incarnated in an activity which supports and expresses them validly, the heart will be filled with a smothered rage, frustration, and a sense of dishonesty."[35]

Daily give-and-take with his young charges and his fellow monks gradually eroded the vestiges of an individualistic notion of the spiritual life and freed Merton to distinguish the authentic Christian tradition from its distortions. In 1964, he would express the insight this way: "Contrary to what has been thought in recent centuries in the West, the spiritual or interior life is not an exclusively private affair. (In reality, the deepest and most authentic Western traditions are at one with those of the East on this point.)"[36]

In retrospect, Merton attributed his recognition of this concept of the interior life, first of all, to his contacts with the scholastics and novices and, secondly, to communication with people outside the monastery in their suffering. Speaking of his changed horizons in *New Seeds of Contemplation*

(1961), Merton compared this revision to the original *Seeds of Contemplation* (1949):

> When the book was first written, the author had no experience in confronting the needs and problems of other men. The book was written in a kind of isolation, in which the author was alone with his own experience of the contemplative life. And such a book can be written best, and perhaps only, in solitude. The second writing has been no less solitary than the first: but the author's solitude has been modified by contact with other solitudes; with the loneliness, the simplicity, the perplexity of novices and scholastics of his monastic community; with the loneliness of people outside any monastery; with the loneliness of people outside the Church.[37]

Without doubt, Merton's appreciation of the interdependence of the spiritual life developed in the context of solitude, but here he stresses the decisive influence of communication with others. It was just such an engagement with people who were searching that convinced Thomas Merton experientially that "truth develops in conversation."[38] Through involvement in the needs and problems of other people (although limited in number), Merton came to discard his earlier view that somehow the individual discovers truth within and by himself and then shares it with others—thereby allowing truth to "develop." Instead, he began to realize that the truth that is within a person could be liberated only "by seeking true liberty for all."[39] This seeking would entail both dialogue with others and commitment to their struggles.

And so Merton's sense of the "political" dimension of the inner life (his own, first of all) grew. He not only understood that one's thought and prayer must be incarnated but also gradually recognized that the individual's spiritual potentialities require some reference to the public domain if they are to be elicited and fulfilled. Merton never interpreted "reference to the public domain" in a univocal sense. Although living the spiritual life demands a relationship to the public sphere, that does not mean each person must exercise his or her political responsibility in the same manner. Merton was adamant in insisting on that. His own contribution was to preserve his "monastic perspective" and his personal exercise of political responsibility would take the form of writing on the moral issues at stake in American society. Writing was Merton's way of expressing his conviction that "the public and political realm is that where issues are decided in a way worthy of free men: by persuasion and words, not by violence."[40]

Thomas Merton's realizations and decisions to act on public ethical issues were already embedded in his "basic experience" with the novices and scholastics, from which he had been able to "recover hope for the other dimension of man's life, the political."[41]

Political Responsibility as Religious Duty

By the late 1950s Merton would be engaged in criticism of American society and national politics precisely as a religious duty incumbent on him as a monk. As we have seen, his own everyday experience prepared the way for taking up the prophetic burden. But Merton's developed understanding of what that responsibility entailed was significantly shaped by Mohandas Gandhi, the moral leader he regarded as "a model of integrity whom we cannot afford to ignore."[42] Gandhi's view of the relationship of spiritual life to public activity proved central to Merton's thinking, and it was the Hindu's teaching on nonviolence that the Christian monk appropriated as the basis for his social ethic. Gandhi profoundly affected the direction of Merton's moral development and the form its mature expression assumed.

Merton's respect for Gandhi went back as far as young Tom's school days in England.[43] Although Merton's earlier writings make little or no mention of Gandhi, several entries in *Conjectures* indicate that Merton was avidly reading and reflecting on him after 1956.[44] Clearly what drew Merton to Gandhi was his "fundamentally religious view of reality, of being and of truth."[45] In contrast to the West's shallow pragmatism, a fragmented vision of life and frenetic preoccupation with "results," Gandhi represented the ability to see things whole and to act with total detachment for the sake of an objective moral good. He provided Merton with a concept of meaningful human action—and an example of it lived out publicly—in keeping with Merton's contemplative concern as well as with the New Testament.

Studying Gandhi during the 1950s crucially influenced Merton's development, opening up to the Trappist monk an interpretation of action that could license the involvement for which Merton was already ripe. "Political action," in the Gandhian sense, is not by definition secular or unspiritual, but rather "a means of witnessing to the truth and the reality of the cosmic structure by making one's own proper contribution to the order willed by God."[46] Such an understanding would be eminently congenial to a man such as Thomas Merton, who ever sought a religious context for making sense of activity.

Gandhi, in fact, suggested a religious context for political action that had cosmic dimensions as well as profound human significance. Merton perceived this meaning particularly in Gandhi's teaching that only an act done with detachment from results can have spiritual power. Gandhi's insistence on the "truth-force" of detached action impressed Merton deeply. Such action undertaken in the public sphere would not be a matter of "tactics" for achieving certain sectarian or partisan goals, but rather a way of manifesting the truth of man's inner being in the practical order of social relationships. "One could thus preserve one's integrity and peace, being detached from results (which are in the hands of God) and being free from the inner violence that comes from division and untruth."[47]

Gandhi's message was one Merton needed and wanted to hear; it was perfectly consonant with his contemplative orientation toward being and truth, yet justified action to eradicate the evils in American society from which so many people suffered. Gandhi helped to convince Thomas Merton that he not only *could* enter the public arena and be faithful to his vocation as a monk but indeed that he *must* do it as a sacred duty. What Gandhi called *satyagraha,* his vow of nonviolent dedication to the truth, Merton recognized as the New Testament injunction "to do the truth in charity."[48]

In fidelity to his vow, Gandhi had undertaken symbolic deeds (fasts and marches) that were both religious acts of worship and political means for awakening and educating people. Merton "did his truth" in another fashion, but one no less symbolic. He chose to remain in the monastery as an explicit form of *noncooperation* with an unjust, disordered society, and to uncover its falsehood—as well as his own—from this standpoint. Merton would be a guilty bystander. His writing would reflect the perspective of this protest and affirm the reality of the truth that is "the law of our being." A journal jotting stresses the point: "For my own part, I am by my whole life committed to a certain protest and non-acquiescence, and that is why I am a monk."[49] Merton had come to regard his monastic vocation itself as a kind of political action, a nonviolent assertion against a violent society caught in its collective illusions.

Merton's comments in *Conjectures* adumbrate what his most developed essay on Gandhi makes clear about the Trappist's debt to him. Gandhi's grasp and expression of the spiritual unity of all life articulated for Merton exactly what his own intuitions, aspirations, and experiences pointed toward. Merton summed up this meaning in two principles. First, "political action" (in Gandhi's sense) must spring from "an inner realization of spiritual unity" and be "the fruit of inner freedom." National liberty will only be the consequence of overcoming and healing divisions within the person. Second, "the spiritual life of one person is simply the life of all manifesting itself in him."[50] The individual cannot achieve his or her own inner freedom, in fact, apart from the struggles of his or her people and the quest for true liberty for all people.

More than anyone else, Gandhi helped Merton cut through too facile distinctions between private and public, sacred and secular. For Merton, it was convincing that "Gandhi . . . did not identify the 'private' sphere with the 'sacred' and did not cut himself off from public activity as 'secular.' "[51] Rather, for him the public domain was sacred. Even his days of silence and retirement were not merely "private," but for Gandhi "they belonged to India and he owed them to India, because his 'spiritual life' was simply his participation in the life and *dharma* of his people."[52]

This feeling for the *oneness of life*—of the person's inner spirit and outward acts, of the individual's organic relationship with his or her people, of humanity as a whole with the cosmos—Merton acquired in considerable measure from Gandhi. Not that it was something utterly new to Merton; his own temperament and instincts disposed him to such a vision, as did his theological preferences for the Greek Fathers, Augustine, and mystics such as Eckhart. But Merton learned from the great Hindu leader as one kindred spirit does from another: by recognizing what he already possesses but what needs the other to be evoked and given shape. The precise shape Gandhi could give Merton's sense of the unity of life was that of political responsibility.

To be a Christian, a monk, a writer in mid-twentieth-century America, Merton became convinced that he must assume his role in the *polis*. He felt called on to enter into dialogue with his brothers and sisters in the world and take up the nonviolent struggle against the untruth of division within the human heart and the division among peoples. Merton was, as he perceived it, living in the time of the greatest crisis of civilization: "Into this crisis I was born. By this crisis my whole life has been shaped. In this crisis my life will be consumed—but not, I hope, meaninglessly!"[53]

Indeed, Thomas Merton's life was not consumed meaninglessly. He responded to the crisis of his times with a sustained, ever-deepening moral commitment to seek ways of healing divisions with the strong medicine of truth. The intensity and quality of his response was consistent from the early days of Merton's religious conversion to the end of his life. The way in which he understood and expressed this commitment, however, changed in the course of time under the pressure of experience and because of Merton's ability to assimilate and move on.

The young Tom Merton had already grasped that contemporary problems were symptomatic of people's spiritual alienation and went off to the monastery as the place for this particular man to meet the crisis in its full dimensions. There he developed perspective on the world and himself as part of it, learned how to ground more solidly his ethical convictions, and gained facility in acting with detachment from results but with acceptance of consequences. In short, Merton's experience in the monastery effected a transformation in his capacity to deliberate, to decide, to do. This meant he could take a position and follow it through.

As a mature monk, Merton grew to realize that what is truly spiritual may have many manifestations. Political action could be—would be—one of them if the action were nonviolent and the fruit of one's inner unity and unconditional devotion to truth. Merton took it as a duty incumbent on him precisely as a man given to the spiritual quest to participate in the struggle for peace, racial justice, and freedom against totalitarian or technological control. He engaged in the fight by reconfirming his own monastic calling but redefining it, in relation to the specific evils of modern society, as *noncooperation*. In his writing, Merton addressed himself to the concrete issues that divided groups and nations, attempting to bring to light the falsity on which hatred and alienation are inevitably based.

Merton may have dwelt behind the front lines of particular battles, but he spoke from the cutting edge of insight into what was really happening and ultimately at stake in Vietnam, Birmingham, or Madison Avenue. The essays and poems from the late 1950s and after displayed a trenchant criticism of social situations, but gave evidence of Merton's trust in God and hope for humankind. They testified to his belief in the power of truth and his courage to speak what he lived and to live what he spoke. Somewhere near the time Merton took up the prophetic task, he wrote in his journal,

> In a time of drastic change one can be too preoccupied with what is ending or too obsessed with what seems to be beginning. In either case one loses touch with the present and with its obscure but dynamic possibilities. What really matters is openness, readiness, attention, courage to face risk. You do not need to know precisely what is happening, or exactly where it is all going. What you need is to recognize the possibilities and challenges offered by the present moment, and to embrace them with courage, faith, and hope. In such an event, courage is the authentic form taken by love.[54]

The courage of Thomas Merton in the last decade of his life was expressed by challenging his fellow citizens and Christians to come to grips with their complicity in the violence threatening American society, Western civilization, and humankind itself. In "Vietnam—an Overwhelming Atrocity," for instance, he protested that not only our national unity but our very humanity was at stake:

Our external violence in Vietnam is rooted in an inner violence which simply ignores the human reality of those we claim to be helping. The result of this at home has been an ever mounting desperation on the part of those who see the uselessness and inhumanity of the war, together with an increasing stubbornness and truculence on the part of those who insist they want to win, regardless of what victory may mean.[55]

And in "Toward a Theology of Resistance" Merton uncovered the nature of the characteristic form of contemporary violence. "Violence today is *white-collar violence,*" he insisted, *"the systematically organized bureaucratic and technological destruction of man."*[56] Merton castigated "our antiquated theology myopically focused on *individual* violence," and showed that modern violence is "abstract, corporate, businesslike, cool, free of guilt-feelings, and therefore a thousand times more deadly than the eruption of violence out of individual hate."[57] It would not be an easy message to hear for Merton's conventional readers—largely "good Catholics," upright citizens, white, and middle class:

The population of the affluent world is nourished on a steady diet of brutal mythology and hallucination, kept at a constant pitch of high tension by a life that is intrinsically violent in that it forces a large part of the population to submit to an existence which is humanly intolerable. Hence murder, mugging, rape, crime, corruption. But it must be remembered that the crime that breaks out in the ghetto is only the fruit of a greater and more pervasive violence: the injustice which forces people to live in the ghetto in the first place. The problem of violence, then, is not the problem of a few rioters and rebels, but the problem of a whole social structure which is outwardly ordered and respectable, and inwardly ridden by psychopathic obsessions and delusions.[58]

Violence was not the only issue Merton addressed, but it was his most pervasive concern and the underlying theme of his reflections on contemporary events. Ideology (whether of the communist or the capitalist variety) is an assault on the individual's ability and right to think for him- or herself and a manipulation of the person by a system. Media culture and advertising similarly attack our reasonableness and demand a cheap surrender of freedom. Technology becomes the master of its makers and reshapes humanity in its own image. Racism systematically denies the rights of others and refuses to acknowledge the reality and goodness of groups different from those in power and enjoying privilege. For Merton, some form of violence is the source and the expression of every social sin. It is the spiritually destructive force that thrives on the illusion that power can sustain or change any situation. Violence is untruth about human nature; it betrays our only real possibilities for transforming the world and ourselves being transformed by love.

The alternatives to violence, as Merton understood it, are a commitment to truthfulness and reasonable dialogue, a profound respect for one's own freedom and that of others, and an unyielding conviction that (as he learned from Gandhi) "love is the law of our being."[59]

We have already observed how Merton saw his monastic life as a form of nonviolent resistance in the 1960s: "It is my intention to make my entire life a rejection of, a protest against the crimes and injustices of war and political tyranny . . . I am saying NO to all the concentration camps . . . I make monastic silence a protest against the lies of politicians, propagandists and agitators."[60] He was a guilty bystander. Merton acknowledged his share in the world's guilt and willingly took on himself the guilt of others, believing that sacrificial love could assist in their, as well as his, redemption. What he wrote in "Blessed Are the Meek" pertained to a theology of nonviolence and was not said of himself. But we could read it as an affirmation of that to which Thomas Merton's life aspired:

> Non-violence must be realistic and concrete. Like ordinary political action, it is no more than the "art of the possible." But precisely the advantage of non-violence is that it lays claim to a *more Christian and a more humane notion of what is possible.* Where the powerful believe that only power is efficacious, the non-violent resister is persuaded of the superior efficacy of love, openness, peaceful negotiation, and above all of truth. For power can guarantee the interests of *some men* but it can never foster the good of *man.* Power always protects the good of some at the expense of all the others. Only love can attain and preserve the good of all.[61]

Merton appropriated a religious philosophy of nonviolence from Gandhi that articulated a rationale for the Gospel precepts in which he already believed. Gandhi himself had rediscovered his own Hindu tradition on nonviolence by reading the New Testament as a law student in England. Through reading Gandhi, Merton recovered an understanding of the centrality of the Sermon on the Mount. And he was prodded to study Christian history with new eyes and uncover the perennial strand there of a theology of nonviolence.

Merton's brilliant essay, "From Pilgrimage to Crusade," charts the rise of Christian practice and justifications of violence. The Crusades epitomized the perversion of that sacred journey to the holy place, the pilgrimage: "the Crusades introduced a note of fatal ambiguity into the concept of pilgrimage and penance. What was intended as a remedy for sins of violence, particularly murder, now became a consecration of violence."[62] That same terrible fusing of the holy quest and the desire for conquest has profoundly marked American history. "The European white man set foot on the shores of America with the conflicting feelings of an Adam newly restored to paradise and of a Crusader about to scale the walls of Acre."[63] Merton prescribed reversing the movement from pilgrimage to crusade; we must stop our crusades and return to going on pilgrimage:

> Our task now is to learn that if we can voyage to the ends of the earth and there find *ourselves* in the aborigine who most differs from ourselves, we will have made a fruitful pilgrimage. That is why pilgrimage is necessary, in some shape or other. Mere sitting at home and meditating on the divine presence is not enough in our time. We have to come to the end of a long journey and see that the stranger we meet there is no other than ourselves—which is the same as saying that we find Christ in him.[64]

The guilty bystander himself would go on pilgrimage, literally and figuratively. He turned to the East to study its philosophy and religion; eventually he journeyed there to experience firsthand what the traditions talked about. The man who had learned how to assume political responsibility was still looking for something more. Thomas Merton sought the "way of wisdom." He had long since been on that path, but he needed and wanted to go further:

> Thus, far from wishing to abandon this way, the contemplative seeks only to travel further and further along it. This journey without maps leads him into rugged mountainous country where there are often mists and storms and where he is more and more alone. Yet at the same time, ascending the slopes in darkness, feeling more and more keenly his own emptiness, and with the winter wind blowing cruelly through his now tattered garments, he meets at times other travelers on the way, poor pilgrims as he is, and as solitary as he, belonging perhaps to other lands and other traditions.[65]

Merton would become a poor pilgrim in the company of other seekers of wisdom from the Eastern traditions.

CHAPTER

5

A Poor Pilgrim

Writing the preface for the Japanese edition of *Seeds of Contemplation* in 1965, Thomas Merton explained the book and presented himself to an Asian audience:

> It must be admitted that this book was written in a monastery. And the author remains in the same monastery nearly twenty years later, still convinced of the reality of the way he seeks to travel, still seeking to understand better the illusions that are met with in this way but not in order to abandon the way.[1]

He went on to characterize himself as one of many "poor pilgrims" from other lands who travel the solitary way of wisdom, and expressed deep affinity with those from the Far East, especially of the Zen tradition.

> Indeed, the author of this book can say that he feels himself much closer to the Zen monks of ancient Japan than to the busy and impatient men of the West, of his own country, who think in terms of money, power, publicity, machines, business, political advantage, military strategy—who seek, in a word, the triumphant affirmation of their own will, their own power, considered as the end for which they exist. Is not this perhaps the most foolish of all dreams, the most tenacious and damaging of illusions?[2]

That sense of identifying with those of the Eastern contemplative traditions was strong in Merton by the 1960s. The guilty bystander's confrontation with the problems of American society convinced him that the root of the West's fragmentation and brokenness was its "invincible illusion of the isolated ego-self, setting itself up in opposition to love, demanding that its own desire be accepted as the law of the universe, and hence suffering from the fact that by its desire it is fractured in itself and cut off from the loving wisdom in which it should be grounded."[3] The East offered some alternative ways of seeing the self in relation to other selves and to the cosmos; moreover, it possessed ancient meditative and monastic disciplines that schooled their practitioners to overcome such illusion.

Merton sought to contact these traditions as a humble, open, receptive learner. In a talk given in India to monks of many different religions, he expressed the attitude that had informed his study of the East and shaped his purpose for traveling there:

> I speak as a Western monk who is preeminently concerned with his own monastic calling and dedication. I have left my monastery to come here not just as a research scholar or even as an author (which I also happen to be). I come as a pilgrim who is anxious to obtain not just information, not just "facts" about other monastic traditions, but to drink from ancient sources of monastic vision and experience. I seek not only to learn more (quantitatively) about religion and monastic life, but to become a better and more enlightened monk (qualitatively) myself.[4]

To be a pilgrim means to undertake a sacred journey. "In the traditions of all the great religions," Merton wrote, "pilgrimage takes the faithful back to the source and center of the religion itself, the place of theophany, of cleansing, renewal, and salvation."[5] Merton adopted the posture of the poor pilgrim, searching to vivify his own quest by touching base with what enlivened others:

> I think we have now reached a stage of (long-overdue) religious maturity at which it may be possible for someone to remain perfectly faithful to a Christian and Western monastic commitment, and yet to learn in depth from, say, a Buddhist or Hindu discipline and experience. I believe that some of us need to do this in order to improve the quality of our own monastic life and to help in the task of monastic renewal which has been undertaken within the Western Church.[6]

What Merton was looking for as a pilgrim in the East was not a new set of doctrinal beliefs; he remained a convinced and committed Christian. Rather, he sought dialogue with "those in the various religions who seek to penetrate the ultimate ground of their beliefs by a transformation of the religious consciousness."[7] The pilgrim was seeking "true self-transcendence and enlightenment . . . the transformation of consciousness in its ultimate ground, as well as in the highest and most authentic devotional love."[8]

Merton's interest in different forms of spirituality throughout his monastic life inevitably pointed him eastward. He felt that the West, as we have already observed, had betrayed its own rich sapiential heritage and become a "one-eyed giant" possessing science without wisdom.[9] He looked for hope to the great civilizations of Asia with their contemplative traditions. The desire to drink from these springs motivated his trip to the East in 1968—but the thirst had been acquired as far back as 1937.

Aldous Huxley's *Ends and Means,* which Merton read before his conversion at Columbia, had sparked a sudden enthusiasm in him for Eastern mysticism as an antidote to Western materialism. "The most important effect of the book on me was to make me start ransacking the university library for books on Oriental mysticism,"[10] Merton commented in his autobiography. Around the same time, his friendship with the little Hindu monk, Bramachari, who had come to New York aroused a sincere respect for the spiritual character of the Indian tradition in comparison with the crudeness of so much American religion.[11]

Although Merton's fascination with Asian religion and philosophy began during college days, it really developed through long years of study and meditation in the monastery. His understanding grew organically and matured leisurely. In the 1940s, the seeds already planted were germinating; in the 1950s, shoots sprouted and some blossoms appeared; in the 1960s, the fruit of Merton's reflection would ripen.

The knowledge the Trappist acquired of the different Asian traditions was broad, but his depth of understanding specific ones was indeed uneven. Generally he was less concerned with Indian religions than those of China and Japan. Nonetheless, Merton was certainly informed regarding both Hinduism and Islam. He was especially fascinated by the Sufis, the mystic ascetics of Islam from India and Persia.[12] He was familiar with Confucian humanism and ethics, especially of the Ju school. He meditated deeply on the teachings of Kung Tzu (Confucius) and studied the writings of Meng Tzu (Mencius), whose "Ox Mountain Parable" he much admired.[13] Understandably, Merton was very fond of Lao Tzu, the mystic and father of Taoism. The legendary author of the *Tao Te Ching* was a teacher after his own heart.[14]

But it was Chuang Tzu who most intrigued Merton and whose writings provided his principal contact with Taoism. Merton's book on this ancient Chinese philosopher-recluse, *The Way of Chuang Tzu,* was the result of long and arduous labor. He spent five years reading, meditating on, and annotating the texts. Regarding Chuang Tzu as "the greatest of the Taoist writers whose historical existence can be verified," Merton was always careful not to confuse the Taoism of Chuang Tzu with "the popular degenerate amalgam of superstition, alchemy, magic, and health-culture which Taoism later became."[15]

More than Merton's appreciation of Taoism was owed to Chuang Tzu. The writings of the ancient sage deeply affected Merton's view of solitude, and he felt he shared with the Chinese recluse "a monastic outlook which is common to all those who have elected to question the value of a life submitted entirely to arbitrary secular presuppositions."[16] Chuang Tzu also provided a link with Zen for Merton:

> There is no question that the kind of thought and culture represented by Chuang Tzu was what transformed highly speculative Indian Buddhism into the humorous, iconoclastic, and totally practical kind of Buddhism that was to flourish in China and in Japan in the various schools of Zen. Zen throws light on Chuang Tzu, and Chuang Tzu throws light on Zen.[17]

Buddhism in general, and Zen in particular, held the indisputable sway over Merton's reading, writing, and affection regarding the Eastern traditions. While never an "academic" Buddhist scholar, Merton had read widely, discussed seriously, and was genuinely knowledgeable in the field.[18] He enjoyed a considerable correspondence with several noted Asian scholars such as John C. H. Wu and Daisetz T. Suzuki. The latter was undoubtedly the single most important influence in shaping Merton's understanding of Zen Buddhism. The dialogue with Suzuki had begun in 1959 when Merton sent him a copy of *The Wisdom of the Desert* with a note that he might be interested in the Desert Fathers because of their similarity to some of the Japanese Zen Masters. The ensuing exchange of views marked a turning point in Merton's involvement with Zen Buddhism.

Even before this contact with Suzuki, however, Merton was interested in Buddhism and considerably informed about it. Scattered references in his writings from the late 1940s and throughout the 1950s indicate he was reading and thinking about Buddhism, especially Zen, over the years at Gethsemani.[19] But once his dialogue with Suzuki was initiated, Zen became one of Merton's major passions and remained so until the time of his death in Asia.

What prepared Merton to plunge into the way of Zen? Besides his increasing familiarity with the Buddhist tradition itself, what had contributed during the first two decades of Merton's monastic life to the mature concern with Zen that showed itself in the last one? In brief, it was the direction of Merton's study of and convictions regarding Christian contemplation, as well as his experience of it.

Merton's youthful orientation to Scholastic and Neo-Scholastic thought would eventually point him toward Zen (perhaps not without some irony!), because it was a concern with the nature of Being as such that drew him to both traditions, divergent though they be. Even more important was Merton's exposure to "apophatic" (negative—what cannot be said) theology during his formative years in the monastery. His early books displayed a decided preference for the Christian mystics of "darkness."[20] The theological conceptions and practical advice Merton appropriated from such masters as Pseudo-Dionysius, Gregory of Nyssa, Tauler, Ruysbroeck, and, above all, John of the Cross would later serve his Zen-ward gravitation.[21] Merton's early book on mystical theology, *The Ascent to Truth*, clearly reflects a distrust of conceptual knowledge. The accent on *experience* and *intuition* of reality is unmistakable, and his language at the beginning of the 1950s is not far distant from Merton's first essays on Zen at the close of that decade:

> There are times when we seem suddenly to awake and discover the full meaning of our present reality. Such discoveries are not capable of being contained in formulas and definitions. They are a matter of personal experience, of uncommunicable intuition. In the light of such an experience it is easy to see the futility of all the trifles that occupy our minds. We recapture something of the calm and balance that ought always to be ours, and we understand that life is far too great a gift to be squandered on anything less than perfection.[22]

Merton's own practice of contemplation was informed by a Zen-like perception. In a 1952 journal entry, he described his experience while working in the woods near the monastery:

> When your tongue is silent, you can rest in the silence of the forest. When your imagination is silent, the forest speaks to you, tells you of its unreality and of the Reality of God. But when your mind is silent, then the forest suddenly becomes magnificently real and blazes transparently with the Reality of God: for now I know that the Creation which first seems to reveal Him, by the same concepts, finally is revealed in Him, in the Holy Spirit: and we who are in God find ourselves united, in Him, with all that springs from Him. This is prayer, and this is glory![23]

A meditation from 1953 or 1954 reflects a similar approach to the Zen emphasis on the direct experience of being as that which transcends the subject–object division:

> My knowledge of myself in silence (not by reflection on my self, but by penetration to the mystery of my true self which is beyond words and concepts because it is utterly particular) opens out into the silence and the "subjectivity" of God's own self.[24]

By the middle of the decade, Merton was more and more disposed to find Zen congenial. Zilboorg's personal advice to him in 1956 (that Merton become less "verbalogical" and stop substituting words for reality) could only be a push in the direction of Zen. An even more persistent impetus, however, would be Merton's reading and thinking about the monastic tradition. In his conferences as Master of Novices, Merton dealt with some very Zen-sounding themes ("emptiness," "discovery of the true self," "overcoming illusion"), although he had encountered these notions in the monastic fathers of the Western tradition. In particular, Cassian's idea of *puritas cordis* provided an important point of contact with Zen thinking.[25] Later, in his dialogue with Suzuki, Merton would draw an explicit comparison between Cassian's "purity of heart" and the Zen meaning of "emptiness." But Cassian himself had picked up the idea from the Desert Fathers, and it was Merton's encounter with them that undoubtedly was the most significant influence from within the Christian tradition impelling the Trappist toward Zen.

Collecting and translating the "sayings" of the Desert Fathers (monks and hermits of the fourth and fifth centuries in Egypt, Palestine, Arabia, and Persia) during the late 1950s provided Merton the opportunity to get to know intimately perhaps the most Zen-like collection of people in the history of Christianity. For Merton, producing *The Wisdom of the Desert* proved not so much a task of scholarly research as the enjoyable experience of making friends with his monastic relatives and spiritual kin.[26] He discovered in these men an expression of his personal attitude to life, and Merton recognized through them his own profound affinities with Zen—as well as theirs. What he admired in these first Christian hermits was their emphasis on solitude, simplicity, poverty, emptiness, compassion, and peace. Merton delighted in their unconventional posture toward the world and appreciated "their fabulous originality."[27] For him, these were the "sane" men possessed of a paradoxical wisdom: "With the Desert Fathers, you have the characteristic of a clean break with a conventional, accepted social context in order to swim for one's life into an apparently irrational void."[28] Reflecting on the Desert Fathers reinforced the thrust of Merton's development of political responsibility, and this too facilitated his gravitation toward Zen. Merton discerned a common approach in the Desert Fathers and the Zen Masters regarding how a person might paradoxically love his or her brothers and sisters by leaving their world "to help save it in saving oneself."[29] He understood this attitude as anything but individualistic; it was, rather, the expression of compassion born of insight and entailed the acceptance of social responsibility. The example and teachings of the Desert Fathers supported Merton's judgment about how he should respond to the crises of the time. A similar spirit pervaded the Zen Masters, and he found guidance in their off-beat little stories.[30]

Merton believed that the Desert Fathers had much to teach contemporary people about moral responsibility and the spiritual quest: "We need to learn from these men of the fourth century how to ignore prejudice, defy compulsion and strike out fearlessly into the unknown."[31] And it was the qualities that Merton so respected in these Christians that he discovered in the Zen Masters of China and Japan. Both groups of teachers entered significantly into the life of Thomas Merton around the same time: toward the end of the 1950s. The language in which he described the striving and goal of the Desert Fathers exhibits how far along the Zen road Merton had come:

> The proximate end of all this striving was "purity of heart"—a clear unobstructed vision of the true state of affairs, an intuitive grasp of one's own inner reality as anchored, or rather lost, in God through Christ. The fruit of this was *quies:* "rest." . . . The "rest" which these men sought was simply the sanity and poise of a being that no longer has to look at itself because it is carried away by the perfection of freedom that is in it. . . . Rest, then, was a kind of simple no-whereness and no-mindedness that had lost all preoccupation with a false or limited "self." At peace in the possession of a sublime "Nothing" the spirit laid hold, in secret, upon the "All"—without trying to know what is possessed.[32]

Beginning in 1959, the dialogue with Suzuki represented the step from Merton's moving toward Zen to setting foot on the Zen way itself.

The Way of Zen

In the last decade of his life, Merton moved steadily and seriously into Zen. Journal reflections on that subject were abundant and suggested he was much occupied with it.[33] Merton was writing prodigiously on Zen and various aspects of Buddhism. He published nearly twenty-five essays on these or related topics and devoted several books to them. Few men would give so much time and effort to something they studied just as detached observers—certainly not Thomas Merton! Such literary output from him could only bespeak an involvement from the inside (of both himself and that about which he wrote). How then did Merton understand the nature of what he was doing with respect to Zen?

In "Wisdom in Emptiness: A Dialogue by Daisetz T. Suzuki and Thomas Merton," the Christian monk made a good start on the way to

Zen, although he perhaps had gotten off on the wrong foot. Looking back on that dialogue nearly ten years later when including it in his collection of Zen writings, *Zen and the Birds of Appetite,* Merton acknowledged his mistake. The editor in him remarked in the "Postface" of the book:

> I was tempted to cut out my own "final remarks" in the dialogue because they are so confusing. Not that they are "wrong," in the sense of "false," or "erroneous," but because any attempt to handle Zen in theological language is bound to miss the point. If I leave these remarks where they are, I do so as an example of how *not* to approach Zen.[34]

Merton had searched for correspondences between Zen terms and language from the Christian theological tradition. For example, John of the Cross' "night" and Cassian's "purity of heart" appeared similar to Zen "emptiness."[35]

Merton's earlier attempt "to handle Zen in theological language," and therefore "to miss the point" assumed that Suzuki was speaking about Zen as a structure of thought or a system of language. If Zen were conceived that way, then terms from other systems might be used to "translate" it. By the time of Merton's later Zen essays, however, he had become aware of that assumption and rejected it. For instance, in "A Christian Looks at Zen" (1967), Merton explained what he now understood Suzuki to be doing in using the fourteenth-century Rhineland mystic, Meister Eckhart, in the Zen scholar's well-known book, *Mysticism: Christian and Buddhist.* "He was not comparing the *mystical theology* of Eckhart with the Buddhist philosophy of the Zen Masters, but the *experience* of Eckhart, ontologically and psychologically, with the *experience* of the Zen Masters."[36] Merton came to think that comparing the experiences of Christian mystics and Zen meditators "is a reasonable enterprise, offering some small hope of interesting and valid results,"[37] while the effort to compare Christianity and Zen is a fruitless and pointless task. "The truth of the matter is that you can hardly set Christianity and Zen side by side and compare them. This would almost be like trying to compare mathematics and tennis."[38]

In his most recent essay included in *Zen and the Birds of Appetite,* Merton clearly distinguished two ways of considering Zen. First, it might be studied as a historical and cultural phenomenon, part of a complex religious and social structure. "But in that case what fits into a system is *Buddhism* rather than *Zen.* The more Zen is considered as Buddhist the more it can be grasped as an expression of man's cultural and religious impulse."[39] Second, Zen may be regarded as "outside all particular structures and distinct forms," simply as "consciousness unstructured by particular form or particular system, a trans-cultural, trans-religious, trans-formed consciousness."[40] In this sense, Zen is "the quest for direct and pure experience on a metaphysical level, liberated from verbal formulas and linguistic preconceptions."[41] Put more simply, Zen, as distinct from Zen Buddhism, may be understood as "a basic natural attitude of mind, a kind of elemental simplicity and sanity which is not necessarily bound to any one religious creed or metaphysic."[42] Seen in this light, Zen neither denies nor affirms any specific set of ideas, beliefs, or practices. It has no "message." As the saying of the Zen Masters goes, "Zen teaches nothing."[43] Throughout most of the 1960s, Merton was principally concerned with Zen in this second way of approaching it. Once he had discovered his initial mistake, Merton observed the distinction between Zen Buddhism as a religious system or conceptual structure and Zen as a "way" that is paradoxically "not a way."[44]

Following the dialogue with Suzuki, Merton's facility for making the distinction—as well as his preference for the latter approach—was helped along from several sources. His old friend, Dom Aelred Graham, brought out a book whose very title suggested that Zen could be extracted from its Buddhist context: *Zen Catholicism*.[45] Merton acknowledged the value of Graham's work and registered agreement with this point of view. He said of Graham's writing what others would say of Merton's: "It represents a wide and intelligent reading of the plentiful Zen literature now available in English, but it always remains informal and personal."[46]

More important was Merton's continued reading of the Zen Masters, which was sparked by the dialogue and notably guided by Suzuki's preferences. Merton was especially impressed with the seventh-century Chinese Master of Zen, Hui Neng (Southern School): "For Hui Neng all life was Zen. Zen could not be found merely by turning away from life to become absorbed in meditation. Zen is the very awareness of life living itself in us."[47] By the time he had worked through Hui Neng (with the assistance of books such as Suzuki's *The Zen Doctrine of No-Mind*), Merton would disagree with R. C. Zaehner that Zen is "passive mysticism" and with Heinrich Dumoulin that it should be called a "natural mysticism."[48] Such terms as *mysticism* and *religion* simply did not apply to what Merton now understood by "Zen":

> The word "Zen" comes from the Chinese *Ch'an*, which designates a certain type of meditation, yet Zen is not a "method of meditation" or a kind of spirituality. It is a "way" and an "experience," a "life," but the way is paradoxically "not a way." Zen is therefore not a religion, not a philosophy, not a system of thought, not a doctrine, not an ascesis.[49]

This view remained constant through Merton's later essays. If any-thing, he became more explicit in cautioning Westerners not to think of Zen as any kind of system (unless they mean Zen Buddhism):

> Zen is not a systematic explanation of life, it is not an ideology, it is not a world view, it is not a theology of revelation and salvation, it is not a mystique, it is not a way of ascetic perfection, it is not mysticism as this is understood in the West, in fact it fits no convenient category of ours.[50]

This affirmation of what Zen is *not* was the basis for Merton's conviction that "Zen is perfectly compatible with Christian belief and indeed with Christian mysticism (if we understand Zen in its pure state, as metaphys-ical intuition.)"[51] And there is the key to what Zen can be said to be: metaphysical intuition of being. At the heart of Zen is an incommunicable insight. "One might say," Merton paradoxically said of the ineffable, "that Zen is the ontological *awareness of pure being beyond subject and object,* an immediate grasp of being in its 'suchness' and 'thusness.' "[52]

Such a state of mind is not easy to name and even harder to character-ize. "For want of a better term," Merton says of this awareness that is "not reflexive, not self-conscious, not philosophical, not theological . . . we may call it 'purely spiritual.' " Because of this "purely spiritual quality" of ontological awareness, Zen does not make statements *about* the meta-physical structure of being. "Rather it points directly to being itself, with-out indulging in speculation." Thus "the Zen Masters staunchly refuse to rationalize or verbalize the Zen experience."[53]

Merton may have admired the Zen Masters for this refusal, but he did not follow their lead. Unlike them, Merton was not content simply to "point" by means of poems, anecdotes, and *koans* (although indeed he loved and did employ such methods). He wrote about Zen in an exposi-tory manner. In fact, frequently enough he tried to explain it in philosophi-cal terms and with analytical procedures, even though Merton himself asserted that Zen is "in some sense an anti-language, and the 'logic' of Zen is a radical reversal of philosophical logic."[54] There was thus a discrep-ancy between what Merton acknowledged as the incommunicable nature of Zen and his use of conceptual apparatus and verbal formulations to speak about it. He was not unaware of that disparity. In part, at least, Merton excused it as endemic to the human situation. "The human di-lemma of communication is that we cannot communicate ordinarily with-out words and signs, but even ordinary experience tends to be falsified by our habits of verbalization and rationalization."[55] Merton recognized that in attempting to elucidate Zen he was caught in the same paradox as apophatic theology: how speak of that which is beyond language.[56] The Zen Masters might "point" and remain silent, but for all his efforts to emulate them, Thomas Merton was a highly verbal Westerner impelled to speak about what he experienced or tried to understand. In that respect, he was a *poor* pilgrim—not keeping to the true path.

Insofar as he sought to express the inexpressible, Merton strayed from the Zen way and not infrequently got lost in conceptual jungles and linguistic labyrinths. Yet even these excursions led him more surely—if roundaboutly—toward what the pilgrim was seeking. There is a Zen-like irony about Merton's efforts to understand and to articulate the Zen experience. His very failure to maintain silence about it engaged him in a process that pushed him back on himself as a conscious subject. And the breakthrough to awareness of one's subjectivity is what Zen is all about.[57]

A contemporary philosopher and theologian, Bernard Lonergan, spells out subjectivity as that unique presence-to-self that constitutes a human person. He shows how this self-presence is revealed and structured in the ways we experience and understand the world and then go on to take a position toward it in the judgments and decisions we make.[58] In these terms, we can see how Merton's struggle to grasp and interpret Zen forced him back on himself as an inquiring subject and enabled him to appropriate his own subjectivity as the ground of all conscious operations.[59]

It was inevitable that a mind so acute as Merton's would employ Zen in a manner directed to clarifying its own processes. But more than that was accomplished. Zen disclosed to Merton the limits of rational consciousness and reenforced his long-standing view of illusion as *sin*, rather than merely intellectual misconception.

Merton had always regarded reason as insufficient for knowing reality, as his voluminous writings on faith, mysticism, and apophatic theology testify. In that sense, Zen told Merton nothing new. What it did accomplish, however, was a *graphic exemplification* for him of the distinction between what *can* be said and what *cannot* be articulated verbally but expressed only in a mode of life. Call it the distinction between "reason and faith," the "metaphysical and the spiritual," "problem and mystery," or what have you. Merton's terms were not always clear and certainly not consistent, but we cannot miss the point: rational consciousness must be transcended and transformed if one is to attain the fullness of human possibility.

The influential modern philosopher Ludwig Wittgenstein has said, "That which expresses *itself* in language, *we* cannot express by language.

. . . What *can* be shown cannot be said."[60] For Merton, Zen was an experience underscoring Wittgenstein's dictum. Even more, Zen affirmed Merton's fundamental conviction "that the heart of Catholicism, too, is a *living experience* of unity in Christ which far transcends conceptual formulations."[61] As the Trappist monk understood Zen, it showed what cannot be said. In this sense, Zen might be thought of as pointing toward the God who revealed himself in the mystery of Christ.

> In the first two chapters of the first Epistle to the Corinthians St. Paul distinguishes between two kinds of wisdom: one which consists in the knowledge of words and statements, a rational, dialectical wisdom, and another which is at once a matter of paradox and of experience, and goes beyond the reach of reason. To attain to this spiritual wisdom, one must first be liberated from servile dependence on the "wisdom of speech" (1 Cor. 1:17). This liberation is effected by the "word of the Cross" which makes no sense to those who cling to their own familiar views and habits of thought. . . . But when one has been freed from dependence on verbal formulas and conceptual structures, the Cross becomes a source of power."[62]

Besides displaying the limits of rational consciousness, Zen—and in this instance, especially Zen *Buddhism*—reminded Merton that illusion is not an intellectual mistake, but a falsified relationship to the whole of reality:

> What the Buddhists call *Avidya.* . . . is an invincible error concerning the very nature of reality and man himself. It is a disposition to treat the ego as an absolute and central reality and to refer all things to it as objects of desire or of repulsion. Christianity attributes this view of man and of reality to "original sin."[63]

Thus for Merton, "illusion" equals "sin," for illusion is "a basic inauthenticity, a kind of predisposition to bad faith in our understanding of ourselves and of the world." It implies a certain willfulness to make things other than they are and to make them subserve our desire for pleasure and power. "As long as this 'brokenness' of existence continues, there is no way out of the inner contradictions that it imposes upon us."[64] At the heart of the "brokenness of existence" is "a persistent and invincible illusion of the isolated ego-self" that is the source of our endless and futile desires, for the "isolated individual ego constitutes itself in opposition to love and being."[65]

The Buddhist answer to the radical problem of illusion, as Merton puts it, is to follow the Buddha's teaching and example, seeking as a disciple:

to apprehend the real nature of his existence and to patiently rediscover his real roots in the true ground of all being. When man is grounded in authentic truth and love the roots of desire themselves wither, brokenness is at an end, and truth is found in the wholeness and simplicity of *Nirvana:* perfect awareness and perfect compassion. *Nirvana* is the wisdom of perfect love grounded in itself and shining through everything, meeting with no opposition.[66]

The Christian answer is to die and rise with Christ—to put to death the "old man" and to be reborn in the life of the Spirit. "The 'death of the old man' is not the destruction of personality but the dissipation of an illusion, and the discovery of the new man is the realization of what was there all along, at least as a radical possibility, by reason of the fact that man is the image of God."[67]

Overcoming the fundamental condition of illusion-sin, for the Christian, is not merely the result of moral effort. It is a divine gift and requires an openness to receive it on the part of the person. "Openness is not something to be acquired, but a radical gift that has been lost and must be recovered."[68] That gift has been called by many names: "dying and rising in Christ," "the indwelling of the Spirit," "grace," "the experience of God's presence." Whatever one names this reality, Merton was certainly talking about a transformation that goes beyond the level of rational consciousness. Zen and Zen Buddhism provided him with another vocabulary for understanding the process of liberation from illusion as transcendent. "Enlightenment" or *"Nirvana,"* like the Christian conception of regeneration in Christ, are not simply psychological experiences that an individual can "have." The Zen Buddhist understanding of "experience" that is "beyond experience" proved useful to Merton for articulating a central truth of Christian theology:

> If an experience is something which one can "have" and "grasp" and "possess," if it can be an object of desire, a content of consciousness, then it is not *Nirvana.* In a sense *Nirvana* is beyond experience. Yet it is also the "highest experience" if we see it as a liberation from merely psychological limitations. The words "experience of love" must not be understood in terms of emotional fulfillment, of desire and possession, but of full realization, total awakening— a complete realization of love not merely as the emotion of a feeling subject, but as the wide openness of Being itself, the realization that Pure Being is Infinite Giving, that Absolute Emptiness is Absolute Compassion. This realization is not intellectual, not abstract, but concrete. It is, in Christ's words, "Spirit and Life." It is then not simply the awareness of a loving subject that he has love in himself, but the awareness of the Spirit of Love as the source of all that is and of all love.[69]

Merton's intellectual pilgrimage into Zen gave him a way of interpreting the Gospel without the pitfalls of what he regarded as the disastrous consequences of the "Cartesian consciousness" for Christianity and the West. He was speaking of the appeal of Zen in general—but the comment in *Conjectures* applied most of all to Thomas Merton himself:

> The taste for Zen in the West is in part a healthy reaction of people exasperated with the heritage of four centuries of Cartesianism: the reification of concepts, idolization of the reflexive consciousness, flight from being into verbalism, mathematics, and rationalization. Descartes made a fetish out of the mirror in which the self finds itself. Zen shatters it.[70]

Zen led Merton to an alternative conception of human consciousness and its fulfillment over against the Cartesian type of isolated self-consciousness surrounded by objects. Merton speaks of "pure consciousness" rather than "consciousness of" this or that, even of self:

> It starts not from the thinking and self-aware subject but from Being ontologically seen to be beyond, and prior to the subject-object divison. Underlying the subjective experience of the individual self there is an immediate experience of Being. This is totally different from an experience of self-consciousness. It is completely nonobjective. It has in it none of the split and alienation that occurs when the subject becomes aware of itself as a quasi-object. The consciousness of Being . . . in an immediate experience that goes beyond reflexive awareness. It is not "consciousness of" but *pure consciousness,* in which the subject as such disappears.[71]

With such consciousness, a person is aware of him- or herself only as a self that is to be lost in God. Merton calls the fulfillment of this process "transcendent experience." The self ceases to be aware of itself as a distinct subject, experiences itself as "no-self." In an important essay comparing the approaches of Zen, Sufism, and Christian mysticism, Merton answers the question, "What is meant by *transcendent experience?"* thus:

> It is an experience of metaphysical or mystical self-transcending and also at the same time an experience of the "Transcendent" or the "Absolute" or "God" not so much as object but Subject. The Absolute Ground of Being . . . is realized so to speak "from within"—realized from within "Himself" and from within "myself," though "myself" is now lost and "found" "in Him." These metaphorical expressions all point to the problem we have in mind: the problem of a self that is "no-self," that is by no means an "alienated self" but on the contrary a transcendent Self which, to clarify it in Christian terms, is metaphysically distinct from the Self of God and yet perfectly identified with that Self by love and freedom, so that there appears to be but one Self. Experience of this is what we here call "transcendent experience" or

the illumination of wisdom *(Sapientia, Sophia, Prajna)*. To attain this experience is to penetrate the reality of all that is, to grasp the meaning of one's own existence, to find one's true place in the scheme of things, to relate perfectly to all that is in a relation of identity and love.[72]

A radical and revolutionary change takes place in the subject who undergoes the transcendent experience—what Merton calls a "transformation of consciousness." From an awareness of one's "empirical self" ("ego-self" and "false self" are synonyms Merton employs), the individual comes to an awareness of the "transcendent self" (also referred to as the "person" or "true self"). No longer conscious of himself or herself as an isolated ego, the person experiences the self in its deepest Ground of Being and as absolutely dependent on it. "In the Christian tradition," Merton notes, "the focus of this 'experience' is found not in the individual self as a separate, limited and temporal ego, but in Christ, or the Holy Spirit 'within' this self. In Zen it is Self with a capital *S,* that is to say precisely *not* the ego-self. This Self is the Void."[73]

Specifically for the Christian, transcendent experience is always a participation in "the mind of Christ," who "emptied himself . . . obedient unto death" (Phil. 2:5–10). Merton elaborates that theme:

> This dynamic of emptying and of transcendence accurately defines the transformation of the Christian consciousness in Christ. It is a kenotic transformation, an emptying of all the contents of the ego-consciousness to become a void in which the light of God or the glory of God, the full radiation of the infinite reality of His Being and Love are manifested.[74]

Writing a preface to the Japanese edition of *The Seven Storey Mountain* in 1963, Thomas Merton expressed that same theme, but here in a Zen idiom and with reference to himself and his own story:

> The ALL is nothing, for if it were to be a single thing separated from all other things, it would not be ALL. This precisely is the liberty I have always sought: the freedom of being subject to nothing and therefore to live in ALL, through ALL, for ALL, by Him who is ALL. In Christian terms, this is to live "in Christ" and by the "Spirit of Christ," for the Spirit is like the wind, blowing where He pleases, and He is the Spirit of Truth. The "Truth shall make you free."
>
> But if the Truth is to make me free, I must also let go my hold upon myself, and not retain the semblance of a self which is an object or a "thing." I, too, must be no-thing. And when I am no-thing I am in the ALL, and Christ lives in me.[75]

Merton went on to affirm his commitment to the monastic way, in characteristically personal terms, and with more than a hint that this poor pilgrim knew the transcendent experience from the inside:

I am still in the monastery, and intend to stay there. I have never had any doubt whatever of my monastic vocation. If I have ever had any desire for change, it has been for a more solitary, more "monastic" way. But precisely because of this it can be said that I am in some sense everywhere. My monastery is not a home. It is not a place where I am rooted and established on the earth. It is not an environment in which I become aware of myself as an individual, but rather a place in which I disappear from the world as an object of interest in order to be everywhere in it by hiddenness and compassion. To exist everywhere I have to be No-one.[76]

The Pilgrim Goes to Asia

Thomas Merton had begun his novitiate in becoming "No-one" by undertaking a hermit's life at Gethsemani. That venture represented a deliberate step in his interior journey—something of "an exercise in ascetic homelessness."[77] When the opportunity came for him to travel to Asia, the Trappist who had remained in his monastery for twenty-seven years was a practiced pilgrim. He had, at least vicariously, gone to the sacred "places" of Buddhism, Taoism, Hinduism, and Sufism. Through the years he had read assiduously, corresponded extensively, and meditated frequently on these and other Eastern religious traditions. Merton studied their sacred texts, read their philosophical and practical expositors, contemplated the characteristic art forms, talked with scholars or simple followers when he could, and even tried his own hand at translations or free interpretative readings or calligraphy. His trip to Asia in 1968 was not a vacation, not a tour. It was a pilgrimage in the richest sense of the word. Someone might have said of Merton's journey to Asia what he had once written of the travels of the earliest Celtic monks:

> The pilgrimage of the Celtic monk was not then just endless and aimless wandering for its own sake. It was a journey to a mysterious, unknown, but divinely appointed place, which was to be the place of the monk's ultimate meeting with God.[78]

Merton's well-documented essay, "From Pilgrimage to Crusade," showed that there are several types of pilgrimages in various religious traditions and at different periods of Christian history. In one sort, the pilgrim "seeks to return to a mythical source, a place of 'origin,' the 'home' where the ancestors came from."[79] There is another kind of pilgrimage to the geographical source or historical center of a religion: Jerusalem, Rome, or Mecca. Or pilgrims visit "sites of repentance and healing . . . tombs of saints, places of hierophany and of joy."[80] The Celtic monks of the sixth and seventh centuries developed their own peculiar kind of pilgrimage: "Peregrinatio, or 'going forth into strange countries,' was a characteristically Irish form of asceticism. The Irish *peregrinus,* or pilgrim, set out on this journey, not in order to visit a sacred shrine, but in search of solitude and exile."[81]

From his own experience as a solitary explorer, Merton appreciated the relationship of the inner journey of contemplation and an actual pilgrimage to a holy place or for the spiritual experience of exile. He observed how "St. Gregory of Nyssa was writing his life of Moses, which is in fact a description of the mystical itinerary and ascent of the monk to God in 'dark contemplation' "[82] and noted that this writing took place in the fourth century when large numbers of anchorites from the deserts of Egypt and Palestine were journeying to Mount Sinai. Perceiving this connection allowed Merton to link his own life as a hermit with a desire to travel in the Far East: "The geographical pilgrimage is the symbolic acting out of an inner journey. The inner journey is the interpolation of the meanings and signs of the outer pilgrimage. One can have one without the other. It is best to have both."[83]

And what Merton wrote elsewhere about a Zen Buddhist monk whose life is seen as a pilgrimage also applied to this monk of Gethsemani. "The purpose of *angya* or pilgrimage is to convince the monk of the fact that his whole life is a search, in exile, for his true home."[84] Thomas Merton was writing an essay called "Zen Buddhist Monasticism," but the comments, *mutatis mutandis,* could belong in one of his own journals:

> The Buddhist monastic life is essentially a life of pilgrimage *(angya).* It is as a pilgrim that the newcomer presents himself at the monastery door. . . . This pilgrimage, let us repeat it, does not end at the monastery gate. When his period of training has ended, the monk will once again take to the road and continue his search, though now, we hope, it will have a totally new dimension. His whole monastic life is a pilgrimage, and his stay in the monastery is only one of the incidents in his journey. Not even the monastery and the training, the discipline, and the teaching and the observance, are permitted to become ends in themselves. However, in practice, it is no longer possible or usual for Zen monks to live the true pilgrimage life that was led by their fathers. Yet, if they return to the world, they must live in it with the mentality of pilgrims.[85]

The paradoxical themes of homelessness and finding one's true home come together for Merton in the metaphor of the pilgrim. The wandering is a return, the going out a coming back, the seeking a finding. Merton's trip to Asia was but a continuation of his journey into solitude, which was always a seeking for God. His first lyric journal entry (October 15, 1968) when departing for the Far East captured the pilgrim's sense of destiny, the poet's gift for images, and the puckish cloistered monk's delight to be *en route* in a world he loved:

There was a delay getting off the ground at San Francisco: the slow ballet of big tailfins in the sun. Now here. Now there. A quadrille of planes jockeying for place on the runway.

The moment of take-off was ecstatic. The dewy wing suddenly covered with rivers of cold sweat running backward. The window wept jagged shining courses of tears. Joy. We left the ground—I with Christian mantras and a great sense of destiny, of being at last on my true way after years of waiting and wondering and fooling around.

May I not come back without having settled the great affair. . . .

I am going home, to the home where I have never been in this body, where I have never been in this washable suit (washed by Sister Gerarda the other day at the Redwoods).[86]

Later that month, in an informal talk at the Temple of Understanding in Calcutta, the pilgrim tried to identify himself to his audience:

First, let me struggle with the contradiction that I have to live with, in appearing before you in what I really consider to be a disguise, because I never, never wear this (a clerical collar). What I ordinarily wear is blue jeans and an open shirt; which brings me to the question that people have been asking to a great extent: Whom do you represent? What religion do you represent? And that, too, is a rather difficult question to answer. I come with the notion of perhaps saying something for monks and to monks of all religions because I am supposed to be a monk. . . . I may not look like one.[87]

Merton employed another metaphor for himself, one related to that of the solitary explorer, the guilty bystander, and the poor pilgrim: a marginal person. He had borrowed it from the American Marxist theorist, Herbert Marcuse, but it aptly fit Merton's purposes in presenting himself as a monk to monks of other traditions. "In speaking for monks," he said, "I am really speaking for a very strange kind of person, a marginal person, because the monk in the modern world is no longer an established person with an established place in society. . . . He is a marginal person who withdraws deliberately to the margin of society with a view to deepening fundamental human experience."[88]

In his prepared paper for that Calcutta conference, "Monastic Experience and East-West Dialogue," Merton asked for a dialogue with other marginal people, with other poor pilgrims like himself—an exchange that would take place "under the true monastic conditions of quiet, tranquility, sobriety, leisureliness, reverence, meditation and cloistered peace."[89] He pointed out what was needed to institute an authentic monastic dialogue: the development of a "kind of lingua franca of religious experience."[90] Merton discussed the levels of such communication, and the reality beyond communication: communion. "The kind of communication that is necessary on this deep level must also be 'communion' beyond the level of words, a communion in authentic experience which is shared not only on a 'preverbal' level but also on a 'postverbal' level."[91] Merton called attention to what, in his estimation, is really essential to the monastic quest: "This, I think, is to be sought in the area of true self-transcendence and enlightenment. It is to be sought in the transformation of consciousness in its ultimate ground, as well as in the highest and most authentic devotional love."[92]

The American, Catholic, Cistercian pilgrim told his fellow monks in the Far East that "monastic training must not form men in a rigid mold, but liberate them from habitual and routine mechanisms." The true monk in the contemporary world "must be not merely a punctilious observer of external traditions, but a living example of traditional and interior realization. He must be wide open to life and to new experience because he has fully utilized his own tradition and gone beyond it."[93]

Thomas Merton certainly was wide open to the life and new experiences he encountered in Asia. His copious writings on Christian and monastic living attested a full utilization of his tradition, and *The Asian Journal,* along with other books and articles on the East, indicated that he had gone beyond the tradition from which he came. He had "gone beyond it" not in the sense that Merton ever rejected, set aside, or outgrew his Christian faith or particular monastic heritage. Rather, he was able to reinterpret them in the light of what he learned from other traditions and could assimilate new insights and experiences within the framework of his commitments. This man was an instance of what the Persian psychoanalyst, Reza Arasteh, called "final integration." Merton had written on Arasteh's book, *Final Integration in the Adult Personality,* and was especially interested in it because the psychoanalyst incorporated in his study material from the mystical tradition of Sufism. Commenting on the outcome of the human task of maturation and self-discovery that Arasteh develops, Merton says,

> Final integration is a state of transcultural maturity far beyond mere social adjustment, which always implies partiality and compromise. The man who is "fully born" has an entirely "inner experience of life." He apprehends his life fully and wholly from an inner ground that is at once more universal than the empirical ego and yet entirely his own. He is in a certain sense "cosmic" and "universal man." He has attained a deeper, fuller identity than that of his limited ego-self which is only a fragment of his being. He is in a certain sense identified with everybody: or in the familiar language of the New Testament . . . he is "all things to all men."[94]

Arasteh's work, which Merton was so taken with, was a psychological, not a theological investigation. But Merton immediately grasped the theological implications of the notion of final integration and did not hesitate to make applications to the great religious traditions with which he had become familiar:

> The state of insight which is final integration implies an openness, an "empti-ness," a "poverty" similar to those described in such detail not only by the Rhenish mystics, by St. John of the Cross, by the early Franciscans, but also by the Sufis, the early Taoist masters and Zen Buddhists. Final integration implies the void, poverty and nonaction which leave one entirely docile to the "Spirit" and hence a potential instrument for unusual creativity.[95]

I have suggested several times that frequently Merton was writing about himself when he was not intending to write about himself. His comments on Gandhi, Chuang Tzu, the Celtic monks were uncannily appropriate as descriptions—at least in some respects—of Thomas Merton. Perhaps that is most true of his description of the finally integrated person-ality:

> The man who has attained final integration is no longer limited by the culture in which he has grown up. "He has embraced *all of life*. . . . He has experienced qualities of every type of life": ordinary human existence, intellectual life, artistic creation, human love, religious life. He passes beyond all these limiting forms, while retaining all that is best and most universal in them. He accepts not only his own community, his own society, his own friends, his own culture, but all mankind. He does not remain bound to one limited set of values in such a way that he opposes them aggressively or defensively to others. He is fully "Catholic" in the best sense of the word. He has a unified vision and experience of one truth shining out in all its various manifestations, some clearer than others. He does not set these partial views up in opposition to each other, but unifies them in a dialectic or an insight of complementarity. With this view of life he is able to bring perspective, liberty and spontaneity into the lives of others. The finally integrated man is a peacemaker, and that is why there is such a desperate need for our leaders to become such men of insight.[96]

Merton the pilgrim had become "fully 'Catholic' in the best sense of the word." He could embrace all of life, accept all sorts of people and cultural embodiments of human values. Thus far we have traced his development as a writer, a monk-autobiographer, a solitary, a social commentator, an explorer of Eastern philosophical and religious traditions. In each of these areas of his life, Merton was able to grow progressively, leaving behind inadequate conceptions or limiting practices, while retain-ing what was authentic and life-giving. He was utterly faithful to life as a journey into the unknown, confident that God would lead him to a fullness beyond imagining.

An Icon for the Poor Pilgrim

A few hours before he died, as he closed his last talk in Bangkok, "Marxism and Monastic Perspectives," Merton asked his audience of Christian contemplatives to reflect on a traditional representation from Buddhist iconography. The Buddha sits in the lotus posture, with one hand pointing to the earth, and holding a begging bowl in the other. Merton explained that the Buddha points to the earth in witness that he has just obtained enlightment by sitting on it. He has overcome the illusion of being alienated from the earth. And "the begging bowl of the Buddha represents . . . the ultimate theological root of the belief not just in a right to beg, but in openness to the gifts of all beings as an expression of the interdependence of all beings."[97] That Buddhist icon served as a self-image for Thomas Merton. He saw himself in his monastic vocation as a poor pilgrim with his begging bowl held out to whoever and whatever could give him some portion of the boundless Truth for which he hungered with all his soul.

His final public words expressed Merton's conviction that this posture of the pilgrim was not only appropriate, but imperative, for him and his fellow Catholic monks. Referring to the Buddhist icon as a model from which Christians could learn, he noted that "when the monk begs from the layman and receives a gift from the layman, it is not as a selfish person getting something from somebody else. He is simply opening himself in this interdependence, this mutual interdependence, in which they all recognize that they all are immersed in illusion together."[98] This view of reality affirms that "if you once penetrate by detachment and purity of heart to the inner secret of the ground of your ordinary experience, you can attain to a liberty that nobody can touch, that nobody can affect, that no political change of circumstances can do anything to."[99] Merton insisted that Christian and Buddhist monasticism had in common "the belief that this kind of freedom and transcendence is somehow attainable."[100] He made a strong plea that his Christian audience at the Bangkok conference remember what their own monastic life is all about by becoming more open to the great monastic traditions of the Asian religions:

> Whenever you have somebody capable of giving some kind of direction and instruction to a small group . . . attempting to love and serve God and reach union with him, you are bound to have some kind of monasticism. This kind of monasticism cannot be extinguished. It is imperishable. It represents an instinct of the human heart, and it represents a charism given by God to man. It cannot be rooted out, because it does not depend on man. It does

not depend on cultural factors, and it does not depend on sociological or psychological factors. It is something much deeper.

I, as a monk—and, I think, you as monks—can agree that we believe this to be the deepest and most essential thing in our lives, and because we believe this, we have given ourselves to the kind of life we have adopted. I believe that our renewal consists precisely in deepening this understanding and this grasp of that which is most real. And I believe that by openness to Buddhism, to Hinduism, and to these great Asian traditions, we stand a wonderful chance of learning more about the potentiality of our own traditions, because they have gone, from the natural point of view, so much deeper into this than we have. The combination of the natural techniques and the graces and the other things that have been manifested in Asia and the Christian liberty of the gospel should bring us all at last to that full and transcendent liberty which is beyond mere cultural differences and mere externals—and mere this or that.[101]

If the image of holding a begging bowl represented for Merton the monk's ideal of openness and receptivity to all life, the Buddha pointing to the ground on which he sits and where he has obtained enlightenment suggested the attitude of a true contemplative. The enlightened Buddha figure does not float in some ethereal space; he is in contact with the earth—the primal stuff of nature. His relationship to the earth is at once the source of illusion and the necessary condition for seeing through illusion. Enlightenment is the attainment of "Buddha mind," which is "an insight into being in all its existential reality and actualization" and "the awareness of full spiritual reality, and therefore the realization of the emptiness of all limited or particularized realities."[102]

The iconography of which Merton spoke in Bangkok, like the great statues of the seated and reclining Buddhas he had encountered a few days earlier in the temple garden at Polonnaruwa, symbolized for him the true mystical state. He beheld "the silence of the extraordinary faces. The great smiles. Huge and yet subtle. Filled with every possibility, questioning nothing, knowing everything, rejecting nothing."[103] These were visual images for what Thomas Merton thought to be, and experienced as, the Christian contemplative's characteristic condition—what he would elsewhere call "a mind awake in the dark."[104]

A Mind Awake in the Dark

He was at home—"this is not a hermitage—it is a house. ('Who was that hermitage I seen you with last night?')"[1]—and, in a sometimes playful, sometimes solemn mood, writing "Day of a Stranger" in the mid-1960s. Anguishing over the world's violence, Merton nonetheless seemed at peace in his deepest center. Solitude was teaching him the limits and the possibilities of freedom:

> I have seen the SAC plane, with the bomb in it, fly low over me and I have looked up out of the woods directly at the closed bay of the metal bird with a scientific egg in its breast! A womb easily and mechanically opened! I do not consider this technological mother to be the friend of anything I believe in. However, like everyone else, I live in the shadow of the apocalyptic cherub. I am surveyed by it, impersonally. Its number recognizes my number. Are these numbers preparing at some moment to coincide in the benevolent mind of a computer? This does not concern me, for I live in the woods as a reminder that I am free not to be a number.
>
> There is, in fact, a choice.[2]

Although he had not yet set out on his journey to the East, Merton was living as a pilgrim in the Kentucky hills, discovering different traditions in "the reassuring companionship of many silent Tzu's and Fu's; Kung Tzu, Lao Tzu, Meng Tzu, Tu Fu. And Jui Neng. And Chao-Chu. . . . Here also is a Syrian hermit called Philoxenus. An Algerian cenobite called Camus."[3] Merton felt part of a "mental ecology . . . a living balance of spirits in this corner of the woods."[4] He was in touch with the simple realities of life: "Rituals. Washing out the coffee pot in the rain bucket. Approaching the outhouse with circumspection on account of the king snake who likes to curl up on one of the beams inside."[5] He could hear

"many other songs besides those of birds . . . Rilke, or René Char, Mon-
tale, Zukofsky, Ungaretti, Edwin Muir, Quasimodo, or . . . feminine
voices from Angela of Foligno to Flannery O'Conner, Theresa of Avila,
Juliana of Norwich . . . Raïssa Maritain."[6] Thomas Merton was possessed
of an identity, vibrantly alive, relaxed. "What I wear is pants. What I
do is live. How I pray is breathe,"[7] the hermit insisted.

And pray he did. One of the vignettes in "Day of a Stranger" conveyed
the feel of Merton at prayer in his hermitage. The images suggest his
understanding of contemplative prayer more powerfully than Merton's
theological writings could:

> I am out of bed at two-fifteen in the morning, when the night is darkest
> and most silent. Perhaps this is due to some ailment or other. I find myself
> in the primordial lostness of night, solitude, forest, peace, a mind awake in
> the dark, looking for a light, not totally reconciled to being out of bed. A
> light appears, and in the light an ikon. There is now in the large darkness a
> small room of radiance with psalms in it. The psalms grow up silently by
> themselves without effort like plants in this light which is favorable to them.
> The plants hold themselves up on stems which have a single consistency,
> that of mercy, or rather great mercy. *Magna misericordia.* In the formlessness
> of night and silence a word then pronounces itself: Mercy. It is surrounded
> by other words of lesser consequence: "Destroy iniquity," "Wash me," "Pu-
> rify," "I know my iniquity." *Peccavi.* Concepts without interest in the world
> of business, war, politics, culture, etc. Concepts also often without serious
> interest to ecclesiastics.[8]

Prayer is both dark and light, silence and word, solitude and communion.
To pray is to experience oneself as lost and found, as bent by one's
own weight yet supported by another's gift. For Merton the solitary,
Merton the seasoned contemplative, prayer does not resolve contradictions; it allows one to accept them. Praying acknowledges one's capability
for alertness of the highest order, coupled with the sense of perpetual
drowsiness regarding what really matters. To pray is to know oneself
as a sinner who is forgiven and a person called to an awareness that
shatters one's mundane preoccupations. To pray is to be and to become
"a mind awake in the dark, looking for a light, not totally reconciled to
being out of bed."[9]

If he spoke of praying as an act of the mind, Merton did not mean
to exclude the body or to imply that it is only an intellectual function.
In fact, by the 1960s he was very critical of such a "pseudo-spiritual"
view:

> The very idea of "spirituality" tends to be unhealthy in so far as it is divisive
> and itself makes total response impossible. The "spiritual" life thus becomes
> something lived "interiorly" and in "the spirit" (or worse still in the "mind"—

indeed in the "imagination"). The body is left out of it, because the body is "bad" or at best "unspiritual." But the "body" gets into the act anyway, sometimes in rather disconcerting ways, especially when it has been excluded on general principles.

So we create problems that should never arise, simply because we "believe" with our mind, but heart and body do not follow.[10]

Merton's language about "a mind awake in the dark" intended to relate contemplative prayer not to a specific faculty, however noble, but rather to that reality indicated by the metaphor of "the ground of our being." He saw a similarity between the Zen meaning of "mind" and what the fourteenth-century Rhineland mystics meant by the "ground." The Zen notion of "mind" *(h' sin)* is not simply a psychological concept.

Nor is it equivalent to the scholastic idea of the soul as "form of the body." Yet it is certainly considered as a principle of *being.* Can we consider it a spiritual essence? I think not.

Suzuki says that "mind" in this sense is "an ultimate reality which is aware of itself and is not the seat of our empirical consciousness. This "mind" for the Zen masters is not the intellectual faculty as such but rather what the Rhenish mystics called the "ground" of our soul or of our being, a "ground" which is not only entitative but enlightened and aware, because it is in immediate contact with God. . . . The New Testament term that might possibly correspond to it [Zen "mind" and mystics' "ground"], though of course with many differences, is St. Paul's "spirit" or "pneuma."[11]

Merton appropriated such a meaning when he spoke of contemplative prayer as a state of "mind."

The description of himself when engaged in contemplation as "a mind awake in the dark" was not meant to conjure up a bodiless specter. Thomas Merton wanted this metaphor to suggest that praying brings to awareness the preconscious or supraconscious reality of our contact with God. In prayer, the person becomes aware of, alert to, and attentive regarding God's presence and activity. This awareness is not "knowledge" in the strict sense; one is conscious without possessing warrants for what one "knows." Thus "in the dark," "darkness," "knowing darkly" are common metaphors for awareness of the divine.

Bernard Lonergan's technical distinction between consciousness and knowing, as that distinction pertains to religious experience, is helpful for understanding Merton's more imaginative language. Lonergan argues that being in love with God is a conscious dynamic state, but this reality is not known:

To say that this dynamic state is conscious is not to say that it is known. For consciousness is just experience, but knowledge is a compound of experience, understanding, and judging. Because the dynamic state is conscious without being known, it is an experience of mystery. . . .

It is conscious on the fourth level of intentional consciousness. It is not the consciousness that accompanies acts of seeing, hearing, smelling, tasting, touching. It is not the consciousness that accompanies acts of inquiry, insight, formulating, speaking. It is not the consciousness that accompanies acts of reflecting, marshalling and weighing the evidence, making judgments of fact or possibility. It is the type of consciousness that deliberates, makes judgments of value, decides, acts responsibly and freely. But it is this consciousness as brought to a fulfillment, as having undergone a conversion. . . . So the gift of God's love occupies the ground and root of the fourth and highest level of man's intentional consciousness. It takes over the peak of the soul, the *apex animae.*[12]

For Merton, "contemplation reaches out to the knowledge and even to the experience of the transcendent and inexpressible God."[13]

Clearly Merton is not using the term *knowledge* in the strict philosophical sense Lonergan does. Merton is speaking metaphorically; contemplation is a very peculiar kind of "knowing." "It is awakening, enlightenment and the amazing intuitive grasp by which love gains certitude of God's creative and dynamic intervention in our daily life. Hence contemplation does not simply 'find' a clear idea of God . . . contemplation is carried away by Him into His own realm, His own mystery and His own freedom."[14] Merton's "mind awake in the dark" is Lonergan's dynamic state on the fourth level of intentional consciousness.

In Thomas Merton's language, contemplation "knows God by seeming to touch Him. Or rather it knows Him as if it had been invisibly touched by him."[15] Trying to explicate this metaphor of being "touched by God," Merton goes on to describe the consciousness that comes from contemplative prayer:

Contemplation is a sudden gift of awareness, an awakening to the Real within all that is real. A vivid awareness of our contingent reality as received, as present from God, as a free gift of love. This is the existential contact of which we speak when we use the metaphor of being "touched by God."[16]

Awakening to the Real, discovering oneself as loved by the very Power that constitutes all reality as well as one's own contingent self, brings about a state of mind that mystics everywhere have called "ecstasy." Merton was familiar with the descriptions of this extraordinary form of consciousness as it is presented in many different religious traditions:

There are documents of all kinds which say that the highest and most "biophilic" expression of man's extraordinary capacities is precisely in this *ecstasis* in which the person is at once totally full, realizing himself in unity not only with all being(s) but with the very source and finality of Being. It is the paradox of D. T. Suzuki's formula that zero equals infinity, or the *todo y nada* of St. John of the Cross.

Hence I want to say that the highest form of life is this "spiritual life" in which the infinitely "fontal" (sourcelike) creativity of our being in Being is somehow attained, and becomes in its turn a source of action and creativity in the world around us. The common jargon of religions tends to speak of this sometimes as "contemplation," sometimes as "liberation," sometimes as "salvation," sometimes as "divination."[17]

Merton constantly stressed the paradoxical nature of contemplative consciousness: full and empty, dark and light, happy yet painful.

God touches us with a touch that is emptiness and empties us. He moves us with a simplicity that simplifies us. . . . Our mind swims in the air of an understanding, a reality that is dark and serene and includes in itself everything. Nothing more is wanting. Our only sorrow, if sorrow be possible at all, is the awareness that we ourselves still live outside of God.[18]

The mind that has awakened in the dark of contemplation experiences an impossible tension: awareness of the unity of all things in their source does not obliterate the normal human sense of infinite multiplicity in the world and divergences within oneself. Nor does *ecstasis* dull the anxiety that accompanies recognition of one's contingency; in fact, that distressing perception of the creature's nothingness is intensified. These tensions can be endured and made fruitful, however, because contemplation plunges the person into the real and yields an overpowering insight into it. "Contemplation is at once the existential appreciation of our own 'nothingness' and of the divine reality, perceived by ineffable spiritual contact within the depths of our being," Merton affirms. "Contemplation is the sudden intuitive penetration of what really IS. It is the unexpected leap of the spirit of man into the existential luminosity of Reality Itself."[19]

Passing through the Center

Needless to say, no one metaphor captures Merton's understanding of contemplative prayer. If it is the activity of a mind awake in the dark, contemplation is also a leap of the spirit and a journey. Merton spoke of contemplation as an inner journey on which one passes through the center of his or her soul. A key text from *The New Man* announces the themes related to this metaphor:

If we would return to God, and find ourselves in Him, we must reverse Adam's journey, we must go back by the way he came. The path lies through the center of our own soul. Adam withdrew into himself from God and then passed through himself and went forth into creation. We must withdraw ourselves (in the right and Christian sense) from exterior things, and pass through the center of our souls to find God. We must recover possession of our souls, we must learn to "go out" of ourselves to God and to others by supernatural charity."[20]

Merton's meaning of "soul" in this passage is functionally equivalent to "mind." The "soul" is the self, our true self that lives in and from God. The term is metaphysical, not psychological. What Merton speaks of as the "soul" refers to our immanent point of contact with the creative source of life. Elsewhere he says that "God's will for us is, before all else, that we should find ourselves, find our true life, or, as the Vulgate text has it, find our *souls*."[21] The discovery—rather, the recovery—of this reality can only come about in prayer.

To "pass through the center of our souls to find God" is one of Merton's metaphorical ways of describing the contemplative process of locating the divine presence and activity within the self. Passing through the center implies that someone comes to know the self as God's dwelling place and penetrates "beyond" the self as a particular entity into the all-embracing God who grounds the self. "We would not seek God unless He were not already 'in us,' " Merton insists in his typically paradoxical language, "and to go 'beyond ourselves' is just to find the inner ground of our being where He is present to us as our creative source, as the fount of redemptive light and grace."[22] Because God constitutes the self, to find the center of the soul or of the self is to recover one's true self. To pass through the center of the soul is to find God, for God himself is that center.

Already in *The Seven Storey Mountain* Merton had spoken of God as the center toward which one is drawn in prayer as though by a gravitational pull. He reflected on what was happening to him at the time of his Baptism and First Communion:

Now I had entered into the everlasting movement of that gravitation which is the very life and spirit of God: God's own gravitation towards the depths of His own infinite nature, His goodness without end. And God, that center, Who is everywhere, and whose circumference is nowhere, finding me, through incorporation with Christ, incorporated into his immense and tremendous gravitational movement which is love, which is the Holy Spirit, loved me.[23]

If the center is found by entering into a movement that draws one to it, Merton also characterizes prayer as the very opposite of motion: "This is a country whose center is everywhere and whose circumference is nowhere," he remarks in *Seeds of Contemplation*. "You do not find it by travelling but by standing still."[24] But whether contemplative prayer is described by active or passive metaphors, Merton thinks of it as that which puts one in touch with God who is the center of the self:

> Contemplation is a mystery in which God reveals Himself to us as the very center of our own most intimate self—*intimior intimo meo* as St. Augustine said. When the realization of His presence bursts upon us, our own self disappears in Him and we pass mystically through the Red Sea of separation to lose ourselves (and thus find our true selves) in Him.[25]

Thus for Thomas Merton, to find one's own center is to find God— or to put it conversely, to find God is to know him as the source of one's being and the power that creates and redeems one's self. This "finding God" is the sort of "knowing" him that comes through contemplative prayer. It is very different from knowledge *about* God. In prayer, "we know him in so far as we become aware of ourselves as known through and through by him."[26] This is a mode of knowing that transcends the subject–object relationship that is operative in our ordinary acts of knowing. The knowledge of God that is possible in prayer is

> a knowledge not of him as the object of our scrutiny, but of ourselves as utterly dependent on his saving and merciful knowledge of us. . . . We know him in and through ourselves in so far as his truth is the source of our being and his merciful love is the very heart of our life and existence.[27]

What Merton sometimes calls "monastic prayer" or "the prayer of the heart" as synonyms for "contemplative prayer" is meant to engender such awareness. (He disliked the term "mental prayer" because of its too cerebral connotations.) "Monastic prayer begins not so much with 'considerations' as with a 'return to the heart,' finding one's deepest center, awakening profound depths of our being in the presence of God who is the source of our being and our life."[28] Such prayer does not employ reasoning, although it is, indeed, a search. The searching, the seeking entailed in this prayer involves not only the intelligence but also one's whole being. It is not a quest for understanding, so much as a longing to rest in the existential truth of God as the center of the self. Merton puts it this way:

> In the "prayer of the heart" we seek first of all the deepest ground of our identity in God. We do not reason about dogmas of faith, or "the mysteries." We seek rather to gain a direct existential grasp, a personal experience of the deepest truths of life and faith, *finding ourselves in God's truth*.[29]

The process of finding ourselves in God's truth goes by many metaphorical names in Merton's writings. To "pass through the center of our souls to find God" suggests the unity of the contemplative quest. As one who engages in it, Thomas Merton asserts:

> There is only one problem on which all my existence, my peace and my happiness depend: to discover myself in discovering God. If I find Him, I will find myself and if I find my true self I will find Him.[30]

In even bolder theological language, Merton speaks of the discovery of personal identity as the experience of God as one's other self:

> My discovery of my identity begins and is perfected in these missions [of the Father, Word, and Spirit], because it is in them that God Himself, bearing in Himself the secret of who I am, begins to live in me not only as my Creator but as my other and true self.[31]

Such a discovery is possible only in and through prayer of the heart.

Recovering Our True Selves

Whatever Merton calls the seeking for one's identity that is for him the substance of contemplative prayer, the process implies a liberation by grace and the restoration of a reality that has been lost, or at least diminished, by sin. Merton often used the traditional theological language of restoring or perfecting the "image" of God in the human person and was especially indebted to St. Augustine's classic conception. But Merton preferred to speak of finding or recovering the "true (real) self" as the task of the spiritual life. "We must withdraw ourselves . . . from exterior things, and pass through the center of our souls to find God. We must recover possession of our true selves by liberation from anxiety and fear and inordinate desire."[32] Another passage from *The New Man* displays his meaning:

> The image of God is the summit of spiritual consciousness in man. It is his highest peak of self-realization. This is achieved not merely by reflection on his actual, present self: one's actual self may be far from "real," since it may be profoundly alienated from one's own deep spiritual identity. To reach one's "real self" one must, in fact, be delivered by grace, virtue and asceticism, from that illusory and false "self" whom we have created by our habits of selfishness and by our constant flights from reality. In order to find God, Whom we can only find in and through the depths of our own soul, we must therefore first find ourselves. To use common figures of speech, we must "return to ourselves," we must "come to ourselves."[33]

Merton used a plethora of synonyms for both the "true self" and the "false self." He spoke of the "true self" variously as the "deep self," "our hidden identity," "the ordinary self recovered," "the new self," "the true person," "indestructible and immortal person," "the true 'I' who answers to a secret name," "the empty self which is our true reality in the eyes of God," "a self that is 'no-self,'" "myself as lost and found in God," and "my true face." He wrote about the "false self" with an equally variegated and colorful vocabulary: the "shadow self," "mask," "outer self," "ego-identity," "false identity," "the empirical self," "the illusory person or self," "our private self," "ego-self," "external self or outward self," "imaginary self," "worldly self," "the 'I' that works, thinks, speaks," "the separate, external, egoistic will," "the slave of fantasy," "the contingent ego," "my superficial ego—this cramp of the imagination," "our vulnerable shell," "our fictitious identities," "his exterior identity, with his passport picture of himself," and "this evanescent shadow or shadow person."

Although many of Merton's terms for the true and false self sprang from his own fertile imagination, he attributed the basic concepts to St. Bernard. In his early study of Cistercian history and spirituality, *The Waters of Siloe,* Merton explained the notion of asceticism inherited from him and the school of Clairvaux:

> In St. Bernard's language, our true personality has been concealed under the "disguise" of a false self, the *ego* whom we tend to worship in place of God. To the worldling, who knows no other "self" than this shadow of himself, the Cistercian life will evidently spell the destruction of everything he is accustomed to think of as his real personality. But the monk who has given himself, without return, to God and to the formation prescribed by the Rule soon discovers that monastic obedience and penance are rapidly delivering him from the one force that has prevented him all his life from knowing his true self.[34]

A few years later, in an essay called "The Sacrament of Advent in the Spirituality of St. Bernard," Merton spoke of the emergence of the true self as a liberation that frees a person from the inside:

> To find the word [which the Lord speaks to us] in our heart we must enter into ourselves not so much by *introspection* as by *compunction.* This is important. The inward movement of compunction is not so much a matter of hiding ourselves within ourselves, as a liberation of ourselves, which takes place in the depths of our being, and lets us *out* of ourselves from the inside. This liberation from concentration on ourself is the beginning of a conversion, a *metanoia,* a real inner transformation.[35]

But such inner transformation, although begun and assisted by ascetical practices, could never be accomplished by them. That is the work of contemplative prayer. Monastic obedience and penance provide the conditions for displacing the false self but of themselves cannot awaken the true self. The recovery of one's true self can happen only in contemplation. Through the prayer of the heart, *metanoia* is possible, because the true self comes to know itself over against its superficial and external disguises. A passage from *New Seeds of Contemplation* sums up Merton's teaching and sketches the range of his metaphors for the true and the false self:

> There is an irreducible opposition between the deep transcendent self that awakens only in contemplation, and the superficial, external self which we commonly identify with the first person singular. We must remember that this superficial "I" is not our real self. It is our "individuality" and our "empirical self" but it is not truly the hidden and mysterious person in whom we subsist before the eyes of God. . . . It is at best the vesture, the mask, the disguise of that mysterious and unknown "self" whom most of us never discover until we are dead. Our external, superficial self is not eternal, not spiritual. . . . Contemplation is precisely the awareness that this "I" is really "not I" and the awakening of the unknown "I" that is beyond observation and reflection and is incapable of commenting upon itself.[36]

The recovery of the true self is the experience of finding God. Contemplative prayer yields the realization of God's presence in one's own presence of the true self. For Thomas Merton, passing through the center of our souls and recovering our true selves are two metaphors for the same reality—the discovery of authentic personal identity and the discovery of God through contemplation. "In knowing that I am, if I penetrate to the depths of my own existence and my own present reality, the indefinable 'am' that is myself in its deepest roots, then through this deep center I pass into the infinite 'I Am' which is the very Name of the Almighty."[37]

If Merton had a predilection for speaking of the true self, he certainly did not neglect the notion of the human person as the image of God— or more precisely in our context, the role of contemplation in recreating the person in God's image. He appropriated the language of the Greek Fathers, St. Augustine, and St. Thomas, using it creatively. For Merton, recovering the true self and restoring the divine image are different expressions for describing one process of realization.

That process, as we have already noted, begins with ascetical practices but is sustained and completed through contemplative prayer. "Cistercian asceticism," Merton says of his own monastic tradition, "is simply the recovery of our true self. . . . It is the purification, and liberation of the divine image in man hidden under layers of 'unlikeness.' Our true self is the person we are meant to be—the man who is free and upright, in the image and likeness of God."[38]

Merton draws heavily on Augustine's theology of perfecting the image of God in the person through contemplation—which includes both illumination and love. "At the summit of his own self-realization, which he calls the *memoria,* Augustine finds not only himself but also the light by which he sees himself as he really is. And in this light he is aware of God from whom the light comes. His awareness of God instantly broadens out into love."[39] Love springs from illumination and carries Augustine to "the God who is enthroned in the very summit of his own personal being: the *apex mentis* or the 'spark' of the soul."[40] In this important essay, "Image and Likeness," Merton develops his understanding of Augustine's teaching on the restoration of the divine image:

> The image of God is found in the soul's structure—awareness, thought, love. But the "likeness" of God is effected in the soul when these powers receive their own fulfillment and super-actualization in a spiritual experience of Him Whose image they are. When the awareness of *"memoria"* becomes consciousness of God, when the intelligence is enlightened in a spiritual understanding of God and when the will raises the whole soul above itself in an ecstasy of love for God, then the "image" is perfected in likeness. . . . And so St. Augustine says "In this image (which is the soul) *the resemblance of God* will be perfect when the vision of God is perfect."[41]

For Merton, it is in and through the prayer of the heart that we "remember" God. As he remarks elsewhere, "if we continue in our prayer, we 'remember' Him, that is to say, we become conscious, once again, of Who He really is. And we see that He has found us. . . . It is a new experience, and it makes us new men."[42]

Like Augustine, Thomas Merton was primarily interested in concrete experience rather than theoretical possibilities. Contemplative prayer is not an abstract relationship; it affects the quality of one's life in all dimensions. "The recovery of the divine image in our souls, in so far as it is experienced by us at all, is an experience of a totally new manner of being. We become 'new men' in Christ."[43] Merton emphasizes that the tangible sign of living as this "new man" in Christ is that there is a profound change in one's manner of knowing God. "He is not known as an 'object' since He is not contained in a concept. On the contrary, the mystical knowledge of God, actualized in the mirror of His image within us, mysteriously coincides with His knowledge of us. . . . We apprehend Him by the love which identifies itself, within us, with His love for us."[44] Merton's conclusion is identical with Augustine's and Aquinas' position: "What will be fully realized in the beatific vision is realized inchoatively in contemplation even in this present life."[45]

Merton liked the way Aquinas articulated the notion of the nature and function of the divine image in the human soul:

> St. Thomas gives us a concrete and thoroughly existential intuition of the divine image when he says that it is not only a static "representation" of something in the divine essence, but a *dynamic tendency* that carries us toward union with God. It is a kind of gravitational sensitivity to the things of God.[46]

To recognize and to recover the image of God in ourselves, it is certainly not enough to engage in introspection, let alone theological speculation. It is insufficient to realize "that the spirituality of our nature makes us potentially god-like. The potentiality must be actualized. How? By knowledge and love: or, more precisely, by a knowledge of God that is inseparable from an experience of love."[47] Merton put in his own language the implications of St. Thomas' teaching that God's image is in the soul according to the knowledge of God the soul conceives and according to the love flowing from such knowledge:

> Self-realization in this true religious sense is then less an awareness of ourselves than an awareness of the God to whom we are drawn in the depths of our own being. We become real, and experience our actuality, not when we pause to reflect upon our own self as an isolated individual entity, but rather when transcending ourselves and passing beyond reflection, we center our whole soul upon the God Who is our life. That is to say we fully "realize" ourselves when we cease to be conscious of ourselves in separateness and know nothing but the one God Who is above all knowledge.[48]

Passing through the center of our souls, recovering possession of our true selves, or realizing the divine image in the depths of our being are but several metaphorical descriptions of an experience of God that can happen only through contemplative prayer.

Going Out of Ourselves to God and Others

The recognition of one's true self, recreated in the divine image, is thus an awakening to the fullness of one's humanity. That awareness comes in the solitude of contemplation, but it necessarily includes other people. For Merton, in fact, the recovery of one's true self precisely enables a woman or man to love all others in Christ. "And when we have gained possession of our souls," he says, "we must learn to 'go out' of ourselves to God and to others by supernatural charity."[49] Merton's language should not be construed to imply a temporal sequence: first we find our true selves, and then we go on to discover how to love others. Nor should it be thought that he is talking about two different kinds of functions— one contemplative, having to do with knowing and loving God and one's true self in prayer, and the other active, concerned with ministering to people's needs, whether spiritual or material. For Merton, rather, the actualizing of one's capacity to love others in Christ is coincidental with recovering possession of one's true self and the discovery of God as the center. *"A man cannot enter into the deepest center of himself and pass through that center into God, unless he is able to pass entirely out of himself and empty himself and give himself to other people, in the purity of selfless love."*[50]

Certainly Thomas Merton did not underestimate the value of concrete service to others. Supernatural charity, like all authentic love, must express itself in specific, immediate, and tangible acts of ministration. As a follower of a Lord who washed the feet of his disciples, Merton was convinced that Christian love demanded external acts as well as a certain inner disposition. As a young monk, of course, he tried to be considerate of his brothers in the monastery at all times and to pray for the good of people in the world. Merton the Master of Novices exercised his responsibilities toward his young charges as a loving service. Merton the social critic fought violence and injustice in society as an expression of love for both the oppressed and the oppressors. He saw his own writing and his work with and for others as a response to Christ's command to love one another:

> God's will for us is not only that we should be the persons He means us to be, but that we should share in His work of creation and *help* Him to make us into the persons He means us to be. . . . And since no man is an island, since we all depend on one another, I cannot work out God's will in my own life unless I also consciously help other men to work out His will in theirs. His will, then, is our sanctification, our transformation in Christ, our deeper and fuller integration with other men.[51]

But, although Christian love is something one *does,* Merton always regarded acts of fraternal charity as rooted in contemplation. The discovery of God as the center of the soul, the recovery of the true self through contemplative awareness, and the recognition of our relationship to others in Christ are coterminous. "The discovery of ourselves in God, and of God in ourselves, by a charity that also finds all other men in God with ourselves is, therefore, not the discovery of ourselves but of Christ."[52]

As we have seen, for Merton that realization is an experience that comes through contemplation.

Authentic expressions of Christian love flow from this contemplative realization of the unity of God, self, and others:

> The Spirit of God, penetrating and enlightening our spirit from within our-
> selves, teaches us the ways of a freedom by which alone we enter into vital
> spiritual contact with those around us. In this contact we become aware of
> our own autonomy, our own identification. We find out who we really are.
> And having made the discovery we are ready for the love and service of
> others.[53]

By passing through the center of our souls to find God, we discover who others really are. "We can come to understand others only by loving Him Who understands them from within the depths of their own being. Otherwise we know them only by the surmises that are formed within the mirror of our own soul."[54] Knowing others in God, moreover, enables us "to let those we love be perfectly themselves . . . not to twist them to fit our own image."[55] Contemplative prayer is the discovery of God's image in ourselves as the basis of unity among all people:

> His one Image is in us all, and we discover Him by discovering the likeness
> of His Image in one another. This does not destroy the differences between
> us but all these accidentals cease to have much meaning when we find that
> we are really one in His love. It is great praise of Him when people rejoice
> at finding Him in one another—not by effort, not by mere blind acts of faith,
> but by the experience of a charity illuminated, perhaps, by Wisdon—for it
> is "sapience" and fruition of God's reflection in the joy which is His mirror
> in souls.[56]

For Thomas Merton, the realization of the divine image in the human self that comes through contemplation is the source of unity within the self, with God, and with all other persons. "To 'go out' of ourselves to God and to others by supernatural charity" really means returning to the foundation of our being and the springs of life. Contemplative prayer alone offers us the possibility of experiencing "the perfect coalescence of the uncreated Image of God with our created image not only in a perfect identification of minds and wills in knowledge and love but also above all knowledge and love in perfect communion."[57] Merton summed up succinctly his understanding of what contemplation effects: "At the center of our souls we meet together, spiritually, in the infinite source of all our different created lives."[58]

Light in Darkness

If contemplation takes us through the center of our souls to God and oneness with others, the meeting takes place in darkness. The journey to that point of encounter is variously described by the great mystics as an ascent to the summit and a descent into the depths of the soul. But with either metaphor, the way is dark. And the meeting— the experiential contact with God—is the darkest of all, although this darkness is paradoxically light. "It is not so much that we come through darkness to light," says Merton, "as that the darkness itself is light."[59]

"Darkness" was one of Merton's favorite metaphors for describing contemplative prayer. He was most at home with the mystical writers of the apophatic tradition (named from the Greek term *apophasis,* which means "denial" or "negation"). Gregory of Nyssa, the Pseudo-Dionysius, John Scotus Erigena, Meister Eckhart, Jan van Ruysbroeck, the unknown author of *The Cloud of Unknowing,* and John of the Cross, to mention but a few, held that God cannot be known by reason alone and that, because he transcends all creation, he cannot be adequately described. What they call "knowledge" of God is, therefore, really a "knowing by unknowing." The apophatic mystics claim that this "knowing by unknowing" is experiential and comes through a transformation of the self rather than the operations of the intellect. Because God remains unknown by the ordinary criteria of human knowledge, these writers frequently use the metaphor of darkness for God himself and for the process of the soul's coming to him. Sometimes they speak of darkness which is light. Merton assimilated the theology of the apophatic mystics and appropriated their language, giving it his own particular twists.

A thorough study of Merton and the apophatic tradition has been done by John Teahan, who nicely summarized his uses of the metaphor of darkness:

> Merton used the symbol in a general way to describe contemplation. More specifically, he treated the dark nights of the sense and spirit, and the darkness of suffering and dread, as necessary preparations for mystical union. Merton also used the symbol of darkness to characterize the region where God is found, the place where the soul unites with him. Finally, Merton employed this image paradoxically to express the simultaneous presence of darkness and light he discerned in the mystical way.[60]

For our purposes, let us focus on this last usage of the metaphor in Merton's writings—the "luminous darkness" that characterizes for him the experience of God in contemplative prayer.

In his essay on the ascetical and mystical doctrine of St. John of the Cross, "Light in Darkness," Merton argued that a sign of genuine sanctity is the "reconciliation of opposites." Knowing by unknowing and loving with perfect detachment will mark the way of the contemplative who seeks complete union with God. The process of spiritual development toward such union, like the perfected union itself, is experienced as darkness that is light or light in darkness. Merton comments on the teachings of John of the Cross, for which he feels an instinctive affinity:

> Just as we can never separate asceticism from mysticism, so in St. John of the Cross we find darkness and light, suffering and joy, sacrifice and love united together so closely that they seem at times to be identified. It is not so much that we come through darkness to light, as that the darkness itself is light.
>
> > Never was fount so clear, undimmed and bright;
> > From it alone, I know, proceeds all light,
> >   Although 'tis night.
>
> Hence the essential simplicity of his teaching: enter into the night and you will be enlightened. "Night" means the "darkening" of all our natural desires, our natural understanding, our human way of loving; but this darkening brings with it an enlightenment. . . . All must be "darkened," that is to say, forgotten, in order that God Himself may become the light of our soul.[61]

The asceticism of light in darkness for Merton, as for John of the Cross, "seeks in all things to bring the soul into the *interior depths* where love is invisible, and to rescue it from the triviality of the obvious and showy forms of spiritual life which are good only for those who remain on the surface."[62] What brings the soul into the depths, to and through the center, is contemplation.

Fidelity to contemplative prayer eventually leads one through the dark night of the senses and the deeper and darker night of the spirit. Merton insists that "the 'darkness' which St. John teaches is not a pure negation. Rather it is the removal and extinguishing of a lesser light in order that pure light may shine in its place."[63] When the "light" of sensual passions is extinguished, when even the positive "lights" of our ideas and images of God and our holy aspirations for ourselves are darkened, then we are brought into immediate contact with the divine Light. In *New Seeds of Contemplation*, Merton puts it this way:

> The closer we get to God, the less is our faith diluted with the half-light of created images and concepts. Our certainty increases with this obscurity, yet not without anguish and even material doubt, because we do not find it easy to subsist in a void in which our natural powers have nothing of their own

to rely on. And it is in the deepest darkness that we must fully possess God on earth, because it is then that our minds are most truly liberated from the weak, created lights that are darkness in comparison to Him; it is then that we are filled with His infinite Light which seems pure darkness to our reason.[64]

Light and dark are then metaphors for knowing and unknowing, and the luminous darkness suggests that paradoxical knowing by unknowing of which the apophatic mystics speak. Thomas Merton situated himself in that tradition in his first theological work in 1951, *The Ascent to Truth,* when he wrote: "In mystical experience, God is 'apprehended' as unknown. He is realized, 'sensed' in His immanence and transcendence. He becomes present not in a finite concept but in His infinite reality which overflows every analogical notion we can utter of Him."[65] Merton continued to show his affirmation of that tradition in his 1961 revision of *Seeds of Contemplation* called *New Seeds of Contemplation*:

> Contemplation is not vision because it sees "without seeing" and knows "without knowing." It is a more profound depth of faith, a knowledge too deep to be grasped in images, in words or even in clear concepts. It can be suggested by symbols, but in the very moment of trying to indicate what it knows the contemplative mind takes back what it has said, and denies what it has affirmed. For in contemplation we know by "unknowing." Or, better, we know *beyond* all knowing or "unknowing."[66]

And at the very end of his life, Merton was still speaking the same way. In "The Contemplative and the Atheist," he claimed that the contemporary Christian contemplative might be in a position to understand the confusions surrounding the question of "atheism" and the "problem of God" current in the world precisely because the contemplative knows that God remains unknown.

> The Christian contemplative is aware that in the mystical tradition both of the Eastern and Western Churches there is a strong element of what has been called "apophatic theology." This "apophatic" tradition concerns itself with the fundamental datum of all faith—and one which is too often forgotten: the God who has revealed Himself to us in His Word has revealed Himself as unknown in His intimate essence, for He is beyond all merely human vision. . . . The heart of the Christian mystical experience is that it experiences the ineffable reality of what is beyond experience. It "knows" the presence of God, not in clear vision but "as unknown."[67]

Thus in the late 1960s, at a time marked by a massive and widespread experience of the "absence" of God in Western culture, Merton argued that the true contemplative could offer assistance to modern people. Because the authentic contemplative knows darkness (although knows that the darkness is light), he or she is in a position to share something pertinent to the experience of contemporary unbelievers. "While the experience of the atheist may be purely negative, that of the contemplative is so to speak negatively positive."[68] Merton explains what he means by reference to the dark–light symbolism of the apophatic tradition:

> Now, while the Christian contemplative must certainly develop, by study, the theological understanding of concepts about God, he is called mainly to penetrate the wordless darkness and apophatic light of an experience beyond concepts, and here he gradually becomes familiar with a God who is "absent," and as it were "nonexistent," to all human experience. The apophatic experience of God does, to some extent, verify the atheist's intuition that God is not an object of limited and precise knowledge and consequently cannot be apprehended as "a thing" to be studied by delimitation. As St. John of the Cross dared to say in mystical language, the term of the ascent of the mount of contemplation is "Nothing"—*Y en el monte Nada* ["And on the mountain, Nothing"].[69]

Thomas Merton himself appears to have exercised this peculiar "apostolate" to many modern people searching for God but feeling unable to find him. From *The Seven Storey Mountain* to *Zen and the Birds of Appetite*, he testified to going through the experience of darkness and emptiness and discovering light and fullness. His capacity for speaking of God and the contemplative quest in the language of "emptiness" and "nothingness" made him a bridge between Eastern and Western spiritual traditions. Merton's even more characteristic use of the metaphors of darkness and light linked him to the Western mystical tradition and gave his writing about the search for God and one's true self considerable appeal to Westerners seeking the way of wisdom. His prayer was his own, but more than only his: "O Great God, Father of all things, Whose infinite light is darkness to me, Whose immensity is to me as the void, You have called me forth out of yourself because You love me in yourself, and I am a transient expression of Your inexhaustible and eternal reality."[70]

He was a mind awake in the dark—awake to the presence of God in his own depths, awake to his true self, awake to his oneness in God and through Jesus Christ with all other human beings. To be fully awake meant, for Merton, to realize in contemplation and to express in his whole manner of life that realization of God as life-giving love. It was difficult to communicate, but this monk and writer kept on sharing his experience:

> Hard as it is to convey in human language, there is a very real and very recognizable (but almost entirely undefinable) Presence of God, in which we confront Him in prayer knowing Him by Whom we are known, aware of Him Who is aware of us, loving Him by Whom we know ourselves to be

loved. Present to ourselves in the fulness of our own personality, we are present to Him Who is infinite in His Being, His Otherness, His Self-hood. It is not a vision face to face, but a certain presence of self to Self in which, with the reverent attention of our whole being, we know Him in Whom all things have their being.[71]

Merton was convinced that discovering one's true identity in contemplation empowered the person for authentic Christian love and service of others. It seems fair to say that the monastic life, and specifically contemplative prayer, brought him to know who he was. Conscious of his identity, having heard his own secret name from the Lord in the prayer of the heart, Thomas Merton could go on to describe his task in relation to contemporary men and women as "to be what I am." His writing can be understood as the attempt to articulate that effort.

7

To Be What I Am: A Critical Appraisal of Thomas Merton

He died before it was published, but Merton would have liked the *New American Bible's* translation of Matthew 10:39, in which Jesus says, "He who seeks only himself brings himself to ruin, whereas he who brings himself to nought for me discovers who he is." Indeed, Merton understood his monastic vocation as the call to seek more than himself, to reduce the false self to nothing, and to discover his true self in God. And he perceived his mission in the Church and the world primarily as a contemplative enterprise. Toward the end of his life, Merton wrote, "My task is only to be what I am, a man seeking God in silence and solitude, with deep respect for the demands and realities of his own vocation, and fully aware that others too are seeking the truth in their own way."[1]

What he was, who he was—in the deepest sense of self-identity—could be known only to God and to Thomas Merton insofar as he remained faithful to his contemplative vocation. But this monk also happened to be a writer who, through his autobiographical work, shared the self he was and was becoming. Like any other Trappist monk, prayer was his most important "work." Unlike just any other Trappist monk, however, Merton possessed a special gift for writing about his life as a contemplative. So writing, especially autobiographical writing, became his *métier* in the monastery (one can hardly speak of a monk having a "profession"), just as some men worked in the fields and others made cheese.

But there is a richer sense in which we can say that autobiographical writing was Merton's work. The effort to articulate what was happening in his life was for him essential to the process of self-discovery. That enterprise actually served to shape Merton's identity, because writing about himself consciously engaged the man in the task he described as trying "to be what I am."

Writing one's story is not, of course, the same thing as living one's life. The work of expressing the self in a series of actions "makes a life." The work of expressing one's self in words about that life "makes a story." The autobiographical writer inextricably weaves these constructions together.

Thomas Merton certainly was an inveterate autobiographer. He wrote only one formal autobiography, but in most of his work he was writing autobiographically. In his journals, topical essays, poetry, novels, even theological commentary, he was continually telling his own story. Or perhaps it would be more accurate to say that through a multitude of literary forms, Merton was constantly involved in narrating his life story in bits and snatches. That scattered, though sustained, way of writing represents a recognition on the part of a complex man undergoing several different types of development, sometimes sequentially, sometimes simultaneously: Merton came to think of his life as one story made up of many stories. There was a unity to the one story—but neither Merton nor his readers would discern that while his life was still in process.

In *The Seven Storey Mountain,* Merton had tried to weave the various strands of his experience into one cohesive story. But that was written relatively early in the monk's life; other stories were yet to unfold and eventually would need to be told. Merton never again attempted to shape the multiform events of his life into a unified narrative. He would leave it to the Lord to reveal in his own time and his way the "hidden wholeness" of Thomas Merton's life.

He adamantly refused to rewrite the early autobiography. In the preface for the Japanese edition of *The Seven Storey Mountain,* the mature Merton acknowledged both his acceptance of and detachment from that account of his first thirty years of life:

> Nearly twenty years have passed since this book was written. The occasion of a new preface invites the author to reflect once again on the story, his own story, and the way he has told it.
>
> Perhaps if I were to attempt this book today, it would be written differently. Who knows? But it was written when I was still quite young, and that is the way it remains. The story no longer belongs to me, and I have no right to tell it in a different way, or to imagine that it should have been seen through wiser eyes. In its present form, which will remain its only form, it

belongs to many people. The author no longer has an exclusive claim upon his story.[2]

As a more experienced monk and writer, Merton often apologized for the flaws in that autobiography, and in the young man who wrote it during his first five to seven years in the monastery. In his enthusiasm for the contemplative life, he had created "a sort of stereotype of the world-denying contemplative," which, Merton admitted, "is probably my own fault, and it is something I have to try to demolish on occasion."[3]

So the seasoned Merton had learned to accept himself and his writing as less than perfect, and still was able to go on working at his life project and his autobiographical storytelling. Better, *because* he came to accept his flaws, Father Louis, O.C.S.O., could continue to grow.

Grow he did throughout his twenty-seven years as a monk—but it was not just a smooth process of gradual unfolding, like the full flowering of a bud. Merton had to cope with his own potent psychic energy and his gifted, but problematic, temperament. As all people do, he brought certain weaknesses into the monastery with him. Some of his native difficulties were exacerbated by the very form of life he had chosen; others were intensified by the situation he found himself in as a contemplative monk who had become a famous author.

In his Bangkok talk on the day he died, Merton used one of his favorite Zen koans: "Where do you go from the top of a thirty-foot pole?"[4] Twenty years earlier, the young Trappist had been faced with a similar sort of riddle: "Where do you go from the top of a seven-storey mountain?" The task of his life would be to discover how the conversion he had shouted from his "mountain top" in Kentucky could continue to deepen and to become totally effective. His autobiographical writing—the ongoing telling of his story or stories—constituted the work through which Merton explored that relentless question.

Merton's autobiographical writing assumed for him, and can for those of us who read it in relation to our own quest, the paradoxical form of a Zen koan: that is, a riddle whose answer can be reached not by thinking about it, but only by experientially working it through. Indulge for a moment in a little game (of a kind Merton's ironic wit would have enjoyed); read the following passage from his essay on the Zen koan, remembering that I have substituted the words "Merton's autobiographical writing" everywhere he used "the koan":

> The study of [Merton's autobiographical writing] has no codified rules and no precise formal answer. Nevertheless, there is a very definite discipline and procedure to be followed in [Merton's autobiographical writing] study. Nothing is arbitrary or left to chance. One either hits the target or misses it entirely.

Hitting and missing are not indifferent. The student seeks at all costs to reach the heart of the matter in [Merton's autobiographical writing] study. Therefore, he learns to "work through" [Merton's autobiographical writing], to live it as his master has lived it. In fact, the heart of [Merton's autobiographical writing] is reached, its kernel is attained and tasted, when one breaks through into the heart of life itself as the ground of one's own consciousness. It is then that one sees the "answer," or rather one experiences oneself, as the question answered. The answer is [Merton's autobiographical writing], the question, seen in a totally new light. It is not something other than the self. It is a cryptic figure of the self, and it is interpreted insofar as the student can become so identified with [Merton's autobiographical writing] that it revolutionizes and liberates his whole consciousness, delivering it from itself.[5]

For Merton, the answer to the question of who he was, what he was called to be, and how the completion of his conversion was to come about, indeed, was "the question, seen in a totally new light." His fidelity to journal keeping, along with following his temperamental inclination to work out everything on paper, provided the monk with that "new light" in which to see the old question. Thus autobiographical writing "solved" some problems for Merton while it created others. The unresolved tensions in his life showed themselves throughout his autobiographical materials. That writing brought to light two conflicts in Merton's personality. One was the tendency toward hyperverbalization in a man who had chosen a life of silence and who preferred nonconceptual modes of prayer. The other was a need to "keep moving," literally and symbolically, in a man who had committed himself to remain within an enclosed monastery, living a form of life not usually generating dramatic developments (whether external or psychic). These two conflicts—or paradoxes, or koans, as you please—made Thomas Merton something of a riddle to himself, as well as to the world.

Undoubtedly, these very traits were the mainsprings of Merton's literary achievement and even of his spiritual growth. But looked at from another point of view, his verbalizing and restiveness represented the more negative aspects of Merton's character. Such tendencies generated emotional turmoil, constituted his habitual temptations, and exhibited that side of him most resistant to transformation.

"To Remain Myself, and to Write About It"

There is a hint of the ludicrous in Merton's constant writing and talking about silence. No one complained so vociferously about the need for and value of silence as he did. This Trappist monk produced volumes of print and file cases full of tapes denouncing useless words, unnecessary chatter, and continuous verbalizing. Yet he himself could speak quite garrulously and write compulsively.

Anyone who produced the sheer amount of material Merton did in the time he had at his disposal as a monk had to be a compulsive writer. His books and articles are filled with indications that for him writing was sometimes work, sometimes recreation, sometimes psychic and spiritual release—but always *necessary* for Thomas Merton to keep going. My conjecture is that often enough he wrote for reasons not unlike those of people who rely on drugs and alcohol: to assure himself that he was real. I once had the opportunity to hear an incredibly revealing tape that Merton had sent to a good friend in lieu of a letter. He spoke of his compulsions, which he experienced more acutely in the hermitage, and Merton complained to the friend of his constant need "to excrete self-justifications like perspiration." Indeed, some of Merton's writing is nearly that sticky. Certainly no one can write so much under such conditions as Merton did and have it all be good.

Merton himself was certainly aware of his inclination to overproduce and to range widely in the quality of his writing. In 1967, he made a chart listing his books chronologically and rating each according to seven categories: "Best," "Better," "Good," "Fair," "Poor," "Bad," and "Awful."[6] Only *What are These Wounds? The Life of a Cistercian Mystic: Saint Lutgarde of Aywieres* (1950) was deemed "Awful." Only *Exile Ends in Glory: The Life of a Trappistine, Mother M. Berchmans* (1948) was "Bad." *Living Bread* (1956), *Spiritual Direction and Meditation* (1960) and *Seasons of Celebration* (1964) were listed as "Poor." In the "Fair" category were *Figures for an Apocalypse* (1948), *The Waters of Siloe* (1949), *The Ascent to Truth* (1951), *Bread in the Wilderness* (1953), *The Last of the Fathers: Saint Bernard of Clairvaux* (1954), *Life and Holiness* (1963), and *Emblems of a Season of Fury* (1963). There were six books called "Good": *A Man in the Divided Sea* (1946), *No Man Is an Island* (1955), *The Strange Islands* (1957), *Disputed Questions* (1960), *The New Man* (1961), and *Mystics and Zen Masters* (1967). Merton judged thirteen of his books to be "Better"—the greatest number in any single category. These included the autobiography and all the then published journals, some poetry, the social commentary, and an assortment of others: *Thirty Poems* (1944), *The Seven Storey Mountain* (1948), *Seeds of Contemplation* (1949), *The Tears of Blind Lions* (1949), *The Sign of Jonas* (1953), *The Silent Life* (1957), *Thoughts in Solitude* (1958), *The Wisdom of the Desert* (1960), *New Seeds of Contemplation* (1961), *Seeds of Destruction* (1967), *The Way of Chuang Tzu* (1965), *Raids on the Unspeakable* (1966), and *Conjectures of a Guilty Bystander* (1966). Although Merton had said of *The Way of Chuang Tzu* that "I have enjoyed writing this book more than any other I can remember"[7] and had humorously addressed *Raids on the Unspeakable* saying, "*Raids,* I think I love you more than the rest,"[8] he only rated them as "Better." Thomas Merton put nothing at all in the "Best" category.We can only wonder if by the time he died, a year or so after making his hastily scribbled little chart, anything would have been placed there. I doubt it.

In my judgment, Merton overrated his poetry and tended to underrate those collections of provocative essays such as *The New Man, Disputed Questions,* and *Mystics and Zen Masters.* While I am no literary critic, personally I think that none of his poetry is great, that some of the early religious poems are quite good, and that the late poetry may be an imaginative and challenging form of writing, but Merton rightly called it "antipoetry." Generally his poetry lacks form and, ironically, often tends to be rather abstract. Others certainly disagree with me, but I consider Merton's prose richer in images and metaphors than most of his poetry.[9] I would not know where to place on Merton's own scale any of his poems, except probably to lower all of his books of poetry by at least one category.

However, I would put the books he rated as "Good" in the "Better" slot. Essays such as "Promethean Theology" and "Image and Likeness" in *The New Man* represent incisive and imaginative theological writing, and ones such as "The Pasternak Affair" and "Notes for a Philosophy of Solitude" in *Disputed Questions* do precisely what their author hoped for in the preface: "stimulate thought and . . . awaken some degree of spiritual awareness."[10] And I would place the autobiography and journals all in the column Thomas Merton left blank: "Best."

In whatever way Merton himself, I, or a multitude of Merton fans or critics might evaluate his books, most of us would agree that he simply wrote too much and too diversely for his work to be consistently good. Unfortunately, once he had made his name, publishers picked up anything and everything Thomas Merton submitted, doing him a considerable disservice.

Because he lived in a monastery and did not enjoy the daily give-and-take of colleague criticism in an academic setting or the shop talk of professional writers, Merton needed assistance in sorting through his massive output of material. He received reactions and suggestions through the mails, and sometimes in person, from friends with whom he shared drafts of pieces on which he was working. But that is quite different from the day-in and day-out criticism of peers in a university or the often merciless judgments of fellow *littérateurs* at social gatherings. Merton got too much adulation from his readers for his own good. Professional critics either completely ignored him because he was religious and they were not interested in that, forgave him too easily because they did not want to confront a "holy monk," or praised him too lavishly as an extraordinary Christian who could relate his religion to just about anything and anybody.

Merton's own monastic brothers at Gethsemani lived in silence and could not talk with him about books or articles of his which they might have read. His scholastics and novices, if they read Merton at all, were hardly in a position to offer critical advice to their religious superior. Not without irony, perhaps it was Father Louis' own Trappist superiors and censors—those who caused him much frustration as a monk-writer with a vow of obedience—who rendered him more service than his New York editors. If some authorities in the Order or in the Abbey of Gethsemani were much too cautious and narrow in certain respects (for example, suppressing Merton's early writings on peace and social issues), they were judicious in others. When I first learned that the censors insisted Merton cut some sections of *The Seven Storey Mountain,* I simply assumed that a group of conservative prigs had made the young monk cut the "juicy" parts out of the story, for fear of scandalizing the pious public. Actually, if one reads the unpublished sections from the original manuscript,[11] the Trappist censors appear to have exercised nothing but commonsense judgment. The parts that were omitted from the original *Seven Storey Mountain* are from the last part, which describes life in Gethsemani. These sections are tedious, adding nothing to the story but length. The censors were less romantic about life in the monastery than Merton was at thirty.

Especially as a young monk, Merton was ambivalent about his writing. More than once during the first half of his monastic life, Merton "gave it up." He would swear off writing with all the fervor of an alcoholic throwing away the bottle—and with about the same results. Thomas Merton could not not-write. For all his idealization of silence and wariness about words, the process of articulating his experience was intrinsic to the monk's development. He could neither find himself, nor be himself, apart from some form of literary expression. Nonetheless, frequently Merton just said too much, too facilely. His powerful verbal gift could dominate as well as serve him.

Merton was aware of more than he could control. Therein lay his redemption as an excessively verbal contemplative. Like Paul of Tarsus, that loquacious and superactive mystic, Merton might say, "So I shall be very happy to make my weaknesses my special boast so that the power of Christ may stay over me. . . . For it is when I am weak that I am strong" (2 Cor. 12:9–10).

If Merton lacked adequate criticism of his writing from professionals, he did not lack self-criticism, either of his writing or his life. As a monk, however, Thomas Merton was far more interested in giving time and energy to scrutinizing his life rather than his work. Obviously, he took writing seriously; still, whatever Merton produced he regarded as insignificant in relation to his quest for God and his true self. Again, like Paul, Merton would have said, "I look on everything as so much rubbish if only I can have Christ and be given a place in him" (Phil. 3:8).

Merton, the monk, valued the process of writing more than the finished products. That was probably true of everything he wrote but especially of his autobiographical works. For such writing was the mode in which he thought, discerned, decided. In the very process of trying to formulate in words what he grasped about himself, Merton could recognize the truth and be able to acknowledge it. Such writing was not only the way in which Merton came to insights about himself and his behavior; it also provided him with the occasion for making choices to change, modify, discard, or to appropriate certain aspects of himself. Autobiographical writing was, therefore, an essential element in Merton's ongoing development as a human being and a Christian.

He worked out practical decisions in his notebooks. Sometimes Merton consciously tested a possible action by writing about its implications before he actually did anything. Always, he reflected on what he was already doing by writing about it. Writing was for Thomas Merton an activity of assessment—and it led him to make some significant changes in his life. Writing *The Secular Journal* helped him decide to enter Gethsemani; writing *The Sign of Jonas* helped him learn how to live with the paradox of his vocation as a monk-writer; and writing *Conjectures of a Guilty Bystander* helped Merton to make up his mind regarding how he could assume social and political responsibility as a monk.

Autobiographical writing accomplished even more than clarifying his self-understanding and fostering decisiveness. It deeply affected Merton's character as a religious person. Having to tell his story served to monitor Merton's pretentions and laid bare any secret claims to righteousness. The process of putting into words what was happening in his life disclosed to Merton the disjunction between his aspirations and his achievements. It goaded him into humility; over and over again, it taught him to acknowledge his life, his very self, as pure gift.

For all the problems writing caused Thomas Merton, he knew in his heart of hearts that it entered into his self-identity. Writing was, as he came to perceive it, his destiny. He could escape neither his own need to write nor his obligation to do it for the sake of others.

In a poignant passage from *The Sign of Jonas*, Merton captured his emotional ambivalence and the irony of his situation as a Trappist monk who could not stop writing his own story:

> Sometimes I feel that I would like to stop writing, precisely as a gesture of defiance. In any case, I hope to stop publishing for a time, for I believe it has now become impossible for me to stop writing altogether. Perhaps I shall continue writing on my deathbed, and even take some asbestos paper with me in order to go on writing in purgatory. . . .
>
> And yet it seems to me that writing, far from being an obstacle to spiritual perfection in my own life, has become one of the conditions on which my perfection will depend. If I am to be a saint—and there is nothing else that I can think of desiring to be—it seems that I must get there by writing books in a Trappist monastery. . . .
>
> To be as good a monk as I can, and to remain myself, and to write about it: to put myself down on paper, in such a situation, with the most complete simplicity and integrity, masking nothing, confusing no issues.[12]

"I Am Going Home, to the Home Where I Have Never Been"

There is an element of pathos in Merton's habitual verbalizing; so, too, in the intense restlessness of a man with a self-proclaimed vocation to stay in one place and remain still. Merton liked to travel and to explore, to move around, to meet new people, to do many things. Although he committed himself to a quiet contemplative life in one particular monastery, Merton never quite came to grips with that part of himself which wanted to be on the go. Unlike that kindred spirit, Augustine, whose passionate energies were harnessed in a vigorously active life, Merton's restive temperament was denied certain outlets. He felt torn between his conviction that he was called to (indeed, had chosen) the contemplative way, and the demands of his aggressively active instincts. Thomas Merton was a *doer* as well as a *seer,* and, in spite of all his protestations, that side of him sometimes led him around by the nose.

I once asked Morton Kelsey, the well-known Jungian analyst, to comment on the dreams that Merton reported in *Conjectures.*[13] The most notable feature of them, Kelsey felt, was a decided ambivalence about himself and his life. Merton's dreams betrayed an unresolved inner conflict about being still and keeping in motion.

Undoubtedly Merton's prodigious writing and his drive to keep on the go were related. Writing provided a needed therapy for an active, adventurous man who had, with full deliberation, opted for the interior journey. But even that conscious choice seemed unable to quell this monk's literal and figurative wanderlust. One hardly need be an expert in psychohistory to notice that Merton's unstable and geographically displaced boyhood may have left lifetime traces in the form of ambivalent attractions to settle down in one spot and to keep roaming at all costs. In spite of my benign interpretation in an earlier chapter of Merton's trip to Asia as a symbolic expression of the monk's inner journey, I also think that something in Merton just wanted to escape the territorial and psychological confines of Gethsemani by hitting the road again. He was, after all, a physically and emotionally vigorous man in his early fifties who had seldom gone further than Louisville in twenty-seven years.

Even as a boy, Merton had despised tourism. When he was a teenager, Tom had sought opportunities to travel in order to enter into the experience of diverse peoples and to taste different cultures. As *The Seven Storey Mountain* testifies, the young man's physical wanderings exemplified his quest for meaning but also exhibited a certain instability and inability to put down roots. Throughout his life, in fact, there were two sides to Merton's characteristic urge to explore "new territory," geographic or other.

The more positive side of that drive to keep in motion was expressed in Merton's thrust to transcend the limits imposed by culture, social convention, education, personal prejudice, or inertia. He always wanted to realize the broadest range of human possibilities—to become a "universal man." As we have already observed, Merton felt that Reza Arasteh had admirably characterized this ideal as "final integration."[14] The monk of Gethsemani certainly aspired to that. He did not think that travel alone could ever bring about a truly universal perspective, but toward the end of his life Merton's desire to go to the East was definitely linked to his quest for transcultural maturity.

Thanks to Merton's boundless enthusiasm and remarkable adaptability, he could be at home almost anywhere and with anybody. That was true not only of the peripatetic youth in France, England, and America, but also of the mature monk who entertained the idea of moving to New Mexico or Alaska or the Far East. Given his capacity for appreciating diversity, Merton was notably free of parochial attitudes and uncritical attachment to groups with whom he was associated. This very openness, however, had its pitfalls. In seeking to become a "universal man," Merton dangerously courted self-deception. That was the negative side of his inclination to keep moving. There appears to be in Merton a flight from responsibility (at least an unconscious one), and some sort of refusal to accept those limits that permanent human ties establish.

What Merton had once called his "profound instinct to keep clear, to keep free,"[15] might well be construed as unacknowledged escapism. There is more than a hint of that in the autobiographer's retrospective comment: "As a child, and since then too, I have always tended to resist any kind of a possessive affection on the part of any other human being."[16] Under the guise of becoming "all things to all men," Merton risked being able to avoid those few responsible ties at the core of ethical decisions. His temptation may have been to shirk specific involvements in the name of transcending limitations.

One caustic critic of Thomas Merton views him precisely in this negative light in reviewing *The Asian Journal.* Robert Evett of the Washington *Star News* had this interpretation of Merton's trip and what it signaled in the man:

> Merton was a very big shot at the Abbey of Gethsemani, and seems not to have suspected that his life was in many ways as much a great ego-trip as it was an interior journey. . . . The Rule of his order "maintains silence, isolation, fasts, restricted diet and manual labor." Apparently it does not apply to a monk on a junket. . . . A question that is bound to emerge from any sustained reading of Merton is why, if he enjoyed flattery and French cooking so much he became a Trappist. Twenty years ago, a monk I know proposed that it was so he wouldn't have to listen to what anybody else had to say. In any event, for a man meditating on the ultimate emptiness, he was remarkably full of himself.[17]

To say the least, I do not agree with Mr. Evett's reading of the situation. I do think, nonetheless, that Merton played a dangerous game with himself and never fully resolved his conflicting attractions to the quiet life "at home" in the monastery and to the exciting life of travel.

On the plane traveling to the East, Merton made a note in his journal that signaled much more, but surely included some reference to this tension: "The moment of take-off was ecstatic. . . . I . . . [was] at last on my true way after years of waiting and wondering and fooling around. May I not come back without having settled the great affair."[18]

Monastic life itself, I would argue, both restrained and channeled Merton's vagabond inclinations. His experience at Gethsemani offset the temptation to call no place home and no one group his own. The monastery provided him with a healthy sense of rootedness. It made Merton part of a particular place and a given community of particular people, thereby helping him to face the specific and concrete nature of human obligations. In choosing to become a monk, Merton had consciously chosen to remain a "pilgrim." And the asceticism he cultivated was founded on rejecting those snugly secure feelings of belonging to anything or anybody other than God. Nevertheless, as a human being Merton needed some spot to call "home" and some group of persons to whom he "belonged" in a special way—not to offer him cheap comfort, but precisely to elicit from him fidelity and sustained devotion.

Even though he sometimes hankered to leave, in his most lucid moments Merton recognized what his ties with Gethsemani had effected in him:

> Returning to the monastery from the hospital: cool evening, gray sky, the dark hills. Once again I get the strange sense that one has when he comes back to a place that has been chosen for him by Providence. I belong to this parcel of land with rocky hills around it, with pine trees on it. These are the woods and fields that I have worked in, and walked in, and in which I have encountered the deepest mystery of my own life.[19]

Just a few weeks before he died, while considering where he might go to live in order to find more solitude after returning from his Asian trip, Merton commented in his journal:

> I do not think I ought to separate myself completely from Gethsemani, even while maintaining an official residence there, legally only. I suppose I ought eventually to end my days there. I do in many ways miss it. There is no problem of my wanting simply to "leave Gethsemani." It is my monastery and being away has helped me see it in perspective and love it more.[20]

Thomas Merton never "left Gethsemani" (severed bonds with the community), but neither did he "end his days there" (physically remain in his own monastery until he died). Perhaps those two facts embody not only the monk's ambivalence, but his only way of living with it. Merton's chronic weakness of fleeing being tied down was never completely overcome, yet he developed a genuine capacity for commitment. He was experientially aware of the Lord's meaning in addressing Paul, a man pleading for release from his struggle with himself: "My grace is enough for you; my power is at its best in weakness;; (2 Cor. 21:9).

Gethsemani was the right kind of home for Merton because, indeed, it was not a "home" in the conventional sense of the word. "My monastery is not a home," Merton wrote in the preface for the Japanese *Seven Storey Mountain.* "It is not a place where I am rooted and established on earth. It is not an environment in which I become aware of myself as an individual, but rather a place in which I disappear from the world as an object of interest in order to be everywhere in it by hiddenness and compassion."[21] In the measure that Merton was disciplined and chastened by a life that taught him how to be truly free and how rightly to be bound to people and places, he was able to describe his last trip as a journey home—a journey into the unknown. With a light touch that blended the universal implications of what he was undertaking with a sense of the concrete details involved in his excursion to Asia at this time, Merton wrote in his journal while flying over San Francisco Bay:

> I am going home, to the home where I have never been in this body, where I have never been in this washable suit (washed by Sister Gerarda the other day at the Redwoods), where I have never been with these suitcases (in Bangkok there must be a katharsis of the suitcases!), where I have never been with these particular books, Evans-Wentz's *Tibetan Yoga and Secret Doctrines* and the others.[22]

"I, as a Monk"

Throughout his monastic life, Merton was plagued with these two tensions we have been discussing: a compulsive need to write and the psychic urge to keep on moving. In some periods, he felt the difficulties to be resolved, but sooner or later the old conflicts surfaced. And, when they did, Thomas Merton was not above engaging in the devious little games of psychological projection to which human beings resort for handling emotional pressures. For instance, there was almost a childish vindictiveness in Merton's description of Dom Frederic setting him to write in 1946, after the young monk had so magnanimously "renounced" writing.[23] We can only conjecture concerning the extent that people and policies that Merton resisted and/or resented actually served his development. In any event, I believe that the monastic life did for Merton what institutions, laws, and vows are intended to do: provide a stablizing context to protect one against one's own erratic inclinations, ephemeral whims, and evanescent desires.

Although it never eradicated Merton's proclivity to verbalize too much or to keep on the move, the monastic life did defuse the destructive force latent in such tendencies. I suspect that apart from the demands placed on him by monastic discipline, Thomas Merton could easily have become just another literary hack. More tragically, he might have been a chronic expatriate—a man belonging nowhere in particular and living in a perpetual limbo, without concrete ties and specific commitments.

Even within the parameters of the monastic vocation, a man so verbal as Merton was in danger of being victimized by his own uncommon gift for expression. As a monk, at least, he was constantly prodded to be aware of its destructive potentialities and to take seriously the dark side of himself. Already in the autobiography Merton acknowledged the threatening presence of "this shadow, this double, this writer who had followed me into the cloister."[24] Zilboorg's warning about becoming "too verbalogical"[25] made Merton acutely sensitive to his susceptibility for being seduced by words and deceived by his own skill in employing them. The monk meditated long and hard on the ever-present danger of substituting words for reality. But, above all, the experience of solitude refined Merton's understanding of how his powerful talent for self-articulation and for continual exploration rendered him vulnerable to self-deception and to evasion of his real quest in life. That quest was to be "converted from the *conversatio* [conversation, exchange] of the world to that of the monastery, and by the *conversatio* of monastic life [to become] gradually 'converted' or 'transformed' in the likeness of Christ."[26]

When Merton's playful wit thought of naming parts of a journal he kept in 1964–1965 "A Vow of Conversation,"[27] his pun on *conversatio* (the Latin can mean either "conversation" or "conversion") expressed the monk's grasp of the connection between conversation and conversion in his life. Within the context of his monastic vocation—a life dedicated to seeking constant conversion—Merton's conversation (with himself in his journals and with others through the published writings) could become an authentic spiritual exchange.

Without the requirements of a life committed to conversion, (Cistercians take a vow of *conversatio morum,* that is, conversion of life), Merton's glibness undoubtedly would have engaged him in endless, futile "clever conversation." He could easily enough be tempted into that—fooling himself that talking was living, or that sheer productivity signaled literary quality. The very brilliance of Merton's capacity for expression, combined with his passionate desire for discovery, set him up for failing both as a writer and as a religious person. He was painfully prone to squander his creative powers and to lose his soul through a narcissism disguised as interest in everyone and everything. It is not difficult to imagine Merton's facility with words degenerating into pure verbosity and his cleverness into stark cynicism were he deprived of the inherent checks that the monastic life provided. (Imagine for a moment, that the dazzling young author of the Joycean-like early novel, *My Argument with the Gestapo,* might one day find himself doing what his glittering contemporary, Norman Mailer, did in 1973: dissipate his verbal genius on an instant biography of Marilyn Monroe, the tragic Hollywood sex symbol, in order to make a quick buck to meet his multiple alimony payments. Ed Rice's reminiscences of his friend Tom's Columbia days in *The Man in the Sycamore Tree*[28] suggest several obvious affinities between Merton and Mailer. The issue of *Time* that carried the story on Mailer's biography of Monroe[29] also carried a cover picture of Mailer that looked spookily like the Griffin closeup of Merton, facing the Prologue and used on the cover of *A Hidden*

Wholeness. The *Time* article carried a caption that—but for circumstances and the grace of God—might have fit Thomas as well as Norman: "The Grand Middle-Aged Man of American Letters at 50. Tinsel, thunder, and a global superstar.")

But Thomas Merton, Father Louis (affectionately called "Louie" by his brothers at Gethsemani), was saved from being destroyed by his own gifts. In the austere setting of the monastery and later in the quiet of his hermitage, Merton learned not only to face his pretensions as a man but also to develop a healthy distance from himself as a writer. Although he would, must, always write, the monastic life taught him both how to value his writing and how to subordinate it to something greater. He told the monks he was addressing in Bangkok:

> The essential thing . . . is the formation of spiritual masters who can bring it [freedom and transcendence] out in the hearts of people who are as yet unformed. Wherever you have somebody capable of giving some kind of direction and instruction to a small group attempting to do this thing, attempting to love and serve God and reach union with him, you are bound to have some kind of monasticism. . . .
>
> I, as a monk—and, I think, you as monks—can agree that we believe this to be the deepest and most essential thing in our lives, and because we believe this, we have given ourselves to the kind of life we have adopted. I believe that our renewal consists precisely in deepening this understanding and this grasp of that which is most real.[30]

The value of Merton's conversation about his ongoing conversion—with a small group in person and with a vast audience through his autobiographical writing—might be assessed by its conversion potential. So long as Thomas Merton sought to be a "true monk," his speaking and writing would be fruitful, contributing toward his own interior growth and that of others "who are as yet unformed." It was autobiographical writing, I think, that made him a spiritual master for many, many people.

"To Be What I Am"

There is no doubt that Thomas Merton's autobiographical writing possesses a dramatic power that renders it fascinating to others. The stories of his initial and continuing conversion, apparently, have brought about some sort of religious conversion in numerous persons. Although one could scarcely document that, it is fairly common testimony among Merton readers.

To cite only my own limited experience (in teaching, lecturing, and writing about Merton over the past ten years) more people than I could count have contacted me to say what a difference Merton made and still makes in their lives. There are those, generally middle-aged or older, who describe how they decided to become Catholics because they read *The Seven Storey Mountain*. There are others who tell me that, although they were cradle Catholics, reading that autobiography opened up a whole new world of religious meaning to them. (I can most easily identify with this group, being one of them. I read *The Seven Storey Mountain* as a high school student in the early 1950s and felt it transformed my whole understanding of Catholicism and religious living.) There are college students who talk about discovering or rediscovering Christianity, even the institutional Church, perhaps through *Conjectures* or *Mystics and Zen Masters*. There are the Quakers who say that *Faith and Violence* has renewed their hope in and commitment to nonviolence. There are the religious studies professors who may argue about the accuracy of Merton's interpretation of various Eastern traditions yet who claim that *The Way of Chuang Tzu* or *Zen and the Birds of Appetite* shows the possibilities of rapproachement for Christians in a powerful, poignant way. There are the members of active religious communities now living in houses of prayer or hermitages, permanently or periodically, who attribute the change in their own living patterns (and the approval of such change granted by their congregations) to Merton. There are the monks at Gethsemani who let it be known that they came to the monastery—or stayed there—thanks to Thomas Merton. And there are the unbelievers who remain unbelievers but read Merton because they share some of his questions; there are alienated Christians whose one link with the traditions or institutions they have rejected is Merton's ironic antipoetry; there are the unsettled conservative Catholics who find solace in *Seeds of Contemplation* and *The Sign of Jonas* and the disaffected liberals who might not survive within the Church except for *Raids on the Unspeakable* and *The Asian Journal of Thomas Merton*.

Merton's writings, even when they are obviously dated, seem to possess an immediacy, an efficacy, a power to transform people and their lives. That was true during the twenty years that Thomas Merton was a prominent Catholic writer, perhaps the most popular spiritual writer in America, and one of the most influential advocates of social justice and ecumenical openness. It is all the more true some ten years after the monk's untimely death in the Far East. His autobiographical writings, evidently, bring all sorts of people to life. Reading his stories of open-ended conversion, people are disturbed, given hope, jolted, calmed, awakened, and prodded. New and unanticipated vistas are opened up. Merton forces us to confront ourselves and to answer to our God, who makes unimagined and new demands as we live and grow.

Do Merton's writings shed light on the dynamics of Christian growth? They do, I think, although not in the sense of offering information or yielding any laws about the process of ongoing conversion. We cannot distill from his autobiographical accounts a universally applicable set of principles concerning how religious transformation comes about, or what course its development will take. Like every human being, this man is more than an instance of a general law. His story cannot be understood merely as a variation on a common theme.

But, if he is not a repeatable type of continuing religious development, Merton *is* a unique exemplification of a process—a story—that one might say has a form rather than a predictable pattern. The story is that of his lifelong journey into the unknown depths of himself, into an unrealized expanse of love for others in Christ, into the unfathomable mystery of God. Merton presents himself to us in all his particularity and with utterly specific features as *this* man, progressively opening up to new and richer possibilities of life. A person of greater potentiality than most of us, Merton never put himself forth as a paradigm. He resisted presenting his life as a model. In his autobiographical writings, Thomas Merton offered "only" himself.

But that self, that story, is fascinating and inspiring to many whose lives are very different from Merton's. People who feel awed by his talents and amazed by this man's achievements find themselves, nonetheless, identifying with him in his continuing search to know himself. Merton comes through in the human measure. His autobiographical writings reveal a person not unlike the rest of us: ambivalent, uncertain, frustrated, inconsistent, struggling, undergoing continual growing pains. For all his strength, Merton appears as a fragile human being—although one remarkably unafraid to display his vulnerability. Perhaps his attractiveness lies precisely in this gift for disclosing our common humanity to all of us by faithfully recounting his own story. Thomas Merton gives us courage and hope in our search for self-identity. His life shows that those who undertake it will discover not one's own, but God's transforming power.

More than any other contemporary religious personality and writer, I think, Merton has taught us to appreciate the theological significance of the quest for self-identity. He reintroduced and legitimized the use of "I" in religious inquiry—not just the "I" that represents the individual ego asserting various opinions and making certain claims but also the searching, probing, receptive, loving "I" that passionately seeks to discover God in the self, in every person, in the whole of creation. The literary context for articulating this quest for and by the true self is, of course, autobiographical narrative.

Thomas Merton was constantly engaged in the process of telling his story—his stories of conversion, "seven" in the biblical sense of an indeterminate number signifying infinity. Paul, Augustine, Dante, John of the Cross, and Kierkegaard had done it, and Merton returns us to that rich tradition of theological discourse. Merton understood his task in life as "only to be what I am." He carried it out by accepting his limitations and affirming God's grace working through them and transforming him. And he carried it out by writing, writing, writing about what he was doing and what God was doing in and through him.

Most of Merton's favorite religious mentors were poetic autobiographers or autobiographical poets who knew how to characterize themselves and their vocations in appropriate metaphors. Paul called himself "the least of the Apostles." Augustine spoke of his "restless heart." Dante presented himself as "the pilgrim poet." John of the Cross was "the beloved" responding in "darkness." Kierkegaard identified himself as "this definite individual." And then there was a Cistercian monk in the middle of the twentieth-century in the backwoods of Kentucky who wrote about himself as "the solitary explorer."

Thomas Merton was, like those other great Christian personalities and writers from whom he learned, a theologian who intuitively understood that the only linguistic device for trying to express the inexpressible is metaphor. Merton used metaphors superbly. They were the means through which he reconstructed his past, got bearings on the present, and imagined his future.

Dorothy L. Sayers had a marvelous comment on Dante's image of the good pagans in Limbo in the First Circle of Hell:

> After those who refused choice come those without opportunity of choice. They could not, that is, choose Christ; they could, and did, choose human virtue, and for that they have their reward. (Pagans who chose evil by their own standards are judged by these standards—cf. Rom. ii, 8–15—and are found lower down.) Here again, the souls "have what they chose"; they enjoy that kind of after-life which they themselves imagined for the virtuous dead; their failure lay in not imagining better.[31]

Merton began telling his life story by describing himself in hell and finding his way out of it to the seven-storey mountain of purgatory. Until the day he died, he continued to describe the never-ending climb up that mountain of continuing transformation, the ascent that Dante (and all Catholic theology) portrays as preliminary to the vision of God. Where Thomas Merton ended, we can only conjecture. My calculated guess is that it is not in any limbo. This man's sins never included "failure . . . in not imagining better."

Notes

The following abbreviations have been used for the works of Thomas Merton most frequently cited.

AT   *The Ascent to Truth.* New York: Harcourt Brace, 1951.

AJ   *The Asian Journal of Thomas Merton.* Edited from his original notebooks by Naomi Burton, Brother Patrick Hart, and James Laughlin. New York: New Directions, 1973.

CGB   *Conjectures of a Guilty Bystander.* Garden City, N.Y.: Doubleday Image Books, 1966.

CWA   *Contemplation in a World of Action.* Garden City, N.Y.: Doubleday Image Books, 1971.

CP   *Contemplative Prayer.* New York: Herder and Herder, 1969.

DQ   *Disputed Questions.* New York: Farrar, Straus & Giroux, Noonday Books, 1976.

FV   *Faith and Violence: Christian Teaching and Christian Practice.* Notre Dame, Ind.: University of Notre Dame Press, 1968.

GNV   *Gandhi on Non-Violence: a Selection from the Writings of Mahatma Gandhi.* Edited and with an introduction by Thomas Merton. New York: New Directions, 1964.

MJ   *The Monastic Journey: Thomas Merton.* Edited by Brother Patrick Hart. Kansas City: Sheed, Andrews and McMeel, 1977.

MZM   *Mystics and Zen Masters.* New York: Dell, Delta Books, 1968.

NM   *The New Man.* New York: Farrar, Straus & Giroux, 1978.

NSC   *New Seeds of Contemplation.* New York: New Directions, 1961.

NMI   *No Man Is an Island.* New York: Dell, Dell Books, 1957.

RU   *Raids on the Unspeakable.* New York: New Directions, 1966.

SCel *Seasons of Celebration.* New York: Farrar, Straus & Giroux, Noonday Books, 1977.

SC   *Seeds of Contemplation.* New York: Dell, Chapel Books, 1960.

SD   *Seeds of Destruction.* New York: Macmillan, 1967.

SSM   *The Seven Storey Mountain.* New York: Harcourt, Brace, Jovanovich, Harvest Books, 1978.

SJ   *The Sign of Jonas.* Garden City, N.Y.: Doubleday Image Books, 1956.

SL   *The Silent Life.* New York: Farrar, Straus, & Giroux, Noonday Books, 1975.

TMP   *Thomas Merton on Peace.* Edited and with an introduction by Gordon C. Zahn. New York: McCall, 1971.

TMR   *A Thomas Merton Reader.* Edited by Thomas P. McDonnell, revised edition. Garden City, N.Y.: Doubleday Image Books, 1974.

TS   *Thoughts in Solitude.* New York: Farrar, Straus & Giroux, Noonday Books, 1976.

WS   *The Waters of Siloe*. Garden City, N.Y.: Doubleday Image Books, 1962.

WCT   *The Way of Chuang Tzu*. New York: New Directions, 1965.

WD   *The Wisdom of the Desert: Sayings from the Desert Fathers of the Fourth Century*. Translated by Thomas Merton. New York: New Directions, 1970.

ZBA   *Zen and the Birds of Appetite*. New York: New Directions, 1968.

PREFACE

1. Thomas Merton, "The White Pebble," in *Where I Found Christ,* ed. John A. O'Brien (New York: Doubleday, 1950), p. 243.

CHAPTER 1: Writing as Temperature

1. Thomas Merton, "Writing as Temperature," *Sewanee Review,* 77 (1969): 537.
2. Thomas Merton, *The Sign of Jonas* (Garden City, N.Y.: Image Books, 1956), p. 228. Hereafter *SJ.*
3. Merton, "Writing as Temperature," 537–38.
4. Merton's will, made a few years before his death, is very restrictive about letters and unpublished materials. He designated certain manuscripts for eventual publication, pending further editing. His private notebooks, however, are not available to anyone except the official biographer appointed by the Merton Legacy Trust until twenty-five years after Merton's death.
5. Robert Lowell, "The Verses of Thomas Merton," *Commonweal* 42 (1945): 240–42.
6. Thomas Merton, *The Seven Storey Mountain* (New York: Harcourt Brace Jovanovich, 1978), pp. 422–23. Hereafter *SSM.*
7. Quoted on the back cover of the first paperback edition of *SSM* (New York: Signet Books, 1952).
8. Quoted on the first-page blurb of the Signet Books *SSM.*
9. Naomi Burton, *More Than Sentinels* (New York: Doubleday, 1964), p. 245.
10. New American Library, Signet Books; Doubleday Image Books: Harvest Books, Harcourt Brace Jovanovich.
11. Francis X. Connolly, *Thought* 24 (1949): 10–14.
12. Y. H. Kirkorian, "The Fruits of Mysticism," *New Republic* 121 (1949): 17–18.
13. Aelred Graham, "Thomas Merton, a Modern Man in Reverse," *Atlantic Monthly* 191 (1953): 70–74.
14. "Benedictine v. Trappist," *Time,* February 2, 1953, pp. 72, 74.
15. For example, Earl S. Dubbel, "In Defense of Thomas Merton," *Atlantic Monthly* 191 (1953): 20.
16. Frank Dell'Isola, "A Bibliography of Thomas Merton," *Thought* 29 (1954): 574–96. This work was later published as a book, *Thomas Merton: a Bibliography* (New York: Farrar, Straus & Cudahy, 1956).
17. Typical of those who praised Merton as a great Catholic poet was Sister Mary Julian Baird in "Blake, Hopkins and Thomas Merton," *Catholic World* 188 (1956): 46–49. Departing from the general Catholic assessment, John Logan complained of Merton's "painful parochialism" in his review, "Babel Theory," *Commonweal* 66 (1957): 357–58.
18. Sister Therese Lentfoehr, for instance, frequently wrote about Merton's books of this period in glowing terms. See "If You Are Looking . . . Look Inside Yourself," review of *The Ascent of Truth* in *Books on Trial* 10 (1951): 66–67.
19. As the entries in *SJ* later made clear, Merton was a dedicated student of theology. The journal shows that in the late 1940s and 1950s, Merton worked diligently at Aquinas and Scotus, as well as Augustine and Bonaventure. He was especially fond

of the Fathers, and read them extensively in the Latin and Greek. Bernard of Clairvaux and John of the Cross, along with monastic theologians such as Aelred of Rievaulx and William of St. Thierry, were Merton's favorites.

20. Merton's own characterization of his theological approach in the prologue of *SJ*, p. 18.

21. *Ibid.*

22. "Merton's Newest," review of *SJ* in *Newsweek*, February 9, 1953, p. 80; Ben Ray Redman, "In the Belly of a Paradox," *Saturday Review of Literature* 36 (1953): 45–46; Henry Rago, "From the Belly of the Whale," *Commonweal* 62 (1952–53): 526–29.

23. Joseph Landy, for example, recognized "a certain impertinence in publishing a personal journal" and asked if there were any justification for it beyond stylistic excellence. He answered that Merton's journal "will not disappoint his public. In it we find a restatement and further refinement of his message to America." See "The Meaning of Thomas Merton," *America* 138 (1953): 569–70.

24. Aelred Graham, O.S.B., "The Mysticism of Thomas Merton," *Commonweal* 62 (1955): 155. Graham went on to describe those gifts as

> The readability of an accomplished writer, imaginative and intelligent, with a poet's ear for the music of words; an instinctive sense of the orthodox blended with the originality, not of one who must think differently from other people, but of one who thinks for himself. Added to these are perceptiveness, compassion, humility and an abounding common sense which relieves his uncompromising message of any suspicion of extravagance or ill humor.

25. "Prayer for a Miracle," *Newsweek*, February 16, 1959, p. 106.

26. William Michelfelder, "Search Beyond the Self," *Saturday Review of Literature*, 43 (1960): 24.

27. Thomas Merton, *The Wisdom of the Desert: Sayings from the Desert Fathers of the Fourth Century*, trans. Thomas Merton (New York: New Directions, 1960), p, ix. Hereafter *WD*.

28. Leonard F. X. Mayhew, "Mystic and Poet," *Commonweal* 75 (1962): 650–51.

29. Thomas Merton, *New Seeds of Contemplation* (New York: New Directions, 1961), p. ix. Hereafter *NSC*.

30. *Ibid.*, p. x.

31. *Ibid.*, p. xi.

32. "Wisdom in Emptiness: A Dialogue by Daisetz T. Suzuki and Thomas Merton," in *New Directions 17 in Prose and Poetry*, ed. J. Laughlin (New York: New Directions, 1961), pp. 65–101.

33. Thomas Merton, "Classic Chinese Thought," *Jubilee* 8 (1961): 26–32.

34. Thomas Merton, "The Shelter Ethic," *Catholic Worker* 28 (1961): 1, 5.

35. Thomas Merton, "Nuclear War and Christian Responsibility," *Commonweal* 80 (1962): 509–13.

36. Thomas Merton, "Religion and the Bomb," *Jubilee* 10 (1962): 7–13. This is typical of several similar essays published at this time.

37. For example, J. G. Hill, "Nuclear War and Christian Responsibility: Exchange of Views," *Commonweal* 76 (1962): 84–85.

38. Thomas Merton, *Life and Holiness* (Garden City, N.Y.: Image Books, 1964), pp. 7, 10, 8.

39. For example, "Spirituality for the Age of Overkill," *Continuum* 1 (1963): 9–21 and "Christian Morality and Nuclear War," *Way* 19 (1963): 12–22.

40. Thomas Merton, "Neither Caliban nor Uncle Tom," *Liberation* 7 (1963): 20–22; "The Negro Revolt," *Jubilee* 11 (1963): 39–43; "Letters to a White Liberal," *Blackfriars* 44 (1963): 464–77, 503–16.

41. Merton, "Letters to a White Liberal," *Seeds of Destruction* (New York: Macmillan, 1967), p. 41. Hereafter *SD*.

42. Merton, *SD*, p. 13.

43. Martin E. Marty, review of "Letters to a White Liberal," *Book Week* 2 (1965): 4.
44. Richard Horchler, review of *Seeds of Destruction*, in *Commonweal* 81 (1965): 4.
45. For example, "Truth and Violence," *Continuum* 2 (1964): 268–81.
46. The other one was an unexceptional collection of essays on liturgical topics, *Seasons of Celebration* (New York: Farrar, Straus & Giroux, 1977). Hereafter *SCel.*
47. Thomas Merton, *The Way of Chuang Tzu* (New York: New Directions, 1965), pp. 9, 10. Hereafter *WCT.*
48. Thomas Merton, "Mystics and Zen Masters," *Chinese Culture* 6 (1965): 1–18.
49. Thomas Merton, "Rain and the Rhinoceros," *Holiday* 38 (1965): 8.
50. For example, "The Night Spirit and the Dawn Air," *New Blackfriars* 66 (1965): 687–93.
51. Thomas Merton, "Answers on Art and Freedom," *The Lugano Review* 1 (1965): 43–45.
52. "Excerpts from *Conjectures of a Guilty Bystander*," *Life*, August 5, 1966, pp. 60–73.
53. Thomas Merton, *Conjectures of a Guilty Bystander* (Garden City, N.Y.: Image Books, 1966), p. 5. Hereafter *CGB.*
54. *Ibid.*, pp. 5–6.
55. James H. Forest, "Raindrops and Riddles," *Critic* 25 (1967): 72.
56. Thomas Merton, *Raids on the Unspeakable* (New York: New Directions, 1966), p. 1. Hereafter *RU.*
57. *Ibid.*, p. 2.
58. Thomas Merton, "Love and Solitude," *Critic* 25 (1966): 33.
59. Thomas Merton, "Is the World a Problem," *Commonweal* 74 (1966): 309.
60. Thomas Merton, "How It Is—Apologies to an Unbeliever," *Harper's* 233 (1966), 36.
61. Thomas Merton, "The Zen Koan," *The Lugano Review* 1 (1966): 126–39; "Buddhism and the Modern World," *Cross Currents* 16 (1966): 495–99.
62. Thomas Merton, *Mystics and Zen Masters* (New York: Delta Books, 1968), p. x. Hereafter *MZM.*
63. There were about ten such articles; for example, "Ishi—a Meditation," review of *Ishi in Two Worlds* by Theodora Kroeber, *Catholic Worker* 33 (1967): 5–6 and "The Meaning of Malcolm X," *Continuum* 5 (1967): 432–35.
64. Thomas Merton, "The Death of God and the End of History," *Theoria to Theory* 2 (1967): 3–16.
65. Thomas Merton, "Day of a Stranger," *Hudson Review* 20 (1967): 216, 211, 213–14.
66. This originally appeared in *Cimarron Review* (Oklahoma State University), June 1968.
67. Thomas Merton, *Zen and the Birds of Appetite* (New York: New Directions, 1968), p. 4. Hereafter *ZBA.*
68. First published as preface to John C. H. Wu's *The Golden Age of Zen* (Committee on Compilation of the Chinese Library, 1967), pp. 1–27.
69. Merton, *ZBA*, p. 38.
70. *Ibid.*, pp. 19, 21, 17.
71. For example, "Contemplation in a World of Action," *Bloominewman* (Newsletter of the Newman Club of the University of Louisville) 2 (1968): 1–5 or "The Spiritual Father in the Desert Tradition," *Monastic Studies* 5 (1968): 87–111.
72. Thomas Merton, *Contemplation in a World of Action* (Garden City, N.Y.: Image Books, 1971), p. 10.
73. For example, "The Vietnam War: An Overwhelming Atrocity," *Catholic Worker* 34 (1968): 1, 6, 7 and "Rites for the Extrusion of a Leper," *The Kentucky Review* 2 (1968): 26.
74. See "A Catch of Anti-Letters by Robert Lax and Thomas Merton," *Voyages* 2 (1968): 44–56, for an exchange with an old friend, and, for Merton's account of the Buddhist friends he was making in Asia, *The Asian Journal of Thomas Merton* (New York: New Directions, 1973). pp. 320–25 (Hereafter *AJ*).
75. Israel Shenker, "Thomas Merton Is Dead at 53; Monk Wrote of Search for God," *The New York Times*, December 11, 1968, pp. 1, 42.

76. Naomi Burton, "I Shall Miss Thomas Merton," *Cistercian Studies* 3 (1969): 218–25.

77. Ten articles appeared in the Merton commemorative issue, *Continuum* 8 (1969).

78. Thomas Merton, *My Argument with the Gestapo: A Macronic Journal* (New York: Doubleday, 1969), p. 6.

79. Thomas Merton, *The Geography of Lograire* (New York: New Directions, 1969), p. 1.

80. James Forest, "The Frozen Rainbow," *Critic* 28 (1970): 87.

81. For example, "Terror and the Absurd: Violence and Nonviolence in Albert Camus," *Motive* 29 (1969): 5–15.

82. "Is the Contemplative Life Finished," *CWA* (pp. 343–96) is one of several such transcriptions.

83. At least five articles appeared with titles such as "The Life That Unifies," *Sisters Today* 42 (1970): 65–73 or "Prayer, Tradition, and Experience," *Sisters Today* 42 (1971): 285–93.

84. Editorial note, *CWA*, p. 19.

85. *The Time-Life Bible* never materialized. Merton had put much work into writing the introductory essay, and held on to it after the project fell through, anticipating other publication possibilities.

86. Thomas Merton, *Opening the Bible* (Collegeville, Minn.: Liturgical Press, 1970), p. 33.

87. Merton, *AJ*, p. 238.

88. Because of restrictions in Merton's will, there are no plans for preparing a volume of collected letters in the near future. Exchanges with particular individuals will be available.

89. Gordon C. Zahn, ed., *Thomas Merton on Peace* (New York: McCall, 1971). Hereafter *TMP*. Brother Patrick Hart, ed., *The Monastic Journey: Thomas Merton* (Kansas City: Sheed, Andrews and McMeel, 1977). Hereafter *MJ*.

90. John Howard Griffin, *A Hidden Wholeness: The Visual World of Thomas Merton* (Boston: Houghton Mifflin, 1970), pp. 3, 4.

91. Thomas P. McDonnell, ed., *A Thomas Merton Reader* (Garden City, N.Y.: Image Books, 1974). Hereafter *TMR*.

92. *The Collected Poems of Thomas Merton* (New York: New Directions, 1977).

93. From the marginalia collected at the Thomas Merton Studies Center in Louisville and quoted by John Leax in his review of the *CPTM* in *The Merton Seasonal of Bellarmine College* 3 (1978): unpaged.

94. Frank Dell'Isola, *Thomas Merton: A Bibliography* (New York: Farrar, Straus & Cudahy, 1956); *Thomas Merton: A Bibliography* (Kent, Ohio: Kent State University Press, 1975). Marquita Breit, *Thomas Merton: a Bibliography* (Metuchen, N.J.: Scarecrow Press, 1974).

95. These numbers have vastly increased in all categories since 1974. *The Merton Seasonal of Bellarmine College* reports in each quarterly issue new publications by and about Merton. The Winter 1979 issue for instance, listed twenty-one publications by Merton and seventy-three about him that had recently appeared.

96. Thomas Merton, *He Is Risen* (Niles, Ill.: Argus Communications, 1975); *Ishi Means Man: Essays on Native Americans* (Greensboro, N.C.: Unicorn Press, 1976).

97. Between 1976 and 1978, Noonday Press, a division of Farrar, Straus & Giroux, reissued in new paperback format *The Secular Journal, The Silent Life, Thoughts in Solitude, Seasons of Celebration, The New Man,* and *Disputed Questions.*

98. *The Merton Seasonal of Bellarmine College* regularly reports on completed dissertations and theses. A list of all completed studies, as well as works in progress, is available from the Thomas Merton Studies Center, Bellarmine College, Louisville, Kentucky 40205.

99. *The Merton Seasonal* provides full information about books and articles on Merton as they appear.

100. Particular issues of *The Merton Seasonal* are devoted to different language translations of Merton: Fall 1977 features works in Polish, Spring 1978 lists all works in Japanese, Summer 1979 lists German translations, and Autumn 1979 focuses on Portugese.

101. In 1970 there was a gathering at Fordham University of scholars from different disciplines to examine "Thomas Merton: East Meets West." The Newman Campus Ministry of the Diocese of Cleveland put on a "Merton Festival" in the fall of 1972; it moved around to five campuses in Ohio and lasted a whole month. It was a massive attempt to introduce Merton to a new generation of college students. Elsewhere there have been countless programs and lectures on Merton in universities, scholarly conferences, parishes, and retreat houses.

102. The Eighth Cistercian Conference, in conjunction with the Conference on Medieval Studies, at Western Michigan University had a special section on Merton in the Spring of 1978. Around the same time, the Vancouver School of Theology in British Columbia held the "Thomas Merton Symposium" along with "The People's Merton Festival." Some twenty-five scholars presented papers for the symposium, and the festival included liturgies, plays, dramatic readings, music, and assorted celebratory events. In Washington, D.C., the Shalom Center sponsored a commemorative conference in early summer to help people relate their own journey to Merton's life and work. It focused on examining those places where Merton discovered truth: art, theology, culture, and the Church. The most extensive celebration of 1978 was held at Columbia University in the two weeks prior to December 10, the date of Merton's death. This included an academic symposium with an impressive list of scholars, a poetry roundtable, the annual Pax Christi USA meeting, an East-West dialogue, an ecumenical faith celebration, and a conference on contemplation and modern society. A Thomas Merton Center was established at Columbia, and an annual Thomas Merton Lecture series inaugurated there.

103. Merton, "Writing as Temperature," 540–41.

104. Merton, *SD*, p. 162.

CHAPTER 2: Journey into the Unknown

1. Blurb on the jacket of the original *A Thomas Merton Reader*, ed. by Thomas P. McDonnell (New York: Harcourt, Brace & World, 1962).

2. Thomas Merton, *Cistercian Life* (Spencer, Mass.: Cistercian Book Service, 1974), unnumbered pages. Also quoted after the preface in *MJ*.

3. Douglas Berggren, "The Use and Abuse of Metaphor," *Review of Metaphysics* 16 (1962–1963): 472.

4. Thomas Merton, *Contemplative Prayer* (New York: Herder and Herder, 1969), p. 27. Hereafter *CP*.

5. Merton, *SSM*, p. 3.

6. *Ibid.*, pp. 3–4.

7. *Ibid.*, p. 52.

8. *Ibid.*, p. 53.

9. *Ibid.*, p. 85.

10. *Ibid.*

11. *Ibid.*, pp. 122–23.

12. *Ibid.*, pp. 129–30.

13. *Ibid.*, p. 131.

14. *Ibid.*, p. 137.

15. *Ibid.*, p. 180.

16. *Ibid.*, p. 154.

17. *Ibid.*, p. 162.

18. *Ibid.*, p. 165.

19. *Ibid.*, p. 185.

20. *Ibid.*, p. 191.

21. *Ibid.*, p. 215.

22. *Ibid.*, p. 226.
23. *Ibid.*, p. 291.
24. *Ibid.*, p. 253.
25. *Ibid.*, pp. 254–55.
26. *Ibid.*, p. 284.
27. *Ibid.*, p. 294.
28. *Ibid.*, p. 296.
29. *Ibid.*, p. 300.
30. *Ibid.*, pp. 300–01.
31. *Ibid.*, p. 328.
32. *Ibid.*, p. 356.
33. *Ibid.*, p. 363.
34. *Saint Augustine: Confessions,* trans. R. S. Pine-Coffin (Baltimore: Penguin Books, 1961), Bk. 8, p. 176.
35. Merton. *SSM.* p. 365.
36. *Ibid.*
37. *Ibid.*, p. 369.
38. *Ibid.*, p. 370.
39. *Ibid.*, p. 419.
40. *Ibid.*, p. 422.
41. Merton, *SJ,* pp. 20–21.
42. *Ibid.*, p. 20.
43. *Ibid.*, p. 95.
44. Merton, *SSM,* p. 410.
45. Merton, *SJ,* p. 129.
46. *Ibid.*, p. 131.
47. *Ibid.*, p. 181.
48. *Ibid.*, p. 225.
49. *Ibid.*, p. 226.
50. *Ibid.*, p. 227.
51. *Ibid.*, pp. 262–63.
52. *Ibid.*, p. 295.
53. *Ibid.*, p. 323.
54. *Ibid.*, p. 319.
55. *Ibid.*, p. 347.
56. *Ibid.*, p. 351.
57. Merton, *TMR,* p. 15.
58. Griffin wrote this in a letter to me, July 1, 1971.
59. Merton had already indicated his persistent longing for greater solitude in the autobiography. In *SJ,* he revealed how nagging was the conflict during the years covered by this journal.
60. See his essay, first published in 1955, "A Renaissance Hermit: Bl. Paul Guistiniani," in *Disputed Questions* (New York: Farrar, Straus & Giroux, 1976), pp. 151–62. Hereafter *DQ.* His book on the eremitical forms of monasticism also reflects these concerns. See *The Silent Life* (New York: Farrar, Straus & Giroux, 1975). Hereafter *SL.*
61. Merton, *SL,* pp. xiii, 60, 146, 168–70.
62. Merton, *TMR,* p. 16.
63. Merton, *CGB,* p. 7.
64. *Ibid.*, p. 157.
65. *Ibid.*, p. 214.
66. Merton discusses the origins of his relations with Suzuki in *ZBA* where the original dialogue, "Wisdom in Emptiness," appears with a prefatory note, pp. 99–138.
67. John Eudes Bamberger, O.C.S.O., "The Cistercian," *Continuum* 7 (1969): 232.

68. Merton, *CGB*, p. 5.
69. *Ibid.*, p. 219.
70. *Ibid.*, p. 189.
71. *Ibid.*, p. 193.
72. *Ibid.*, p. 263.
73. *Ibid.*, p. 261.
74. *Ibid.*, p. 5.
75. "Author's Preface to the Japanese Edition," in *Nanae No Yama (The Seven Storey Mountain)*, trans. Tadishi Judo (Tokyo: Chuo Shuppansha, 1966), p. 9. Hereafter "Preface Japanese." This also appeared as "Introducing a Book: Introduction to Japanese Edition of *Seven Storey Mountain,"* Queens Work, 56 (1964): 9–10.
76. Merton, "Preface Japanese," p. 11.
77. The following section, except where otherwise indicated, is based on unpublished autobiographical materials of Merton. At the present time, it is not possible for a writer to quote from them, but only to refer to them indirectly.
78. See Zahn, *TMP*, p. xiv, for a discussion of the retreat and a list of the participants. The Bellarmine files contain a mimeographed sheet called "The Spiritual Roots of Protest," drawn up by Merton and outlining the topics he proposed for consideration to the retreatants.
79. See *MJ* for Merton's detailed plan, "Project for a Hermitage," pp. 135–43.
80. Merton discussed his visit with Suzuki in "Learning to Live," an essay in a collection by prominent Columbia University alumni. It also appears in *Love and Living*, ed. Naomi Burton Stone and Brother Patrick Hart (New York: Farrar, Straus & Giroux, 1979), pp. 3–14.
81. Zahn, *TMP*, p. xxxiv.
82. *Ibid.*
83. Merton, *MZM*, p. ix.
84. Thomas Merton, "Apologies to an Unbeliever," *Faith and Violence: Christian Teaching and Christian Practice* (Notre Dame, Ind.: University of Notre Dame Press, 1968), p. 206. Hereafter *FV*.
85. *Ibid.*, p. 213.
86. Merton, "Is the World a Problem?", *CWA*, p. 160.
87. Merton, "The Hot Summer of Sixty-Seven," *FV*, pp. 165, 166.
88. Thomas Merton, "As Man to Man," *Cistercian Studies*, 4 (1969): 90, 92.
89. *Ibid.*, p. 93.
90. This section is based on unpublished materials, and I am bound by the restrictions previously mentioned.
91. Merton, *AJ*, p. 296.
92. *Ibid.*, p. 320.
93. *Ibid.*, p. xxviii.
94. *Ibid.*, pp. 312–13.
95. See Griffin's *A Hidden Wholeness*, pp. 135–43 and *AJ*, pp. 149, 152, and 156 for these striking pictures.
96. Merton, *AJ*, p. 233.
97. *Ibid.*, pp. 233–35.
98. *Ibid.*, pp. 235–36.
99. *Ibid.*, p. 257.
100. *Ibid.*, p. 238.
101. *Ibid.*, p. 257.
102. Merton, *CGB*, pp. 188–89. See Griffin, *A Hidden Wholeness*, pp. 144–46, for this photograph and his reflections on the experience of developing Merton's last role of film, which was in the camera Griffin had given to the monk and was returned to him after Merton's death.

103. A videotape of this conference was made by a Dutch television agency. The film is available at the Thomas Merton Studies Center at Bellarmine College, Louisville, Kentucky 40205. Merton appears animated, in good health, and generally in fine form.
104. Merton, *AJ*, p. 326.
105. *Ibid.*, p. 338.
106. *Ibid.*, p. 340.
107. *Ibid.*, pp. 342–43.
108. *Ibid.*, p. 343.
109. *Ibid.*, p. 4.
110. James Olney, *Metaphors of Self: The Meaning of Autobiography* (Princeton, N.J.: Princeton University Press, 1972), pp. 31–32.
111. Merton, *CP*, p. 26.

CHAPTER 3: The Solitary Explorer

1. Merton, *DQ*, p. 163.
2. *Ibid.*, p. 166.
3. Merton, *FV*, p. 213.
4. Merton, *CP*, p. 29.
5. Merton, *CGB*, p. 245.
6. Merton, *CWA*, p. 118.
7. Merton, *MJ*, p. 159.
8. *Ibid.*, p. 171.
9. *Ibid.*
10. Merton, *FV*, p. 213.
11. Merton, *MJ*, p. 159.
12. Thomas Merton, *Seeds of Contemplation* (New York: Dell, 1960), p. 54. Hereafter *SC*.
13. *Ibid.*, p. 50.
14. *Ibid.*
15. Thomas Merton, *The Waters of Siloe* (Garden City, N.Y.: Image Books, 1962), p. 28. Hereafter *WS*.
16. Merton, *SJ*, p. 97.
17. *Ibid.*, p. 163.
18. Merton, *SL*, p. 8.
19. Merton, *SJ*, p. 251.
20. *Ibid.*, p. 312.
21. Merton, *WD*, p. 17.
22. *Ibid.*
23. *Ibid.*, p. 23.
24. *Ibid.*
25. *Ibid.*
26. Merton, *DQ*, p. 180.
27. Merton, *CGB*, p. 7.
28. *Ibid.*, p. 257.
29. *Ibid.*, p. 47.
30. *Ibid.*, p. 48.
31. Merton, *CWA*, p. 170.
32. Merton, *FV*, p. 256.
33. Merton, *CGB*, p. 48.
34. Merton, *DQ*, p. ix.
35. Merton, "Preface Japanese," pp. 11–12.
36. *Ibid.*, p. 9.
37. Merton, *CWA*, p. 43.

38. Merton, *CGB*, p. 245.
39. Merton, *MJ*, p. xii.
40. Merton, *CWA*, p. 242.
41. Merton, *DQ*, p. xii.
42. *Ibid.*, p. 180.
43. Merton, *CWA*, p. 247.
44. Merton, *RU*, pp. 17–18.
45. *Ibid.*, p. 17.
46. Merton, *DQ*, p. 179.
47. Merton, *FV*, p. 221.
48. *Ibid.*, p. 146.
49. Merton, *RU*, p. 18.
50. Merton, *DQ*, p. 171.
51. Merton, *CWA*, p. 199.
52. *Ibid.*, p. 258.
53. *Ibid.*, p. 242.
54. Merton, *RU*, pp. 14–15.
55. Merton, *CWA*, p. 258.
56. Merton, *MJ*, p. 146.
57. *Ibid.*
58. *Ibid.*, p. 175.
59. *Ibid.*, p. 176.
60. *Ibid.*
61. Merton, *CWA*, p. 242.
62. Merton, *CGB*, p. 250.
63. Merton, *CWA*, p. 349.
64. *Ibid.*, p. 350.
65. *Ibid.*, p. 233.
66. *Ibid.*, p. 232.
67. Merton, *Monastery of Christ in the Desert* (Abiquiu, New Mexico). Unpaged brochure.
68. Thomas Merton, *No Man Is an Island* (New York: Dell, 1957), p. 148. Hereafter *NMI.*
69. Merton, *SL*, p. viii.
70. Merton, *MJ*, p. 13.
71. Merton, *SC*, pp. 30–31.
72. *Ibid.*, p. 31.
73. Merton, *SL*, p. vii.
74. Merton, *MJ*, pp. 12–13.
75. *Ibid.*, p. 13.
76. Merton, *DQ*, p. 163.
77. *Ibid.*, p. 165.
78. *Ibid.*, p. 166.
79. *Ibid.*, p. 175.
80. *Ibid.*, p. 184.
81. Merton, *CWA*, p. 118.
82. Merton, *ZBA*, p. 22.
83. Merton, *SCel*, p. 223.
84. Merton, *MJ*, p. 171.
85. Merton, *CWA*, p. 119.
86. *Ibid.*, pp. 126–27.
87. *Ibid.*, p. 129.
88. *Ibid.*, pp. 130–31.
89. Merton, *MZM*, p. 98.
90. Merton, *AJ*, pp. 312–13.

91. *Ibid.,* p. 317.
92. *Ibid.*

CHAPTER 4: A Guilty Bystander

1. Merton, *CGB,* p. 19.
2. *Ibid.,* p. 7.
3. *Ibid.,* p. 6.
4. *Ibid.,* p. 7.
5. *Ibid.*
6. Thomas Merton, "Peace: a Religious Responsibility," *Breakthrough to Peace: Twelve Views on the Threat of Thermonuclear Extermination* (New York: New Directions, 1962), p. 90.
7. Merton, *SD,* p. 53.
8. Merton, *SC,* p. 65.
9. Merton, *SD,* p. 7.
10. *Ibid.,* p. 8.
11. *Ibid.,* pp. 8–9.
12. Merton, *SSM,* p. 148.
13. *Ibid.,* p. 131.
14. *Ibid.,* p. 132.
15. *Ibid.,* p. 311.
16. *Ibid.,* pp. 311–12.
17. *Ibid.,* p. 312.
18. *Ibid.,* p. 311.
19. *Ibid.,* p. 313.
20. *Ibid.,* pp. 312–13.
21. Merton, *SC,* p. 66.
22. Merton, *SJ,* p. 150.
23. This novel would eventually be published under the title *My Argument with the Gestapo.*
24. Merton, *SJ,* p. 312.
25. *Ibid.*
26. *Ibid.*
27. *Ibid.,* pp. 312–13.
28. *Ibid.,* p. 319.
29. *Ibid.,* p. 326.
30. Thomas Merton, "A Life Free from Care," *Cistercian Studies* 5 (1970): 218.
31. Merton, *SJ,* p. 323.
32. Merton, *SSM,* pp. 118–30.
33. See the observations of John Eudes Bamberger, a scholastic under Merton and later a psychiatrist at Gethsemani, on Merton's development as a social critic within the monastery, in "The Cistercian," *Continuum* 8 (1969): 232.
34. Merton, *CGB,* p. 225.
35. *Ibid.,* p. 278.
36. Thomas Merton, *Gandhi on Non-Violence* (New York: New Directions, 1964), p. 6. Hereafter *GNV.*
37. Merton, *NSC,* pp. ix–x.
38. Merton, *CGB,* p. 218.
39. Merton, *GNV,* p. 6.
40. *Ibid.,* p. 7.
41. Merton, *CGB,* p. 214.
42. Merton, *SD,* p. 164.
43. In "A Tribute to Gandhi," Merton tells how in 1931 he defended the Indian's acts of civil disobedience to his British chums in the dormitory. (See *SD,* p. 156.)

44. Merton, *CGB*, pp. 44, 58–59, 117.
45. *Ibid.*, p. 117.
46. Merton, *SD*, p. 160.
47. *Ibid.*
48. Merton, *CGB*, p. 118.
49. *Ibid.*, p. 48.
50. Merton, *GNV*, p. 6.
51. *Ibid.*, p. 9.
52. *Ibid.*, p. 7.
53. Merton, *CGB*, p. 69.
54. *Ibid.*, p. 208.
55. Merton, *FV*, p. 92.
56. *Ibid.*, p. 6.
57. *Ibid.*, p. 7.
58. *Ibid.*, p. 3.
59. Merton, *GNV*, p. 11.
60. Merton, "Preface Japanese," p. 12.
61. Merton, *FV*, p. 20.
62. Merton, *MZM*, p. 107.
63. *Ibid.*, p. 109.
64. *Ibid.*, p. 112.
65. Merton, *FV*, p. 219.

CHAPTER 5: A Poor Pilgrim

1. Thomas Merton, "Preface to the Japanese Edition of *Seeds of Contemplation*," *Kanso No Tane*, trans. Yahuwo Kikama (Kyoto: Veritas, 1965), p. 1.
2. *Ibid.*, pp. 4–5.
3. Merton, *ZBA*, p. 84.
4. Merton, *AJ*, pp. 312–13.
5. Merton, *MZM*, p. 91.
6. Merton, *AJ*, p. 313.
7. *Ibid.*, p. 311.
8. *Ibid.*, p. 316.
9. Merton, *GNV*, p. 1.
10. Merton, *SSM*, p. 187.
11. *Ibid.*, pp. 194–99.
12. Twenty-four of Merton's conferences to the monks at Gethsemani on Sufism are available on cassette tapes from Electronic Paperbacks, P.O. Box 2, Chappaqua, NY 10514.
13. Merton, *MZM*, pp. 45–68.
14. *Ibid.*, pp. 69–80.
15. Merton, *WCT*, p. 15.
16. *Ibid.*, p. 10.
17. *Ibid.*, p. 16.
18. Brother Patrick Hart tells that Merton had many scholarly books on Asian studies, especially Buddhism, made available to him through friends associated with university libraries. He tried to learn Chinese in the early 1960s, but gave up due to work pressures. Merton commented on his method of working with texts in *WCT*, pp. 9–10.
19. Merton, *SJ*, pp. 195, 237.
20. Thomas Merton, *The Ascent to Truth* (New York: Harcourt, Brace, and Co., 1951) pp. 53, 82, 98, 107, 123–24, 133, 292–93. Hereafter *AT*.

21. Chalmers MacCormick makes an interesting observation about the influence of the apophatic mystics on Merton: "These writers—who were 'safe' theologically and thus bound to preserve and foster Merton's Catholicism—were at the same time, because of marked affinities between their outlook and the outlook of Oriental mystics, ordained to help spark a revival of his Oriental interests." (See "The Zen Catholicism of Thomas Merton, *Journal of Ecumenical Studies* 9 (1972): 806.

22. Merton, *AT*, p. 10.

23. Merton, *SJ*, p. 332.

24. Thomas Merton, *Thoughts in Solitude* (New York: Farrar, Straus & Giroux, 1976), p. 70. Hereafter *TS*.

25. Merton, *SL*, pp. vii–xiv, 1–20.

26. Merton, *WD*, p. ix.

27. *Ibid.*, p. 10.

28. *Ibid.*, p. 9.

29. *Ibid.*, p. 23.

30. For example, the Zen story of "The Great Way," included in *CGB*, p. 199.

31. Merton, *WD*, p. 24.

32. *Ibid.*, p. 8.

33. There are a number of entries in *CGB:* pp. 152, 185, 199.

34. Merton, *ZBA*, p. 139.

35. *Ibid.*, pp. 118–19; 130–33.

36. *Ibid.*, p. 42.

37. *Ibid.*

38. *Ibid.*, p. 33.

39. *Ibid.*, p. 1.

40. *Ibid.*, p. 4.

41. *Ibid.*, p. 44.

42. Thomas Merton, "Zen: Sense and Sensibility," *America* 108 (1963): 752.

43. Merton, *ZBA*, p. 47.

44. Merton, *MZM*, p. 12.

45. Aelred Graham, *Zen Catholicism* (New York: Harcourt, Brace and World, 1963).

46. Merton, "Zen: Sense and Sensibility," p. 752.

47. Thomas Merton, "The Zen Revival," *Continuum* 1 (1964): 531.

48. For Merton's understanding and criticism of Zaehner, see *MZM*, pp. 3–7, 41; for his appreciation of, but disagreement with, Dumoulin, pp. 7–12, 37.

49. *Ibid.*, p. 12.

50. Merton, *ZBA*, p. 35.

51. *Ibid.*, p. 47.

52. Merton, *MZM*, pp. 13–14.

53. *Ibid.*, p. 14.

54. Merton, *ZBA*, p. 48.

55. *Ibid.*

56. *Ibid.*, p. 13.

57. Merton, *MZM*, p. 13.

58. Bernard J. Lonergan, *Method in Theology* (New York: Herder and Herder, 1972), pp. 6–9.

59. *Ibid.*, p. 83.

60. Ludwig Wittgenstein, *Tractatus Logico-Philosophicus* (London: Routledge & Kegan Paul, 1922), 4.12–4.1212.

61. Merton, *ZBA*, p. 39.

62. *Ibid.*, p. 55.

63. *Ibid.*, p. 82.

64. *Ibid.*, p. 83.

65. *Ibid.*, p. 84.
66. *Ibid.*
67. *Ibid.*, p. 118.
68. *Ibid.*, p. 25.
69. *Ibid.*, p. 86.
70. Merton, *CGB*, p. 285.
71. Merton, *ZBA*, pp. 23–24.
72. *Ibid.*, pp. 71–72.
73. *Ibid.*, p. 74.
74. *Ibid.*, p. 75.
75. Merton, "Preface Japanese," p. 11.
76. *Ibid.*
77. Merton, *MZM*, p. 94.
78. *Ibid.*, p. 96.
79. *Ibid.*, p. 91.
80. *Ibid.*, p. 92.
81. *Ibid.*, p. 94.
82. *Ibid.*, p. 92.
83. *Ibid.*
84. *Ibid.*, p. 226.
85. *Ibid.*, pp. 225–27.
86. Merton, *AJ*, pp. 4–5.
87. *Ibid.*, p. 305.
88. *Ibid.*
89. *Ibid.*, p. 313.
90. *Ibid.*, p. 314.
91. *Ibid.*, p. 315.
92. *Ibid.*, p. 316.
93. *Ibid.*, p. 315.
94. Merton, *CWA*, p. 225.
95. *Ibid.*
96. *Ibid.*, pp. 225–26.
97. Merton, *AJ*, p. 341.
98. *Ibid.*, p. 342.
99. *Ibid.*
100. *Ibid.*
101. *Ibid.*, pp. 342–43.
102. Merton, *MZM*, p. 17.
103. Merton, *AJ*, p. 233.
104. Merton, *TMR*, p. 433.

CHAPTER 6: A Mind Awake in the Dark

1. Merton, *TMR*, p. 433.
2. *Ibid.*, p. 431.
3. *Ibid.*, p. 432.
4. *Ibid.*
5. *Ibid.*, p. 435.
6. *Ibid.*, pp. 432–33.
7. *Ibid.*, p. 433.
8. *Ibid.*
9. *Ibid.*
10. Merton, *CGB*, pp. 277–78.
11. Merton, *MZM*, p. 16.

12. Lonergan, *Method*, pp. 106–07.
13. Merton, *NSC*, p. 2.
14. *Ibid.*, p. 5.
15. *Ibid.*, pp. 2–3.
16. *Ibid.*, p. 3.
17. Merton, *FV*, pp. 114–15.
18. Merton, *SC*, p. 139.
19. Thomas Merton, *The New Man* (New York: Farrar, Straus & Giroux, 1978), p. 14. Hereafter *NM*.
20. *Ibid.*, p. 73.
21. Merton, *NMI*, p. 79.
22. Merton, *CWA*, p. 119.
23. Merton, *SSM*, p. 225.
24. Merton, *SC*, p. 52.
25. Merton, *NM*, p. 19.
26. Merton, *CP*, p. 103.
27. *Ibid.*, pp. 103–04.
28. *Ibid.*, p. 34.
29. *Ibid.*, p. 82.
30. Merton, *SC*, p. 23.
31. *Ibid.*, p. 27.
32. Merton, *NM*, pp. 118–19.
33. *Ibid.*, pp. 63–64.
34. Merton, *WS*, p. 366.
35. Merton, *SCel*, p. 70.
36. Merton, *NSC*, p. 7.
37. Merton, *TS*, p. 70.
38. Merton, *SL*, p. 22.
39. Merton, *NM*, pp. 60–61.
40. *Ibid.*, p. 61.
41. *Ibid.*, pp. 61–62.
42. Merton, *NMI*, p. 224.
43. Merton, *NM*, p. 123.
44. *Ibid.*, p. 124.
45. *Ibid.*
46. *Ibid.*, p. 121.
47. *Ibid.*, pp. 121–22.
48. *Ibid.*, p. 122.
49. *Ibid.*, p. 119.
50. Merton, *NSC*, p. 64.
51. Merton, *NMI*, pp. 79–80.
52. *Ibid.*, p. 15.
53. Merton, *NM*, pp. 67–68.
54. Merton, *NMI*, p. 168.
55. *Ibid.*, p. 169.
56. Merton, *SJ*, p. 152.
57. Merton, *NM*, p. 141.
58. *Ibid.*, pp. 142–43.
59. Merton, *DQ*, p. 198.
60. John F. Teahan, "A Dark and Empty Way: Thomas Merton and the Apophatic Tradition," *The Journal of Religion* 58 (1978): 276.
61. Merton, *DQ*, p. 198.
62. *Ibid.*, p. 202.
63. *Ibid.*, pp. 198–99.

64. Merton, *NSC*, pp. 134–35.
65. Merton, *AT*, p. 82.
66. Merton, *NSC*, pp. 1–2.
67. Merton, *CWA*, p. 185.
68. *Ibid.*, p. 186.
69. *Ibid.*
70. Merton, *TS*, p. 71.
71. *Ibid.*, p. 51.

CHAPTER 7: "To Be What I Am"

1. Merton, *CWA*, p. 245.
2. Merton, "Preface Japanese," p. 9.
3. Merton, *CWA*, p. 159.
4. Merton, *AJ*, p. 338.
5. Merton, *MZM*, pp. 235–36.
6. Chart in the files of the Thomas Merton Studies Center, Bellarmine College, Louisville, Kentucky, labeled "Fr. Louis' Own Evaluation of His Books." The chart is in Merton's handwriting. The list of books is not inclusive and the chronology is not exact.
7. Merton, *WCT*, pp. 9–10.
8. Merton, *RU*, p. 2.
9. See my review of *The Collected Poems of Thomas Merton* in *The Notre Dame English Journal* 11 (1978): 71–74.
10. Merton, *DQ*, p. vii.
11. Some unpublished sections of the original *SSM* manuscript appear in *TMR*, pp. 145–51; 155–58.
12. Merton, *SJ*, pp. 228–29.
13. Merton, *CGB*, pp. 15–16; 29–30; 188–89.
14. Merton, *CWA*, p. 225.
15. Merton, *SSM*, p. 57.
16. *Ibid.*
17. Robert Evett, "A Worldly Monk in Search of Truth," *Star News* (Washington, D.C.), August 5, 1973.
18. Merton, *AJ*, p. 4.
19. Merton, *CGB*, p. 257.
20. Merton, *AJ*, p. 149.
21. Merton, "Preface Japanese," p. 11.
22. Merton, *AJ*, p. 5.
23. Merton, *SJ*, pp. 23–24.
24. Merton, *SSM*, p. 410.
25. For a fuller discussion of Zilboorg's criticisms of Merton, see Raymond Bailey, *Thomas Merton on Mysticism* (Garden City, N.Y.: Image Books, 1974), pp. 100–01.
26. Merton, *MJ*, p. 119.
27. Unpublished manuscript available for study only with permission of the Merton Legacy Trust.
28. Edward Rice, *The Man in the Sycamore Tree: The Good Times and Hard Life of Thomas Merton* (Garden City, N.Y.: Doubleday, 1970), pp. 17–45.
29. "Two Myths Converge: Norman Mailer Discovers Marilyn Monroe," *Time,* July 16, 1973, pp. 60–70.
30. Merton, *AJ,*, pp. 342–43.
31. Dorothy L. Sayers, trans., *The Comedy of Dante Alighieri:* Cantica 1, *Hell* (Baltimore: Penguin Books, 1949), p. 95.

Index